An Introductory History of England ...: from the
Earliest Times to the Close of the Middle Ages.
1907
by Charles Robert Leslie Fletcher

Address:
HardPress
8345 NW 66TH ST #2561
MIAMI FL 33166-2626
USA
Email: info@hardpress.net

AN INTRODUCTORY HISTORY OF ENGLAND · FLETCHER ·

AN INTRODUCTORY
HISTORY OF ENGLAND

AN INTRODUCTORY
HISTORY OF ENGLAND

FROM THE EARLIEST TIMES
TO THE CLOSE OF THE
MIDDLE AGES

BY C. R. L. FLETCHER

LATE FELLOW OF MAGDALEN COLLEGE, OXFORD

WITH MAPS

NEW YORK
E. P. DUTTON AND COMPANY
1907

FIRST EDITION . . . . . *July* 1904
REPRINTED . . . . . *August* 1904
SECOND 5/- EDITION . . . . *May* 1905
REPRINTED . . . . . *August* 1907

PRINTED IN GREAT BRITAIN

July 1904
August 1904
May 1905
August 1907

PREFACE

THE presumption of adding another to tl
of Histories of England for boys needs soi
The venture was suggested to me by cert
plimentary young gentlemen (near relatic
own), who were always complaining that
History intolerably dull.

My own view is that English History
an inheritance of childhood; that its lege
romance should grow into our thoughts
early years, and should expand themselve
expansion of our minds; that we should :
and dream of it rather than learn it as a less
is that boy who, having so "grown up witl
of his country, can people the fields and
home with the figures of the past; can hea
of Rupert's horsemen down his village stre
picture the good monks catching baskets-f
in the stream (there were more trout in it
Reformation) wherein he is failing to get a r:

For English History as part of a school "
or as a means of education, I have no suc
all. Education is not the acquisition of infi
those people appear to think who wish to tu:
Winchester into cramming establishments fi
or "useful avenues for commercial life," or,
copies of a German *Realschule*. The sul
Modern History and other "modern subje
great schools for Greek and Latin I regar<

short of an irretrievable calamity. I do not even consider that the immense growth of the History School at
Oxford and of the History Tripos at Cambridge in recent
years is at all a healthy sign for English education.
Such training for the mind as may be derived from
this School and this Tripos is mainly derived from a
certain amount of " Political Philosophy " which is (or
is not) studied concurrently ; to the vast majority of the
students History is merely an easy avenue to a degree.
A man's true " education " in History can only be given
by himself. An exhaustive reading of History (in the
light of " past politics teaching by example ") is indis-
pensable to the statesman and the philosopher ; a wide
reading of it is necessary for every cultivated scholar and
gentleman ; but such reading is a matter for a lifetime,
rather than for those early years in which a young man's
studies should be wholly directed to the stimulation of
the reasoning faculties. What is called the scientific
study of the subject, *i.e.* the determination of the date of
a document by the colour or texture of the parchment,
or of the credibility of a charter by the names of the
signatories, is no doubt one of the most fascinating
studies in the world, but it is necessarily the task of a
very few.

This little book, then, not being designed to pour
information into any one, still less to help any one to
pass any examination, is not fortified with any tables,
summaries, or lists of dates. When I began it I had
foolish hopes that it might be a book which some boys
would take up for amusement ; but I soon discovered
that twenty-three years of teaching had made it impossible for me to do more than smear the powder
with a thin layer of jam. We cannot render our dreams
of the past (however convinced we may be of their
absolute truth) into an intelligible consecutive story.

I do not even con-
'he History School at
: Cambridge in recent
' English education.
ay be derived from
.inly derived from a
;ophy " which is (or
vast majority of the
ivenue to a degree.
y can only be given
of History (in the
:xample ") is indis-
hilosopher ; a wide
tivated scholar and
itter for a lifetime,
iich a young man's
the stimulation of
lled the scientific
ion of the date of
f the parchment,
he names of the
most fascinating
ily the task of a

esigned to pour
help any one to
with any tables,
began it I had
hich some boys
ioon discovered
d made it im-
ar the powder
der our dreams
iy be of their
tive story.

I have no pretensions to be a scholar in the '
document" sense, and I fear it will be very
those who are such scholars to find many mi
detail, as well as to question my conclusion:
only claim to have read the ordinary book:
have reflected a great deal about them.   But
an undergraduate at the feet of Bishop S'
was honoured by the friendship of Samuel
Gardiner ; I have listened to the veteran F
Berlin ; most fortunate of all do I count the c
I paid an accidental visit to Professor N
lecture-room at Cambridge, and straightwa;
view of the Middle Ages was opened to
I have tried to render into familiar langua
of the ideas which these great men and oth
taught me.

I am afraid it is very unfashionable
Mrs. Markham's spelling for Saxon names
cannot bring myself to call Edith Eadgyth, c
Ælgifu ; indeed I have a shrewd suspicion tl
ladies, if asked about the spelling of thei
would reply that " it depended on the t:
fancy of the speller." Still less can I brin
to call an abbot an abbat, as some precisians
these and for other old-fashioned prejudices l
ask pardon of my contemporaries.

A word is perhaps necessary about the i
village which I have tried to depict for my re
is not drawn from any existing model.   The
hundred of Rotherey in Sussex or elsewhere;
five Fyfields, but none in Sussex ; there is
Tubney, and that (happily) is in Berkshire.

My warmest thanks are due to friends v
assisted me with advice and criticism ; first, a
to my father ; then to Mr. A. L. Smith of Ballio

who was good enough to read the manuscript; to Mr. Moreton Macdonald of Largie, to Professor Lodge of Edinburgh, and to Mr. Edward Hilliard of the Inner Temple, who revised the proof-sheets; to Sir James Ramsay of Bamff, to Professor Dicey, and Professor Oman, who have been most kind in answering particular questions.

C. R. L. F.

OXFORD, 1904.

CONTENTS

CHAPTER I

BEFORE HISTORY AND BEFORE ROME

CHAPTER II

ROME

CHAPTER III

THE SAXONS COME AND SETTLE

CHAPTER IV

THE SAXONS DO AFTER THEIR KIND

CHAPTER V

THE DANES COME

CHAPTER VI

SHALL ENGLAND BE DANISH OR NORMAN?

CHAPTER VII

THE REIGN OF WILLIAM THE CONQUEROR

CHAPTER VIII

WILLIAM RUFUS AND HENRY I

CHAPTER IX

STEPHEN AND ANARCHY

CHAPTER X
HENRY II. AND LAW

CHAPTER XI
RICHARD I. AND JOHN

CHAPTER XII
HENRY III. AND THE GERM OF PARLIAMENT

CHAPTER XIII

EDWARD I

CHAPTER XIV

THE LEGAL AND SOCIAL SYSTEM OF THE
THIRTEENTH CENTURY

CHAPTER XV

EDWARD II AND THE BEGINNINGS OF DECADENCE

CHAPTER XVI

THE REIGN OF EDWARD III

CHAPTER XVII

RICHARD II. AND THE GERM OF PROTESTANTISM

CHAPTER XVIII

HENRY IV. AND HENRY V

CHAPTER XIX

HENRY VI. AND CIVIL WAR

CHAPTER XX

THE HOUSE OF YORK AND THE CLOSE OF THE MIDDLE AGES

CONTENTS

b

LIST OF MAPS

A HISTORY OF ENGLAND

FROM THE EARLIEST TIMES

CHAPTER I

BEFORE HISTORY AND BEFORE ROME

MANY thousands of years ago there were men of some sort in Britain. Geologists can tell you, very roughly, the dates of rocks and gravels; and, if you find tools or weapons of any kind deep underground, even in earth known to be 50,000 years old, you may be sure that men left them there.

If you find them in company with bones of animals now extinct, you may be sure that it was a very primitive man who left them there. Now, such tools, made of roughly split flint, are found in many places in our islands, and constantly in company with bones of extinct animals; in some few cases in company with the skulls of the men themselves.

These earliest known men are generally called "Old-Stone men," from the rough implements of flint which they used. And the earliest of them are called "River-drift men," from the gravel in the old river-beds in which these discoveries have been made. They existed before the "great ice age," which we may roughly guess to have begun 50,000 years ago; they lived through it somehow or other, though probably not in Britain, and they continued to exist after it, say

A

10,000 years ago. During that uncomfortable time the high ground of Europe gradually got covered with sheets of ice as thickly as Spitzbergen is now. As the ice-sheet advanced the wild animals gradually moved southwards; the primitive Briton, unhindered by English Channel or Mediterranean Sea, walked after the mammoth and the hippopotamus, shooting at them with wooden arrows tipped with flints. And the grizzly bear and the sabre-toothed tiger walked after the primitive Briton. When you come to think what a feat it is to shoot a mere common lion with a modern express rifle, you must allow that our first ancestors must have been extraordinarily fine all-round sportsmen, or they would have been eaten up very quickly. And gradually the ice-sheet melted back again towards the North Pole, and man and his animal attendants wandered back after it. It was probably at that time that the hippopotamus decided to stay in Africa, a climate more suited to his tranquil habits.

If you ask me what brought on the ice age and what took it away again, I can't tell you any more than I can tell you whence primitive man first reached Britain. I can only guess that the first cradle of the human race was somewhere in Central Asia, and that God has planted in man a divine instinct of going westward, an instinct which successive races of men obeyed :—

> "Westward the course of Empire takes its way;
>   The first four acts already past ;
> A fifth shall close the drama with the day ;
>   Time's noblest offspring is the last."

So wrote a poet who wished to pay a compliment to the United States of America. The first line is undoubtedly true.

Neither can I tell you what this River-drift man

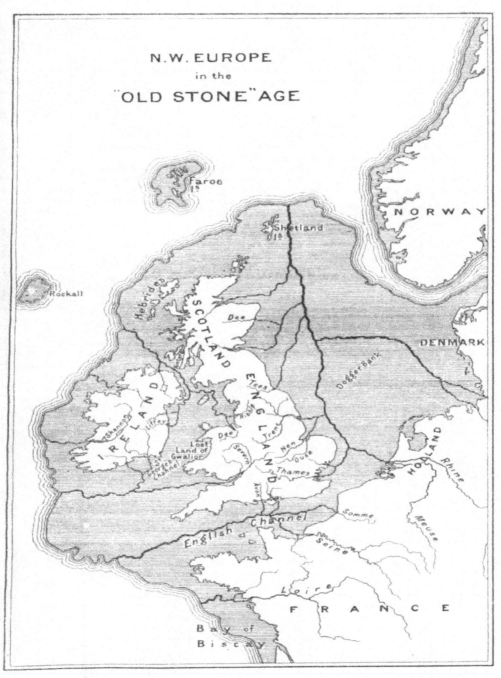

N.W. EUROPE
in the
"OLD STONE" AGE

To face page **2**

was like; possibly he was hairy all over; certainly he was very short in stature, seldom exceeding five feet. His senses of sight and hearing must have been much keener than our own, and his sense of smell amazing. There is little doubt that he would have known by his nose what animal was in front of him and how far off. It is doubtful if he even knew the use of fire, so he probably ate his meat raw.

Before the ice age, and perhaps through the greater part of it, the average level of our islands was some 600 feet higher than it is now. That does not sound very much, but it is enough to make dry land of the English and Irish Channels, the Baltic and the German Oceans. To make an Old-Stone-Age map for yourselves, take a pair of compasses and a map of Northern Europe. Put one point of the compasses on the north corner of Holland and the other point about 50 miles outside the north-west corner of Ireland, and then draw a half circle; it will touch the coast of Norway on the north, and the French coast in the middle of the Bay of Biscay on the south. All within that half circle was probably land 20,000 years ago. The Thames and all the eastern rivers of Britain ran into the Rhine, which ran across the bed of the present North Sea, and finally found salt water near the Faroe Islands. The Hampshire rivers, Test, Itchen, Avon, &c., ran into the Seine, and the Seine ran down the bed of the present English Channel, and emptied itself into the Atlantic 100 miles west of Plymouth; the Severn received the rivers of Southern Ireland and followed a course parallel to the Seine. The Cheshire Dee, the Lancashire Ribble, the Dublin Liffey, and the Scottish Clyde met in one stream, and rolled the bones of mastodons and mammoths between Kintyre and Ireland to some point beyond the Outer Hebrides. And all these rivers were much wider and their banks were much more marshy than at the present day. Whatever was not marsh was dense forest of oak or pine. The climate must have been much more rainy, and our first ancestors must have been at the mercy of the mosquitoes.

But the " River-drift men " have disappeared. They cannot be identified with any living race in the world. That is true ; and yet it would be rash to say that they were wholly exterminated by the next race of men who came to Britain. It is almost impossible to exterminate a wild people in a wild country. But perhaps I was wrong to call them our first ancestors, as there is no evidence that the next comers ever intermarried with them. The evidence is, in fact, against it. The further we go back, the more clear it is that one savage race utterly refuses to have anything to do with a race a little more savage than itself, except in the killing line ; *e.g.* the Red Indians simply killed Esquimaux whenever they met them, but shrank with horror from the idea of trafficking or marrying with them.

Anyhow, the River-drift men had to yield possession of Britain to a new and superior species of Old-Stone-man called the Cave-man. This new race can almost certainly be identified with the still living race of Esquimaux, shoved as they have been by successive waves of more civilised peoples into the remotest habitable corner of the globe, while the poor River-drift men have perhaps been shoved off it altogether.

The remains of the Cave-men have been discovered in the caves in which they undoubtedly lived and died. Their flint weapons are of superior make and much more polished than those of the River-drift men, but still are not worked up to a really sharp edge, and that is why we class them still as Old-Stone men. They also used needles and harpoons of bone. They could draw, and have left to us many specimens of drawings of animals upon bone and tusk. They knew the use of fire and cooked their meat, though they did not know pottery, and so, we presume, could not boil, but only roast it. They probably only lived in their caves in the winter, and encamped in the open in summer. When Cave-men broke up their summer encampment, they often found that a family of hyenas had been occupying their town-house during the summer. Such caves cannot have been very "sweet" places at the best of times ; but primitive man loved strong odours.

These men unquestionably wore skins, and knew how to sew them together, their thread being the sinews of animals. They hunted horses, bisons, bears, stags, and wild cattle, probably also seals and whales. They snared birds and they speared fish. They have left us drawings of all these forms of sport. They wore strings of animals' teeth as necklaces, both for ornaments and also for charms. Very probably they had the idea, common to many savages, that if you killed and ate a certain animal, his qualities passed into you ; thus to eat a bit of a lion would make you fierce, a bit of stag would make you swift of foot. If they had any vestiges of religion, it was probably in the form of magic ; that is to say, a belief that by acting or reciting certain charms, you could bend the powers of nature to your will ; by keeping a fire burning you could compel the sun to shine ; by pouring a bucket of water over a cliff you could compel the rain to fall ; and as the sun and rain generally did perform their normal functions, you felt sure that it was on account of your spells that they did so. But this is different from the next form of primitive religion, in which the savage seeks to propitiate unseen powers who govern the forces of nature with sacrifices and prayers. Probably the commonest form of early religion was some sort of identification of these powers of nature with deceased ancestors ; and a people who had grasped this idea would pay elaborate honours to its dead, and bury or burn them with great solemnity. But the Cave-man, like the modern Esquimaux, was particularly indifferent to the fate of his dead ; he seems generally to have presented them to the hyenas.

If we may judge by the Esquimaux, the Cave-man was also ignorant of the art of war, and as soon as a really war-like race arrived he was gradually driven to the inhos-pitable regions within the Arctic circle, where he has stayed ever since. But this process would take a long time, and he may often have lurked in inaccessible parts of our island and given rise to the legends of "fairies" and "picts" and "little men," of whom our peasants told tales far into the sixteenth century, some belief in whom perhaps lingers at the present day ; for all our civilisation is but skin-deep, and deeply rooted in the minds of the ignorant even to-day are beliefs in magic and witchcraft, though they are seldom seen on the surface.

We must see then who it was who came and hunted the Cave-man out of his cave. Perhaps before the next race came the great geographical changes had already taken place which had made Great Britain and Ireland into two islands separated from the continent of Europe. The islands of Wight and Anglesey may still have been part of England and Wales ; the Wash and the estuaries of the great rivers Thames, Severn, Mersey, Ribble, Forth, Clyde and Tay may still have been dry land. Tradition—probably true—still tells of the lost land of Gwalior, now covered by the sea of Cardigan Bay, and lost by the drunkenness of Prince Seithenyn ap Saidi, who was so busy in "drinking wine from cups of gold " that he neglected to repair the embankment which defended it.

I think we gained greatly by becoming an island or a group of islands ; for not only did we necessarily become a hardy race of sailors, but also none but the hardiest, most enterprising, and valiant races of the world could penetrate to us, and mix their blood with ours — the Saxon pirates, the Norse pirates, and that mighty race of Northerners who delighted to believe themselves Frenchmen and " came over with the Conqueror " in 1066. Moreover, we were distinctly. kept at a distance from the evil influences of continental luxury, and the pernicious habit of living in cities, which has told so heavily against the Latin races, and which will soon begin to tell heavily against ourselves, if we don't take care.

The race who turned out the Cave-men may be called the " New-Stone men " at first. I don't want to put back their coming much more than 5000 years, that is to say, about the time when real Historical Civilisation began in Egypt. Before we give them another name let us see how they differed from their predecessors. Well, they lived in houses of a sort, squared or rounded wig-wams, like beehives, made of logs or wicker-work, and sometimes in huts built out on piles into a shallow lake, no doubt for additional safety against enemies. Then they had domesticated animals ; dog, horse, goat, sheep, cow, pig ; dog probably first of all, for your early hunter would soon discover the dog as his rival in the chase, and would perhaps bring home the puppies to his children as playthings, and these would grow up as dependents and assistants in hunting. I don't mean that the New-Stone man found these animals in Britain and tamed them ; no, he brought them with him in his log canoe ready tamed, wherever he came from. You must accustom yourself to think of very considerable numbers of men migrating in large bands to these islands, for the Channel is a stormy sea, and great numbers of them must have perished on the passage.

To continue: not only had they tamed animals, but they had discovered the use of corn to make bread with, flax to weave into linen, and earthen pots to hold water. They dug deep in the earth to get the proper kind of flints to make their polished axes, saws, and spears, so deep that one might almost speak of "flint mines," and they knew how to give these stone implements a really sharp edge : and with these they, first of men, began to clear the forests of Britain. It is probable that they were the first constructors of those great earthworks, wrongly called "Roman camps," which are so frequent on the hilltops of Southern and Eastern Britain. Such would unquestionably have been necessary not only against a rally of despairing Cave-men, but against each other. For, though originally, no doubt, of one stock, the New-Stone men would be divided into warring tribes long before their migrations to Britain. As for the government of these tribes, we can only guess that war begets kingship of some sort, if only for a time, and so they were probably governed by chiefs or kings. But it is also very probable that a strong religious element entered into all early kingship, and the king would be a sacred man or priest as well as an earthly sovereign. The very elaborate burial customs of this people point to a really religious idea. The great men were buried on the tops of hills in walled stone chambers—now called " barrows "—with trees planted over the grave ; tools and food would be buried with them for their use in the next world. And though such a man undoubtedly went to some other world, yet his spirit stayed and guarded the hilltop for the benefit of his tribe, if proper worship were paid to him and proper rites performed. Among these rites, bloody and even human sacrifices are probable, though not certain ; slaves and wives might be slain at his grave, not only for his future use, but to appease his spirit. In due time such a hero would become a god, and would be identified with some special object of nature which it would be his duty to keep in working order, as the sun, a well or fountain, a sacred tree, the growing corn. I think it is to these New-Stone men that we owe much of our " folk-lore."

We must now try to consider the questions whether (1) the New-Stone men are represented in Great Britain or Ireland by any living descendants to-day, and (2) whether they are of kin to any existing races on the Continent. Both may be fairly answered "yes." To the New-Stone men succeeded the " Bronze men," that is, men using bronze weapons, and these we know for certain to have been of Celtic race ; and we also know that the Celt elsewhere in Europe not only pushed out and supplanted, but also intermarried with and enslaved a small, dark-haired, wiry race, who are identified with the Finns of Finland or the Basques of Northern Spain of the present day. Now, the Celt at his first coming was tall and fair and blue-eyed ; and yet in many out-of-the-way corners of our islands we may see a people much more like Basques and Finns. This is especially the case in Southern Wales and South-Western Ireland. The name now generally given to the dark, small race is " Iberian," and that, I take it, is the name by which we ought in future to call the New-Stone men. We may, moreover, fairly guess them to have been, before the close of the New-Stone age, not altogether averse from trading and intercourse with races more civilised than themselves. The Celts would not very long have pushed the Iberians out of Gaul (modern France) and

Iberia (modern Spain) before turning their attention to the white cliffs of Dover—at first perhaps with the idea of trade in the skins of animals, but soon with the idea of conquest. But of conquest and enslavement this time, not of extermination. It must have begun to dawn upon such comparatively civilised people as the Celts, even in 1000 B.C. (for I do not wish to put the coming of the Celts any earlier than that) that an enemy was much more useful as a live slave than as a nasty dead body. The gods, it is true, might be angry if you did not exterminate him, but after all the gods could be appeased by the sacrifice, say, of every tenth Iberian. And so slavery, which sounds so horrible to us, was originally a merciful institution.

The Celt had no difficulty in his triumph over the Iberian in Britain, for he brought with him a highly superior method of killing his enemies, namely, the bronze weapon. Now bronze is a compound of two metals, tin and copper, and one of them (tin) a rare metal, which is found abundantly in parts of Cornwall, and it may have been the knowledge of this that first attracted the Celts to Britain. I prefer, however, to believe that British tin was not worked till some long time after the coming of the Celts, and that they obtained their bronze elsewhere. But, anyway, bronze at once prevailed over stone, and the Iberians were enslaved. Flint weapons, no doubt, continued to be used by the humbler classes both in hunting and warfare long after the introduction of "expensive" bronze ; how late they may have continued we can hardly say, but there is some evidence of them as late as the Norman Conquest.

Look back for a moment, and see that each succeeding improvement in weapons leads to a new civilisation and the coming of a new race to Britain. Each "age" is infinitely shorter and lives faster than the one before it. We gave the Old-Stone men something less than 50,000 years; we gave the New-Stone men something less than 5000. We shall have to give the bronze age not much more than 800, when it will give way to the iron age, even before the Romans come to teach the Celts their business. And as for the iron age, we are still going on with that, as no one has yet discovered a better metal for killing enemies than steel, which is only tempered iron. Perhaps the iron age will give way at some discovery which will enable us to soar through space ; and we shall then undertake expeditions to distant planets and subdue their inhabitants with new weapons. At any rate, I am sure we shall call it "spreading the blessing of earthly civilisation to those barbarous planets." The Celt, no doubt, told a similar tale to the Iberian when he enslaved him.

The Celt seems always to have been quite ready to mingle with inferior races ; it is only with superior races that he entertains, even occasionally at the present day, an objection to amalgamate : and yet this cannot be attributed to his humility, which is by no means his strong point. And so he undoubtedly absorbed a great deal of Iberian blood, and largely lost his fair hair and his blue eyes. No very great improvement in the arts of peace can be definitely assigned to the Celt as against the Iberian, if we except the art of weaving woollen cloth. His mining industry, which in the last 300 years before Christ was great, he probably learned from Carthaginian or Greek traders ; but, when once taught, the Celts, or their Iberian slaves, became great miners, and dug not only tin and copper, but gold, silver, lead, and finally iron, out of the hills of Britain. It is strange that iron, the most useful of all metals, was the last to be discovered.

The gods of the Celts unquestionably despised the

gods of the Iberians, and called themselves by different and more civilised names, and were worshipped with a more elaborate but perhaps not a less bloody set of rites ; but, after all, I doubt if they were more than deified ancestors and deified objects of nature.   In their honour, however, were reared, some time during the bronze age, the two great Wiltshire monuments to which the Saxons gave the very Saxon names of Stonehenge and Avebury.

Of the former at least enough remains to make us wonder at the people who could have raised these enormous blocks of stone (some of them brought from a great distance) without any machinery but human hands and ropes.   This great temple, whose principal entrance exactly faces the rising sun on midsummer day, was probably devoted to sun-worship, and it is certain that the builders of it had grasped the rudiments of the measurement of time by the sun.   I know few things in Europe that give one so much the impression of the lapse of time and the darkness of early history as a visit to Stonehenge.   But the ritual of the Celtic religion has only been made more mysterious for us by the insistence of the Roman writers and all early historians of England upon the great power of the Druids, the mysterious priests of the Britons, who used to wear white robes and cut mistletoe with golden sickles and speak the oracles of the gods.   Why they cut the mistletoe, and why with a golden sickle, we don't know ; in fact, the truth is that we know nothing at all about the Druids.

A more interesting point is the date of the first contact of Britain with a really civilised and trading race. Tradition is powerfully in favour of the ships of the great merchant cities of Tyre, and of Carthage the colony of Tyre.   These are said to have come to Britain to get tin, and the " tin islands " have sometimes been identified with the Scilly Islands and with Cornwall. Their coming, if ever they did come, may have been as early as 500 B.C., viz. just about the time of the struggle of Greece with the Persians. Very likely these people bought our raw tin with manufactured bronze implements, just as we buy raw Australian wool with large and hideous consignments of ready-made clothing. The voyages of Greek traders to Britain a century and a half later are quite certain, and even that is 200 years before the Roman conquest of Greece. Marseilles was a Greek colony as early as 500 B.C., and there was a regular trade route for pack-horses across Gaul to the shores of the English Channel. These Greek traders were the earliest people to bring coined money to our island, and the influence of coined money as a medium of civilisation can hardly be overrated. Semi-barbarous nations begin to use the coins of their civilised neighbours long before they have any of their own. Next they begin (very badly) to imitate them. Let me try and picture a scene from British history at this time.

You are, we will imagine, a rich Celtic patriarch (I might as well say " Briton " at once, as it is to the Celtic people that the term is first applied by historians), living on the shores of Southampton Water in a beautiful wattled wigwam, surrounded, like Jacob in the Bible, by flocks and herds, and several hundreds of Iberian slaves are tilling the soil for you. Enter to you a Greek ship rowed by oars or driven by sails up the Solent. Your first idea is, of course, to murder the Greek crew as they land, or to seize them to sacrifice to your gods. But upon closer inspection you discover that the Greeks are very completely armed, that they draw up in close formation on the beach, and that they have not the least intention of letting themselves be sacrificed by your half-naked slaves. Your tame Druid comes out of his hut and expostulates with you in the name of his gods; but, unless you can summon a large body of neighbours from many miles away, you are as helpless as the king of a South Sea Island before a company of British soldiers armed with Lee-Metford rifles. For the same reason, to plunder this intrusive Greek is equally out of the question. But your Greek captain is what is nowadays called "a man of the world," and you would very much like to be thought one too, though you are not. So you and the Greek captain decide to try and cheat each other at a bargain instead of coming to blows : the Greek unquestionably gets the better of you at this game, but both of you benefit in some degree. In part payment for your hides, furs, tin, and a few superfluous slaves— "handy fellows, those of yours," he says—he will leave you a lot of glass beads, some highly superior bronze weapons (specially made at Marseilles for the British market), and a few gold or silver coins which he solemnly, and truly, assures you will buy almost anything you want from the next Greek trader who comes that way.

If we were to shift this scene a couple of thousand years on, and for the Greek merchant imagine a British backwoodsman with pack on back and musket on shoulder, and for the British patriarch in skins and woad a Red Indian Sachem at the back of the Alleghany mountains, we should find much the same sort of feelings on both sides and much the same sort of bargain concluded. That is how the "blessings of civilisation" are spread.

Now we have an actual record of one such Greek trader named Pytheas, who in the year 350 B.C. sailed all the way from Marseilles through the Straits of Gibraltar to Britain, Denmark, and Norway, and who spent, both going and returning, a considerable time in Britain.

I think we may assume that it was through some

such channel as this that a knowledge of the use of iron first penetrated to our island.   Iron was still a rarity in Greece in Homer's time (say 800 B.C.), but was in full use in Britain by the time of Cæsar's invasion (55 B.C.). When iron was once discovered its cheapness would lead to the use of defensive armour in war, iron weapons would supplant bronze, and the war chariots of the Britons would be armed with iron scythes sticking out from their sides and have iron tyres on their wheels.

The divisions of the Celtic race were probably tribal, as those of the Iberian race were ; wars between the tribes would be the normal occupation of the people ; successive migrations from Gaul of fresh Celtic tribes, each one rather more civilised than the last, would always be going on ; and so the earliest Celtic settlers would gradually be pushed back to the remoter corners of the island.   It is, therefore, possible that the " Picts," of whom one hears so much in the fourth and fifth centuries A.D., were earlier Celts rather than Iberians or Cave-men ; and it is certain that Ireland was inhabited by a very much earlier race of Celts than those of Southern Britain.   There were also alliances and wars between the latest Celtic settlers in Southern Britain and their kinsmen in Gaul, which were, after all, only (undress) rehearsals of the wars of George II. and Louis XV.

CHAPTER II

ROME

TRIBAL government and war, as we have seen, beget kingship, and one is always reading of British "kings." Shakespeare has laid the scene of one of his last and loveliest plays in the reign of one of these kings, called Cymbeline. But I will not ask you to remember even the romanised version of their barbarous names. They lived, not in cities in the Roman sense of the word, but in wattled stockaded villages, and these were chiefly on the lower slopes of the downs, where the clearing of the forests would be easier than on the swampy low lands. A Briton was richer or poorer, as all early peoples are, according as he had more food-bearing land to support him and his family with corn and cattle; all intertribal wars and all invasions are mainly undertaken with a view to getting more food-bearing lands, so that one may eat and drink better :—

> " The mountain sheep are sweeter,
> But the valley sheep are fatter,
> We therefore deemed it meeter
> To carry off the latter."

That is, after all, the " quintessence of all early war-songs," and the motive of all early wars.

Yes, even of Cæsar's invasion of Britain. Cæsar was busy adding the food-bearing lands of Gaul to the Roman Empire, and in the course of that troublesome job he discovered that the Gauls were being assisted by their British kinsmen. So one fine day he made a raid into Britain, landing somewhere at the corner of Romney Marsh, 54 B.C., but without much effect; and in the next year, with a much larger force, he came again, and drove a confederation of British tribes, which had been formed to oppose him, across the Thames, which he crossed somewhere near Shepperton. He burned a stockaded camp of their "king," whom he called Cassivelaunus. He spent about two months on the island, and received various deceptive promises of submission from native chiefs. He was not plagued with that curse of modern warfare, the special correspondent, so he wrote his own account of the campaign, and a very sensible one it is. He leaves us under the impression that the Britons were a numerous and warlike people, who would always rally again behind the shelter of the dense forests when beaten in the field. But until Gaul was completely made into a Roman province any real Roman "conquest" of Britain was pretty hopeless. Yet from the date of his invasion some barbarous copy of Roman civilisation probably began to spread over Southern and Eastern Britain. "British kings" visited Rome to implore help against other "British kings," much in the same way as one Indian rajah used to travel to Calcutta to ask Warren Hastings to help him against another rajah. Roman coins and Roman traders found their way more freely; more clearings of forests; more corn growing; more wearing of clothes and less painting of faces would be the result : we already read of large sporting dogs being among the exports of Britain. A whole Gaulish tribe, the "Belgae," perhaps migrated to Britain at this time, and founded something like a "city" at Venta Belgarum (Winchester), which afterwards became the first real capital of an united England.

At last, in A.D. 43, the forces of the Roman Empire were bent in earnest to the subjugation of this island.

B

The fat Emperor Claudius came in person; a fort-night of our climate was enough for him, and, as his large army under his able general Aulus Plautius had easily scattered the Britons and planted a Roman city at Colchester, His Majesty was enabled to go home and enjoy a "triumph," and be called Claudius Britannicus. From that time the conquest of Britain proceeded steadily, the future Emperor Vespasian signalising him-self greatly in the process. But this conquest must have been a terrible task, for the forests were an even greater enemy than the Britons who hid in them.

The only approach to the Thames would be by the southern shore of its estuary, for the vast forest of Sussex and Surrey extended almost to London and far into Kent on the east, while on the west it joined trees with the forest of Hampshire, and this again extended far into Dorsetshire. North of the Thames the wood, of which Epping is the sole remnant, covered half Hertford-shire and all Essex except the marshes. Warwickshire, Northampton- and Nottingham-shires, Derbyshire, and the West Riding of Yorkshire were all forest; and so the only routes would be by the river valleys. Eventu-ally the Romans did penetrate and drive roads through the greater part of these forests; but not through the heart of the "Andreds-Weald" (the Sussex forest), though they seem to have set up iron-works in some of its clearings.

Before A.D. 60, we hear of London, Gloucester, Chester, Exeter, Colchester, and Leicester as Roman "cities," i.e. probably at first stockaded forts, but even-tually to be surrounded with walls of stone and Roman brick; the first five are natural places to find forts, for they are on the estuaries of great tidal rivers, but the last is curious, for, though it is near, it is not exactly at the meeting-place of the two greatest Roman roads, Watling Street and the Fosse Way.

After a great revolt of Eastern Britain under "Queen" Boadicea, which was put down by the Roman general Suetonius with great cruelty, we hear of Doncaster, Manchester, York, Lincoln, and Caerleon-on-Usk (in South Wales). Beyond the line of the great roads, however, the barbarism of the Celtic race seems to have been little affected, at least in the first two centuries after the Roman conquest, although the great and good governor Agricola (A.D. 78–85), father-in-law of the Roman historian Tacitus, did his best to foster the arts of peace, and treated the conquered people with careful kindness wherever they would submit to the arms of Rome. But he had plenty of fighting to do as well. After completing the conquest of North Wales, Agricola resolved to attempt the reduction of the whole island.

And for this purpose he made towards the end of his government two expeditions into " Scotland." There are but three practicable routes for this purpose ; on the West by the Cumberland mountains and the valleys of the Eden, Esk, and Clyde, and even there two passes of upwards of 1000 feet have to be crossed, as the North-Western and Caledonian Railways know to their cost ; by the valley of the North Tyne and the Reed and by Carter Fell to the Teviot and Tweed ; and by the East coast, the easiest but longest of all. Agricola went on two occasions by the two first of these routes, and on each occasion he was wise enough to take his fleet alongside of him, to carry supplies and munitions of war, without which he would have been starved and powerless. (Note that Edward I. did the same in his great campaign against Scotland, and would have had no success at all without it.) Agricola's fleet even sailed round the island and discovered the Orkneys. Meanwhile the general himself penetrated beyond the Tay, leaving traces of his march in a series of little forts, and somewhere in Forfarshire he inflicted a terrible defeat on the "Caledonians," whoever they may have been. Carlisle seems to have been the only great Roman city that he added to the list; but he undoubtedly suggested the first building of the celebrated " Roman Wall " or Walls.

Now, you must take the building of these walls as a confession of failure by the Conquerors of the World. The first wall ran, roughly speaking, from Newcastle to Carlisle, *i.e.* from Tyne to Solway, and the second from Forth to Clyde. The execution of Agricola's design was carried out by the Emperor Hadrian (A.D. 120) and his successors. These walls were designed to keep out the barbarous Caledonians, Picts, or whatever you like to call them. But they could effect this only if they were garrisoned by an army much larger than the total Roman force in Britain. And, after all, it would have been a wiser policy not to leave the barbarians of the North unsubdued; but to drive roads and build cities, and to civilise the people right up to the Pentland Firth. But this was too much for the Roman Empire, the already weary Titan, with all the load of all the civilised world upon its shoulders. The walls, no doubt, impressed the barbarians with a sense of the majesty of the power which could carry out such colossal work : it was, no doubt, long before they discovered that the walls were a feeble protection and insufficiently garrisoned, that York, the base of troops and support, was too far off for the outposts on the walls to resist a sudden attack, &c. But they did find it out in time, and then the walls were useless.

There is little trace left of the Northern wall, except in the imagination of venerable antiquaries; but the

Southern one, which was over seventy miles long, consisted not only of a stone rampart twenty feet high, with watch-towers every quarter of a mile, but of a triple earthwork and deep ditch parallel to it. The foundations of all this can still be traced in many places, and much of the wall was still remaining when Field-Marshal Wade in 1746 pulled it down in order to build the modern military road from Newcastle to Carlisle. Once, but once only, after Agricola's time, the Roman arms appeared beyond the Northern wall; that was in 208-9, when the brave old Emperor Severus had himself carried in a litter, at the age of seventy-three, at the head of his legions, on a punitive expedition against the Caledonians, as far as the shores of the Moray Firth, a little north of Aberdeen. Much more frequently these same Caledonians raided the land between the walls for a winter's amusement.

Southern Britain, however, was probably a happy and well-governed province in the second century of our era. It was the age of the "Antonines," the golden age of the Roman Empire, when all the provinces were decently governed. The details of the journeys of two of the Emperors, Hadrian himself and Caracalla, at a distance of about a hundred years apart, have been preserved, and are our chief authority for the topography of Roman Britain. Before the middle of the third century the aspect of the scene had changed. The Empire was too unwieldy to be governed by one man, and we begin to hear of "associated Cæsars." Britain gets included in one "Government" with Gaul and Spain (sufficiently large, you would say, even for an "associated Cæsar!"). And then rebel Cæsars start up everywhere, and get murdered as quickly as they start up; Britain was particularly fertile in such gentlemen. A successful general proclaims himself "Emperor" at

York. What is his first idea ? To get to Rome and repeat the process there ; but he cannot go alone, and so he has to take a legion or legions with him, and so weaken the defences of Britain.

And then the Picts hear of this ; and the Celtic Scots (who live in Ireland till the fifth or sixth century) ; and the terrible Saxons and Frisians from the shore of North Germany : pirates all of them, whether by land or sea. No combined attack is at first made, but you can fancy the distracted condition of a Roman general at York who hears on the 1st September of a landing of Saxons on the coast of Suffolk, and before he has started to chastise them, hears that the Scots have sailed up the Dee and are threatening Chester ; while before the month is out the Picts are over the Southern wall, full steam ahead for York itself.

Valiant efforts at defence are continually made ; one hears of a special officer, called " Count of the Saxon Shore," at the close of the third century ; he is evidently meant to defend our south-east coast. A whole row of Roman fortresses is built along the coast from the Wash to Southampton Water : the mighty Roman walls of York and Lincoln and Colchester are rebuilt ; but it is all in vain. Not Constantius, though he died at York, not Constantine the Great, though he was born and proclaimed Emperor there (306) and became a Christian (325), could avert the fate of Britain or of Rome. Theodosius, called " the Great," had some temporary successes against the Picts in 368, and Stilicho, a great Roman general, drove back the Picts for the last time early in the long reign of Honorius. The last Roman legions were withdrawn by a rebel called Constantine in 407. He came to a bad end, but Honorius refused at the intercession of the defenceless Britons to send them back (410).

The long 360 years of Roman rule had come to an end. Let us pause for a moment and see what the principal effects of this rule had been ; and I would have you note several things.

(1) That we to-day all are, in the best sense of the word, children of the Roman Empire. Rome left few traces on our language, none on our early laws, little on our blood ; but in common with all the nations that she did, and with many that she did not conquer, but only awed from afar both in space and time, we are her children nevertheless. Wherever a civilised language is spoken, men think in the forms and speak the grammar, reason on the principles, and are judged and governed according to the standards of law and good government which have descended to them, either directly from Imperial Rome or from Greece through Roman channels. There were violent interruptions to all this ; the whole early Middle Ages were a violent interruption ; but Rome came to her own at last, and holds us in her mighty grip still.

(2) It is a lesser fact, but still an important one, that the Romans unquestionably started Britain upon a path of material civilisation, which even the ferocious Saxons only succeeded in obliterating for a short time, and of which they and all succeeding Englishmen were and are the ultimate heirs. For the Romans first seriously began to clear the forests, "to drive their roads a nation's length," and to bridge the rivers : and their roads and their bridges were so well built that they largely satisfied the needs of England down to the sixteenth century We, in this over-populated, over-civilised island, have little conception, especially those of us who have the misfortune to live in towns, of the civilising power of roads and bridges. If I were a heathen Roman emperor

I would build the finest temple in the world to the Goddess of Roads and Bridges.

(3) We owe the first introduction of Christianity, if not to the Roman Empire, at least to the protection accorded by Rome to all her citizens, and it is no small claim to honour that the first Christian Emperor, Constantine, was born at York. It is true that we know little of the Romano-British Church, which was entirely destroyed by the heathen Saxons, and true also that the most flourishing offshoot of that Church undoubtedly existed in Ireland, where the Roman arms never penetrated. "Official Christianity," that is to say, religion as a part of the state machinery, seems to have been accepted by the Britons rather as the "proper thing to accept" than with any great enthusiasm; and indeed the whole West-Roman world was in the fourth century in a sort of tolerant, well-bred attitude towards all religions, in which "no one was very sure that anything was true," but there "might be a good deal of truth in all religions." That is a very different condition from the confidence in the gods of Rome which gave the early Roman soldiers the mastery of the world, and the confidence in the Lord of Hosts which gave Cromwell's soldiers the victories of Naseby and Dunbar.

(4) For all good government the governed must pay. We Englishmen are very slow to realise this; and peaceable merchants. will often grumble at, and misguided men in Parliament get up and denounce, the taxation necessary to build the battleships that defend their hearths and homes. The Romans undoubtedly established a severe system of taxation, and have, of course, been called grasping and extortionate wretches because they did so. But it was probably better for the Britons to be taxed by the Romans than to have their houses sacked by the Picts or the Frisian pirates.

(5) The Romans undoubtedly worked up the natural and mineral resources of the island, and improved them by the introduction of foreign trees, crops and animals (including that doubtful blessing the rabbit). But at the same time they systematised and extended slavery, which it taxed all the efforts of the Church in after ages to eradicate. And although one ought not to think of slavery in the ancient world as comparable to the savage system introduced into America in the sixteenth century, yet slavery in its mildest form not only is absolutely contrary to the principles of humanity and Christianity, but does not pay in the long run as a means of cultivating the soil.

(6) Finally, we may conclude that the Roman conquest was incomplete, just as the successive conquests of Ireland by England have been incomplete. It never touched Ireland, never affected Northern Scotland, and never seriously affected Southern Scotland ; and it was undertaken too late in the history of Rome to admit of that part of Britain, which was conquered and occupied, being ever thoroughly organised. Not *enough* forests were cleared, not *enough* roads and bridges built. The Briton of the South accepted Roman customs very willingly, that is so say, he bathed, he learnt Latin, he wore a toga, and he served (somewhat unwillingly) in the Roman army ; but when left to himself he relapsed either into effeminacy or barbarism. The system of the Empire had one great fault, a fault which the British Empire of to-day is trying to avoid : the Romans employed legions raised from British soldiers anywhere but in Britain : the wall of Hadrian was garrisoned by Spaniards or Greeks, or any troops but British ; and so, when the crash came, the warlike strength of the British race had been drawn away elsewhere. If we now employed Sikhs to garrison South Africa, and Boers to

hold Canada, and Haussas from the Gold Coast to garrison India, we might perhaps have a larger, and, on the face of it, a more satisfactory army than we have; but we should never accustom the outlying territories of our Empire to defend themselves for their own sakes as well as for ours.   We have got to show the Sikhs and Ghoorkas—and we do successfully show them—that it is as much their interest as ours to keep India from the hug of the Russian Bear.   But we only show it them by treating them with a proud confidence in their loyalty.

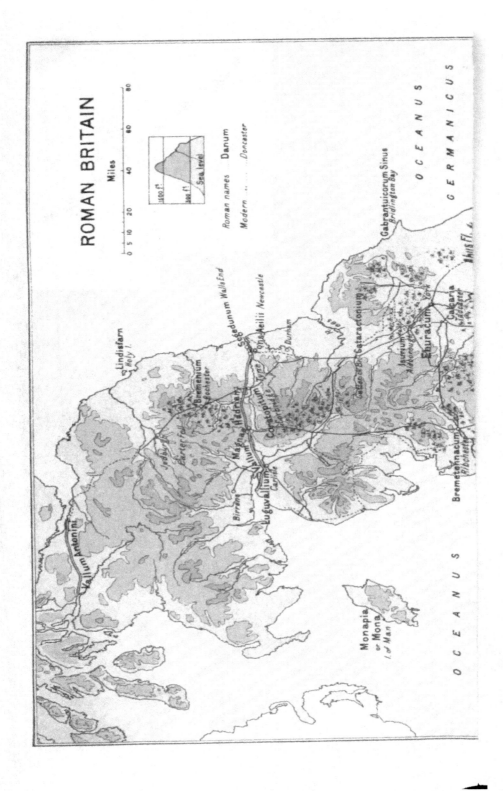

ROMAN BRITAIN

Miles
0 5 10   20   40   60   80

Roman names .... Danum
Modern .. ..Doncaster

1000 ft.
500 ft.
Sea level

O C E A N U S   G E R M A N I C U S

O C E A N U S

CHAPTER III

THE SAXONS COME AND SETTLE

ONE would very much like to think that there was historical ground for believing in the beautiful story of King Arthur and the Knights of the Round Table. In the fifteenth century it was made the subject of the noblest prose poem in the English language, Sir Thomas Malory's "Morte d'Arthur"; and in the nineteenth it gave birth to Tennyson's magnificent "Idylls of the King." The idea of a Christian prince taking up the defence of Britain against the heathen Saxons, and refusing to render obedience to Rome, should indeed be dear to all who love their island ; but unfortunately we must admit that King Arthur and his knights never had any existence outside the limits of romance. Some germ of the story can be traced as early as the ninth century, but it was first actually told by Geoffrey of Monmouth, a famous and amusing story-teller of the twelfth. The fifth and sixth centuries, during which alone Arthur could have played the part ascribed to him, were among the most wretched in our history. The British princes, who squabbled among themselves after the legions were withdrawn, did, no doubt, often fight bravely against the invaders ; and Britain, on the whole, offered a far better resistance to the Saxons than Roman Gaul offered to the Franks, or Roman Spain to the Visigoths. But that was just because she was less civilised than Gaul or Spain ; the forests hindered the Saxons far more than they had hindered the Romans, because these new barbarians had no Roman organisation to help them to conquer; and so it took them one hundred and fifty years to conquer even the eastern half of Britain from the Forth to Dorset-shire.

It is to these interesting pirates that we must now turn our attention. For one hundred and fifty years before the traditional date of the landing of Hengist and Horsa in the Isle of Thanet, the tribes of North-western Germany had been raiding our shores. They came of the only race of Central Europe which had never bowed the knee to Rome, the German—the so-called "Low German," because if you look at a raised map of Europe, you will see that Germany slopes steadily down from the Alps to the Baltic and the North Sea; and these fellows came from that corner of Low Germany which almost touches on the Scandinavian country of Denmark. Probably there was at this time little difference in speech, or religion, or manners between them and those "Danes" and Norsemen who after-wards proved such a terrible scourge to Saxon England.

Rome had left Germany severely alone since A.D. 9, when the half-mythical hero Arminius had swallowed up the Roman General Varus and his legions, in the most disastrous check to the Roman arms since Cannae. It has been conjectured that Tacitus saw something of the tribes of Western-central Germany in his youth, for he wrote a book, called "Germania," in which he magnified their virtues and strength; and in it he seems to speak from personal experience of them. The North German pirates who came to Britain may have differed very largely from Tacitus' friends of three hundred years before; but, after all, they were of a kindred stock, and many of their laws and habits, after they settled in England, can be paralleled with institutions described by Tacitus.

Anyhow, the " Jutes, Angles, and Saxons," as their earliest chroniclers call them, began to come in war bands for mere plunder, on long galleys such as you may still see in the Norwegian fjords, with one tall oblong sail, but also with powerful crews of oarsmen.   And when they saw what a rich and defenceless land Britain was, they sent for reinforcements, and also for their wives, children, and cattle, and a migration arose out of a conquest.   This, too, was no doubt part of that strange, divine impulse of peoples towards the setting sun of which I have spoken above.   The new-comers were of very different race from the Celts, with all the vices and virtues of far more primitive barbarians.   For instance, they preferred killing to enslaving their enemies, and they would not intermarry with them at all.   That is why there is now so little Celtic or Iberian blood left in Eastern England.   For the first hundred and fifty years the war really was a war of extermination, to which the Christianity of the Britons and the savage heathenism of the Saxons only added fuel.   The Celt was much cleverer, much more adaptable ; it would have taken him far less time to learn the lesson that slavery was more profitable than extermination.   Your Saxon was much more stupid ; he feared or hated what he did not understand, and hence he destroyed it if he could. Roman city or dense forest were alike dangerous places to him, probably the abode of demons : give him a nice flat river-bank—the marshier the better—and he was happy, because it was like the cheerless country he had left behind him.   He was also horribly cruel, though human sacrifice does not seem to have been part of his creed.   He was greatly addicted to strong drink and to gambling, both of which vices he in some degree bequeathed to his descendants.

But, on the other hand, he was supremely brave, not

with the fiery red-hot valour of the Celt, which was apt to evaporate, but with the cool, dogged valour which thoroughly realises danger, but thoroughly despises it. He had a high sense of honour and faith, a great reverence for women, and great domestic purity of life. War and agriculture were to him the only occupations worthy of a freeman; and he perhaps of all men came nearest to what the poet Horace fondly believed his own Roman ancestors to have been—

> " Rusticorum mascula militum
> Proles, Sabellis docta ligonibus
> Versare glebas."

To these two occupations of war and agriculture all the simple, deeply-rooted institutions of his race had been directed. And we must now try to understand some of these institutions, because they are directly the parents of much of our strange system of self-government at the present day.

I may appear to be putting the cart before the horse if I try to describe the institutions before writing the history of the conquest; but I think it is better to do so.

Now, by "institutions" we mean those practices and customs by which men live and feed themselves, and also by which they govern themselves or are governed. Our idea of a government is one which has four main duties to perform—(1) To see to the defence of the country; (2) to keep order in the country; (3) to judge or arbitrate between its subjects; (4) to legislate. Very slowly did these "functions of government" develop in Saxon England, yet the germ of them all was there, and was much mixed up with the customs by which men lived and fed themselves. Let us take a concrete instance, and see in what form the settlement was made, what duties devolved on the settlers, and how they performed them.

You must try to think of small bodies of pirates, bound together by some loose tie of *kindred ;* say, some five hundred adult warriors who land on the coast of Sussex in some twenty-five ships. They have their wives and growing children with them ; the grandfathers and babies are left behind. That will roughly give you some two thousand five hundred persons. They have elected a chief for the raid before they left Germany, a man well proved in war. He is for the time merely a leader, and the warriors under him hunt the Britons up and down that narrow strip of Sussex that lies between the downs and the sea, and finally drive the remnant over the downs into the great forest beyond. Having done that, they settle down to their other normal business, agriculture. One must, however, imagine some allotment of the newly-won land among these warriors. It need not be, nay, it is sure not to be, an equal allotment. Some have proved themselves braver than others ; some are of nobler blood within the kindred than others : the shares of these will be larger. The chief will be raised on a shield, and proclaimed a " king" (which word means " head of the kindred "). Such allotment of land, such proclamation of royalty, will be done in assembly of all the freemen-warriors of the tribe, and such " government " as there is is at first vested in that assembly. Every one ought to come to it, and be able to speak in it. The new king is only a sort of president of it. Well, this is self-government, is it not, like our modern parliamentary system? with the sole difference that, as it would be inconvenient for forty million of people to meet all at once, we now elect persons to represent us in a similar assembly.

But from the very first the newly settled tribe seems to have paid little attention to these parliamentary duties. It has to live, and can only do that by unremitting agricultural labour.   Five hundred families may well people fifty villages, and will proceed to do so according to the allotment of land made in the assembly.   The villages will be far enough apart to allow of plenty of land for each family and plenty of room for expansion as population increases.   That is, there will be great tracts of waste land between each village.   You will reckon roughly that each household should have as much land as it can plough, sow, and reap in the year, say 120 acres, which was called a " hide " ; an acre being roughly a day's ploughing.   But these acres were not all allotted to you in one piece.   The lands round the village—let us call it Tubney—are marked off into three enormous open fields, and you will have a greater or lesser number of strips allotted to you in each of these fields.   Oxen are used in ploughing, and it takes a team of eight to draw the very primitive plough.   It is not likely that any of the villagers has as many as eight oxen himself —more likely two or three is the average—and the ploughing will, therefore, be done by a team contributed by several villagers : the convenience of the system of strips, afterwards absurd, thus becomes manifest, the village plough can readily pass from the strip of Higg, the son of Snell, to the strip of Pigg, the son of Troll, no fence dividing their shares in the open fields. If in time either Higg or Pigg becomes rich enough to keep a team of his own, he will probably prefer to plough all by himself ; but until he is so he must either help his neighbours or his lands will lie unploughed. There is no compulsion on him except that of long descended custom, which no primitive man willingly defies.   The custom, further, is that one of these great open fields in turn is left to lie fallow every year ; on one of them wheat or rye or oats is grown for food, and on the third barley for drink.   It sounds a great deal to devote to drink, but I am afraid our ancestors were men who loved to drink themselves very drunk with strong beer. Sheep, beasts, pigs, and horses (there are few of these last) are allowed to graze on the waste outside the open fields, on the fallow field, and on all the fields after harvest. And a pretty poor living they must have picked up, and thin, raw-boned creatures they must have been. Pretty quarrels, too, there must have been between Higg, Pigg, and their kind as to the right time to begin ploughing, &c.

Now we must consider how much time would be left to these gentlemen for fulfilling the other "duties of a citizen," namely, serving the tribe in war and doing justice to each other in the assembly of the tribe or elsewhere. Well, I say that from their very first settle-ment at Tubney these duties must have become a supreme bore. To go to the tribal assembly at Selsey, perhaps fifty miles distant, to discuss the "state of the nation," to be sent (because it was a tribal duty) on a distant foray into the county of Hants, would mean to a man in East Sussex a mere loss of so many days' or weeks' necessary agricultural work. Somebody must, however, do both of these things, and so the doing of them will more and more devolve upon the king and his immediate followers.

For that he had immediate followers, who were not at once settled upon lands, I make no doubt : and pro-vision for the maintenance of the "King and Court" seems in some way to have been incumbent upon Higg and Pigg and all landowners. Such "rents," if one may use the word, would be in kind and not in money. Higg will send the king a barrel of salted eels from the river Rother once a year, Pigg will send him ten bushels of wheat. In due time both of these persons will come to be thought of (by the king at least) as holding their land

C

ly this rent, and as long as they continue to pay it, well. —But if they do not? then the king will come to think he has a right to deprive them of their land. Now, very likely, in order to save himself trouble and to provide for a deserving follower, whom we may now, perhaps, call a "thegn" (the ancestor of the "squire" of our own day), the king will say to this thegn, Edric, "I give you all the rents that are due to me from the village of Tubney."

But he may therewith give Edric something more. The king himself has received at the original allotment a share of land for himself, and very likely a large share scattered about in various villages in the kingdom. From the very first, if there were no slaves, these lands must have been cultivated for the king's benefit by free men, either men whom the king undertook to feed and clothe in return for their labour on his lands, or men who paid him "rent" in labour instead of in kind. There is such a man in Tubney—let us call him Gurth: and the king has a small holding of his own in that famous village.

"Very well then," he says, "I give to you, Edric, my strips of land in the village of Tubney, Gurth's labour thereon, and all the rents in kind that Higg and his friends used to pay me." Don't you see that Edric is in a fair way to become squire of Tubney? "Moreover," says the king to Edric, "you must serve me in war, and in a different fashion from those unwilling villagers. You must come on a horse and bring six stout knaves a-foot with you." Edric will be able (because he lives there) to compel six out of the villagers really to fulfil their military duties to the tribe and king, and the rest will gradually regard themselves as exempt from such duty. At first Higg, and all who get such an exemption, are pleased; they have not got to send their salted eels and their bushels of wheat all the way to Selsey, but only up to the rather superior wooden house which Edric is building for himself in the village. But they gradually come to be less and less free. The king lived a long way off, and, in the rude plenty of his court, did not much mind if the eels were high or not. Edric is much nearer and much more particular. As for Gurth's labour-rent, that is not enough to cultivate Edric's land, and he gets the villagers one by one to pay him labour-rents of some sort. Some of them stand out and refuse, and perhaps appeal to the tribal assembly—sturdy Saxon grumblers who will stand no nonsense. They may even refuse, when the time comes, to have their rent increased or their services made harder by Edric's Norman successor after the Norman Conquest. They will be the ancestors of the yeomen, the sturdy small freeholders who formed the backbone of the old English army in later times. But the majority of them will give way, especially those who after all are only too glad to escape the burden of military service.

And now I must explain another duty which they are glad to shuffle off, and their neglect of which helps Edric's power in the village. To understand this, we must go back to a time before Edric came to Tubney— almost to the time of the migration. We said that one of the functions of government (vested in the tribal assembly of all freemen) was to arbitrate between subject and subject—in other words, to "do justice." Remember that we are dealing with a state of society in which the tie of kindred is very strong. So, if in the year 500 I wrong Higg, I wrong all his kindred, and if I slay him his kindred ought to slay me and my kindred. That is what is called the "blood feud," and was normal both in Teutonic and Celtic tribes. But long before the migration the common sense of the Germans had substituted for the blood feud a system of fines—so many sheep or oxen, or so much money, according to the nature of the wrong done and the rank of the persons concerned. I might, indeed, enjoy the luxury of killing my king if I could pay the totally prohibitory fine at which his royal blood was valued. And one of the main businesses of the tribal assembly, in which the king presided, was to see these fines properly assessed and paid. Murder, wounding, and cattle-stealing were the only crimes common in such a rude state of society, and each offence had its regular tariff. But, anyhow, it was a matter between the wrong-doer and the wronged (or rather between their kindreds), and the king had nothing to say to it. Not till very much later (hardly before the Norman Conquest) did the idea arise that in breaking your head I had broken something more important, viz. the *Law*, or the "King's peace." But soon after the Saxon migration the king began to make us pay for his trouble in presiding over the court or assembly which arbitrated between us, and to take a "fine" from me. And he began to call the tribal assembly where the fines were assessed *his* "court," *his* "Gemot"; and, as such matters were of daily occurrence, he began to hold Gemots, or send officers to hold them, in many different parts of his kingdom. In other words, he broke up his kingdom into small jurisdictions; and there would be a "shire-gemot" or county court held for a whole county, and perhaps forty or fifty "hundred-gemots" in small divisions called "hundreds." Now we will suppose Tubney to lie in a "hundred" called Rotherey.

Before Edric came, Higg and Pigg and the rest all had to attend the hundred court at Rotherey, and the fines were collected by the royal officer who presided at it —say once a month—and sent to the king. They were his reward for sending his royal officer to preside. But that officer was not a judge. All the freemen in the district of Rotherey were the judges, and they assessed the compensation to be paid for all wrongs done, not according to our ideas, by listening to "evidence," but by their knowledge of the weight and importance of the parties in the suit before them. If Pigg has stolen a sheep from Higg, he must pay him four sheep (and a fine to the king, as aforesaid) ; if Pigg will not pay, the only thing is to proclaim him an "outlaw," and "let him slay him for a thief that can come at him" (which, no doubt, Higg and his friends promptly proceed to do on the way home from the court).

But see how these monthly attendances, even at a place so near as Rotherey, especially when coupled with an occasional attendance at the tribal assembly far away at Selsey, also became an intolerable burden. Man after man will be willing to pay the king a higher rent in kind to get exempt from such a burden ; and so, perhaps, there will be only three persons in Tubney who are bound to attend.

But what if the king also should feel it a burden to hold these courts—the fines that come in from them are so small ? What if he should say to Edric, "Hold the hundred court of Rotherey in my stead—you live near there ; take the stupid little fines and pay me annually a cast of hawks instead of them ?" Edric is delighted ; and is in a far better position to get the fines, and even to increase them, than the king had been.

Now look back and consider what sort of a village society we have got, say by the end of the ninth century (for, of course, all these changes only crept in gradually). We have arrived at something like a *feudal* state of society, in which the king has delegated his powers of holding courts, calling out soldiers, receiving royal rents, to a private landowner who pays him services and rents in return.   Higg and Pigg still think they *hold their land* quite freely ; but they don't, though for the written and legal acknowledgment that they hold it of Edric we have to wait till the Norman Conquest.

Was this feudal condition an evil ?   To some extent it was, for it undoubtedly led to the neglect of the duties of a citizen by all but the upper classes ; and its system of labour rents was also apt to weigh heavily on the lower classes.   If all England had really been armed and free and led by a warlike king, England would never have fallen to the Danes and Normans.

From another point of view this feudal condition was not at all an evil, but a convenience all round, for it was to some extent a division of labour.   Edric and his six stout knaves did the fighting for the village, a village smith forged swords and axes for them, a village swineherd kept their pigs and a shepherd their sheep, the ploughmen ploughed and the hedgers and ditchers hedged and ditched, and every one came to have his special work in the village, and life probably became more profitable under such conditions.   The great Domesday Book, drawn up by order of William the Conqueror, which tells us where and why every free-man held his lands and on what tenures, gives us a distinct picture of a society with a great number of gradations of rank and duty kept fairly distinct, yet with each village fairly independent of outside help for the raising of the necessaries of life.

We shall have occasion to refer to this picture again, but must now stop to consider the actual course followed by the various Anglian and Saxon tribes in the first century and a half after the migration (say 450–600).   To guide us in this guess-work we have little but the physical geography of the country, which tells us the lines which the invaders must have taken, or would naturally take. Our only written "authorities" are a Welsh monk called Gildas, who wrote "on the destruction of Britain" from his refuge in Brittany in the middle of the sixth century; the Northumbrian monk Bede, who wrote at Jarrow in the first quarter of the eighth; and the Anglo-Saxon Chronicle, which began to be compiled by King Alfred in the last quarter of the ninth. Now, a mediæval monk may be a credible witness on Church matters, or even on worldly events which happened in his own neighbourhood, but he is not always well informed about events which happened 100 miles from his monastery, which he hardly ever left unless the Saxons or Danes smoked him out. He is almost certain to represent any man who meddled with monks or Church property as an abandoned monster past hope of redemption, and any one who defended the same as next door to a saint. His interest is centred on the things of the next world. Moreover, he has no more idea of numbers than a primitive savage : he will tell you that the West-Saxons "boast themselves to be 200,000 men that draw sword" at a date when there were hardly as many adult males in Britain. He can't help this ; what he means is "an enormous number."

Bede, however, who lived in the most flourishing period of the Northumbrian Church, is likely to know something about that Church and its people, if he is likely to know nothing at all about Sussex. The Anglo-Saxon Chronicle, written by and for West-Saxons, is likely to have preserved some sort of faithful tradition about the occupation by that tribe of the country south of the Thames. We can gather a few further scraps of information from the names of places and modern boundaries of counties.

But in the main our history of the Saxon migration will best be expressed in terms of probability. For instance, the invaders of Kent, the Jutes, would naturally land in Thanet, would spend some time in starving out the defenders of the small fortresses of Richborough and Reculver, would advance along the Roman road from Dover to Canterbury towards London, and fight at the successive passages of the Medway, the Cray, and the Darenth. At least the Britons would be very unwise if they did not make stands at all these places. When beaten from the last of these, the Britons would fly behind the Roman walls of London. To take such a city would be entirely beyond the power of the first invaders, and, as the forest came almost up to London by Wimbledon Common, these would in the end be content with occupying the rich county of Kent. And we do find one definite tribe called Jutes in possession of that county, under a king called Ethelbert, 150 years after the received date of the first landing of the " Kings " Hengist and Horsa.

Wherever you look you must trust to the same vague guidance. The East-Saxons must have sailed up the muddy creeks of Essex, and (how we cannot guess) have taken Colchester, and then been barred from westward advance by the forests which bordered Hertfordshire and Essex, of which Epping is the last remnant. The South-Saxon kingdom can only have been the narrow strip between the downs and the sea, in which we have already hypothetically placed our friends Higg and Edric ; Chichester and Anderida (Pevensey) must have been blockaded or destroyed at some time or other, and then been left waste perhaps for centuries. The middle of England, the district afterwards vaguely called Mercia (or " borderland "), the speech of whose settlers has remained as the basis of our modern English tongue, offers easier entrance, owing to the great fen rivers, Nen, Welland, and Ouse, and to the southern branches of the Humber, Trent, and Don ; and tribe after tribe of Angles must have poured in by these gaps and spread themselves westward to the Severn and northward to the wild dales of Derbyshire. Norfolk and Suffolk would be as easy a country to occupy as you could wish, once you had the Roman legions withdrawn from the coast fortresses. Not even a legend or tradition tells us anything of the fall of Venta Icenorum (Norwich) or of any of the midland Roman cities. Most strange of all, we don't know when London became English ; all we know is that early in the seventh century it was in the possession of a King of Essex, and that it was one of the first places to receive a Christian bishop of its own after the conversion of Kent in 597.

Ida the Angle established himself, according to Bede's legend, at the rock fortress of Bamborough somewhere about 500, and plenty of other Anglian leaders doubtless came and fought before the two branches of the North-umbrian Kingdom, which the monk calls Bernicia and Deira, were established. Whether Bernicians extended to the Forth and Deirans occupied the old Roman capital of York before the days of the first Christian King of Northumbria (Edwin) we don't know. But it seems to have been he who first seized on the rock for-tress at the edge of the Pentlands and called it " Edwin's-burh " or Edinburgh. We do know that just before his time the last great heathen King of Northumbria, called Ethelfrith, had penetrated to Chester and destroyed that old Roman city.

Finally, if the legend is true that the West-Saxons or " Gewissas " landed first in or near Southampton Water, it is probable that they penetrated up the Test and Avon,

and had to fight their way very hard before they reached
the Thames : when they destroyed Venta Belgarum
(Winchester) and all the other rich cities of the South we
don't know.   It does seem, however, pretty certain that
the earliest counties to form part of a kingdom of Wessex
were Hants, Wilts, Berks, and Surrey, and that it was not
till late in the seventh century that Dorset, Somerset, and
part of Devon were added.   As for the names of the
sturdy savages who carved out these kingdoms, I am not
going to bother you much with them.   Milton has been
scolded for calling their struggles "wars of kites and
crows"; and perhaps it was a little disrespectful of him.
We don't even know anything about their weapons or
their methods of fighting, except that they must have
been tolerably efficient.   We can, however, fairly lay
down one or two generalisations.

(1) That within the first two centuries after the with-
drawal of Roman troops they had fairly well conquered
and settled about two-thirds of England, counting from
East to West ; they had penetrated to the tidal Severn
near Gloucester, and the tidal Dee near Chester, and so
had cut up the British kingdoms into three separate
parts, namely, West Somerset, Dorset, Devon, and Cornwall ; Wales ; and Cumbria or Strathclyde, *i.e.* Lancashire north of the Ribble, Cumberland, Westmorland,
and all Galloway.

(2) That "Scottish" pirates coming from Ireland
had begun to do the same to "Caledonia" or Pictland
before the sixth century was over, and had formed a
Christian Kingdom (for these were Christian pirates)
in Argyllshire, with the Holy Island of Iona for its
mission station.   The Picts seem still to have been
heathens.

(3) That though we very seldom hear of the destruction of Roman cities, we have every reason to believe

that, with the exception of York and London, these were destroyed within the Eastern two-thirds of the island, or else left uninhabited; that some of them perhaps began to be reoccupied early in the seventh century.

CHAPTER IV

THE SAXONS DO AFTER THEIR KIND

WHEN all this two-thirds had been occupied and settled, the " kings " of these numerous small kingdoms had nothing to do but fight each other, and so from about 600 to 830 the years are principally occupied with intertribal wars, which the advent and rapid spread of Christianity, from 597 onwards, did little to stop. Consequently during this time the Welsh (as we may now begin to call the Britons) did not lose so much ground as we should have expected. Nay, they were sometimes called in by one English King against another, and were by no means loth to come. It was a Christian Welsh King, Cadwalla, who helped Penda, the last great heathen King of. Mercia, in his struggles against Christian Northumbria. But on the whole the Welsh did lose ground. King Ine of Wessex (685–715) swept up Dorset and West Somerset, and reached Exeter. A century later King Egbert carried West-Saxon arms to the Land's End, and extinguished for good the kingdom of Cornwall. King Offa of Mercia (757–796) extended his boundaries beyond the Severn, and built a dyke from the Dee to the Wye, which made English ground of the modern counties of Hereford and Shropshire. But these were Christian Kings, and the extermination and even the enslavement of the Britons was a thing of the past. An aristocracy of Teutonic race may have been planted in Celtic villages, but, so far as we can judge, Celtic blood probably predominates over Teutonic in

these parts.   Ine's path to the West is not marked by
blood-eagles carved upon the backs of priests of the
White God (with salt rubbed in) as that of his heathen
forefathers had been, but by the great monastic and
episcopal foundations of Sherborne and Malmesbury and
Glastonbury, where, perhaps, he venerated the bones of
Arthur, and plucked a spray from the sacred thorn-tree
said to have been planted by Joseph of Arimathæa.

When the Roman Empire came to an end in Western
Europe no contemporary person could realise the sad
fact.   The city of Rome, plundered and sacked though it
had been by Goth and Vandal, still remained, in the
imagination of men, mistress of the world ; and so the
bishop of that city, who was the only symbol of law and
order left there, had little difficulty in making good his
claim—an entirely unhistorical one as far as early
Christianity is concerned—to a supremacy over all
Western Churches.

But there was one exception ; the hunted remains of
British Christianity in Wales, and the unhunted and
flourishing Church of Ireland were cut off, in the fifth
and sixth centuries, from intercourse with Rome by the
wedge of heathen England thrust in between them and
Europe ; many of their usages and rituals differed from
those of Rome ; and so, at the very time when Saint
Columba was beginning the conversion of the Picts and
Northumbrians to this Celtic Christianity from his new
monastery of Iona, the Bishop of Rome, or the Pope, as
we may now call him, was sending a special mission to
Christianise England.   In the traditionary story of the
origin of this mission Pope Gregory the Great speaks of
England as if it were a barbarian island in the South
Seas of which no one had ever heard before. The leader of
the mission was an arrogant priest called Augustine, who
came and preached quite successfully to King Ethelbert

of Kent, a king who already had a Christian princess to
wife, Bertha, the daughter of a Frankish King.   The ease
with which Ethelbert and his people abandoned their
heathenism is remarkable among such a conservative and
stupid people.   Indeed, nowhere in England did heathenism make any serious stand, if sufficient missionary
zeal were shown against it.   Heathen practices lingered
among all the lower classes, and, as elsewhere in Europe,
heathen holy-days were changed by the Church into
Christian holy-days, *e.g.* Yule into Christmas ; and the
heathen gods became demons whom it was still no
doubt wise to propitiate.   Mercia under Penda (630–
657) led a sort of temporary rally of heathenism in a
struggle against the Kings of Northumbria ; and Sussex,
cut off by the great forest, is said not to have been converted till 680.   But elsewhere the spread of the true
faith was marvellously rapid.   Nay, in the eighth century
English missionaries are found among its foremost ex-
ponents among the still heathen peoples of North
Germany, and English kings were most conspicuous in
their devotion to the Church, zealous in building monasteries and in endowing them with rich lands.

You would have supposed that all this would lead to a
rapid reconciliation and amalgamation with the remains
of the British Church, but it did not.   It stopped the
harmful and cruel pastime of exterminating Britons, but
it did little more ; Rome would have her own terms, or
none.   Augustine was a man who thought more of getting his own claims as first Archbishop of Canterbury
acknowledged by the whole island than of preaching
peace and goodwill among Christians.   He had a meeting with some Welsh bishops on the Severn seashore,
and when they refused to admit his whole claims, he
shook off the dust of his feet against them ; and the Welsh
Church remained apart until after the Norman Conquest.

Canterbury then became the Mother Church of the whole island, although the subordination of the other English Archbishopric, York, founded in 735, has never been quite expressed in law.

Celtic Christianity, which had by this time well begun the conversion of the Picts and penetrated far into Northumbria, made a brief struggle against the Roman form at the Court of Oswy, King of that kingdom ; but in 664, at the Synod of Whitby, Oswy resolved to throw in his lot, as he crudely expressed it, with the Church of St. Peter who held the " keys of heaven." Scotland, however, retained the Celtic form till the end of the eleventh and Ireland till the middle of the twelfth century. Bishoprics were rapidly carved out and endowed all over England, usually on the lines of the old tribal divisions, which were now becoming " shire " or county divisions ; theoretically there should be a bishopric to every shire, but there never have been quite so many in England, and down to the Reformation there were only nineteen of very unequal size. Almost more important were the very numerous foundations of monasteries, at first mainly in very out-of-the-way and uncomfortable places ; for the mediæval idea was, that the more uncomfortable you were the more you were likely to devote yourself to the service of God and to save your own soul. The evil of this idea is the separation made between the service of God and the service of one's fellow-creatures ; and to some extent a rather unpractical form of monkish piety got a firm hold of our Saxon forefathers ; carried to its extreme it led kings to neglect their duty to their peoples, to alienate rich lands and rents and services (which should have been used to defend England against foreign foes) to the ever-growing greed of the Church, and always for the sake of saving their souls. But there was immense good in it too ; for after the Roman conqueror the monk was the next greatest colonist and civiliser. Either his practical common sense refused to allow him to be uncomfortable and idle, or else his own innate dislike of discomfort taught him that he had better set to work to turn his consecrated wilderness into a garden. And so the monasteries became the greatest centres of civilisation in England ; agriculture, learning, and mechanical arts flourished in their domains, while everywhere else little progress was made.

From the time of Archbishop Theodore (669–700)— "the first Archbishop whom the whole English Church obeyed," Bede calls him — date the beginnings of a system of parishes, and so another great agent of civilisation is born, the parish church in every village in the kingdom with its Sunday and saints'-day services, its daily prayers, and its parish school. It is true that in Saxon times most of the churches were of wood and also that the Normans were the great builders of parish churches ; but this is largely because by no means every village had a squire in it till some time after the Norman Conquest.

The struggle between the kingdoms lasted, I have said, till about 830 ; it was in the main a struggle between the three greater kingdoms, and it has left even to our own day a well-marked triple division of the land into Northumbria, Mercia, and Wessex. Kent, Essex, and East Anglia had very short lives as separate kingdoms, being absorbed each by its nearest big neighbour. Of the three great ones Northumbria held its own roughly till about 750. It gave us Bede and several distinguished saints, notably Cuthbert and Wilfrid ; it built great monasteries at Whitby and Jarrow ; it produced several learned men. But it was always hampered by inroads of the Picts ; one of its greatest kings, Egfrith, was killed by them in an attempt to extend its dominions beyond the Forth, and by the middle of the eighth century it had relapsed into an anarchic condition, which the coming Danish invasions contributed much to make worse.

Mercia is definitely supreme only in the reign of Offa (757–796). He seems to have been a great man, if we may judge from the stories told of his corresponding upon equal terms with the great Charlemagne, the reviver of the Empire of the West. " Don't be afraid," Charlemagne is said to have written to the Pope, " it is not true that Offa intends to come to Rome and depose you." Such intention, indeed, was probably very far from Offa's mind, but he seems to have induced the Pope to erect Lichfield into an archbishopric (as a rival to Canterbury and York) — this quickly disappeared after his death. Mercia is, however, the least united of the three great kingdoms, and we know nothing of its organisation or internal condition.

Last, and most fortunate of all, came the supremacy of Wessex, a country well defined by the great geographical boundary of the river Thames, united in itself, not easy to invade, agriculturally rich, nearer than the others to civilised Europe. Its royal race too was, with few exceptions, one of marked ability. Egbert (802–839) had been an exile at the court of Charlemagne during Offa's reign ; one would like to know if he was one of those who saw that monarch on Christmas Day, 800, receive the golden crown of the Cæsars in old St. Peter's Church at Rome, and so " revive the Western Empire." Towards the end of his reign Egbert finally crushed Mercia at the battle of Ellandun (825), received the submission of Northumbria, and made Wessex nominally at least supreme over the whole island. All English kings since that time, with the exception of Canute,

D

Hardicanute, the two Harolds, and the Conqueror, have the blood of Egbert in their veins.

But the supremacy of Wessex meant practical anarchy in the North ; and the claims of the kingdom of Scotland, where all north of the Forth and Clyde was united under Kenneth M'Alpin in the middle of the ninth century, grew at the expense of Northumbria. And it had not yet occurred to any King of Wessex that he was *direct sovereign* of his Mercian and Northumbrian subjects. He was King of the West-Saxons, head of their kindred or tribe, and he was king over other rulers of the other parts of the island ; that is, he was an "emperor," as Edward VII. is of India. Some of the subordinate rulers even kept the title of king ; as " King " Edmund of East Anglia, who was shot to death by the Danes in 870. But that the king was lord of the land and of all men dwelling thereon hardly occurred to any man before William the Conqueror. King Edgar no doubt thought himself a very fine fellow when he steered a six-oared boat rowed by six " kings," with the King of Scots at the stroke thwart, on the Dee at Chester ; but he would have been a wiser man if he had been rowed by six professional watermen with the six kings in chains in the stern-sheets. What mediæval Britain wanted was a sovereign strong enough to make his will law from the Channel to the Pentland Firth, for the defence of the weak against the strong, and for the defence of Britain from external foes. But that she never got.

CHAPTER V

THE DANES COME

BEFORE Egbert's reign was over a fresh wave of foreign invaders had begun to harry England ; at first merely to harry it, but soon to settle in it. These were the celebrated "Danes" or Norsemen, the later counterparts of the Saxon pirates of the fifth century, but immeasurably better armed than they. They have contributed some of the very best blood that has gone to make up our race ; but only in small quantities. Had they been only twice as numerous as they were, it is probable that they would have made an entire conquest and resettlement of the island, and perhaps have made it strong enough to resist their kinsmen the Normans.

When one reads the story of their ravages one is astonished chiefly at the smallness of their numbers. The average crew of a Danish ship is variously stated at thirty-five or eighty-five ; thirty or forty ships is a very large fleet for them to bring, and even half-a-dozen will do great damage. It is clear from this that the English kings had neglected the arming of the country, and, though vigorous defence is occasionally made, it rests entirely upon the quality of the local "sheriff" or "alderman" ; probably one armed man from each village was as much as he could expect to get to help him. But long before even that force could be collected the Danes had swept the country bare of arms and provisions, burnt the church, carved a blood-eagle on the priest's back, stolen all the horses and ridden on to the next county, or else retired to their ships.

These invaders might strike our shores by one of two ways, either along the coast of North Germany to the Humber, the Wash or the Channel ; or straight across from Norway to the Orkneys. Those who chose the latter route would probably go down the west coast of Scotland, where they have left Scandinavian names on every island and strait and cape, and thence to the east coast of Ireland, where they founded settlements that remained flourishing till the twelfth century. Often the fleets from both these routes would meet in a plundering raid on the coast of Southern England or Northern or Western France. The distances and the dangers of their voyages in open boats sound incredible to our ears. Iceland (ninth century), Greenland (tenth), North America (eleventh), are hardly more distant from Norway than the Bay of Biscay and the Mediterranean. Yet they settled or ravaged all of these in the days when to be Vikings and command pirate crews of their own was the noblest dream of all the youths of Denmark and Norway.

There are gaps on our own coasts where we find no Norse names, such as the East coast from the Moray Firth to the Tweed, and Wales, and Cornwall ; but the probable explanation of these gaps is that there was little plunder worth attention in such places. It was the rich churches of Northumbria and Mercia and of Ireland that attracted the pirates most. Their long boats with sixteen oars a side could sail up mere streamlets and were amazingly fast. The raids lasted over fifty years before any considerable body of them had effected a settlement in Southern Britain. By that time raiding had become a great war-game to which all the best blood of Scandinavia continually sent reinforcements.

The kings of Wessex fought valiantly after their lights,

even Egbert's successor, Ethelwulf (839–856), though he seems to have been much under the thumb of the churchmen ; still better, Ethelwulf's three elder sons, who all reigned in succession (856–871) ; most valiantly of all our great King Alfred (871–901). Alfred is the first king who is much more than a name to us, and we hold him in high honour as one of the true founders of the English monarchy, a form of government, mind you, that experience has proved to be about the best, for the defence of the weak against the strong and for resistance to foreign foes. The England that Alfred rescued from the Danes was reduced to a strip lying south-west of a line drawn from Chester to London ; but he rescued it from such slaughter and such terror as it has never known since. That was enough to make Alfred's name a household word ; but besides soldier he was sailor, church-builder, scholar, inventor, organiser, and historian. And all his wonderful gifts and all his strenuous life he devoted to the good of his people. He found them ravaged, disunited, disheartened, and beaten ; he left them starting afresh upon a path from which they have never wholly turned back. All sorts of things which Alfred never did have no doubt been attributed to him ; but that is only posterity's way of saying that the things he did were wonderful.

He began by fighting the Danes in six great battles. They had occupied the whole of England to the Thames, and were engaged in dealing desperate blows at the last defences of Wessex. From a great entrenched camp in Lincolnshire, into which reinforcements from the North were continually pouring, they issued stronger year after year for their final assaults on the last unsubdued part of England. Beaten back from the valley of the Thames in his first six years, Alfred gathered the last remnants of his force in the marshes of the Parret in Somerset, and at last, by superior strategy, managed to overwhelm "King" Guthrum, the Danish leader, somewhere on the borders of Somerset and Wilts, in 878. That was the turn of the tide. Guthrum agreed to receive baptism and to retire behind the line which the treaty, called the Treaty of Wedmore or Chippenham, drew from London to Chester, and to leave Wessex and Western Mercia alone. In much of the land east of this line the Danes actually settled, especially in Lincolnshire and Nottinghamshire.

Whether their first energy was spent or their numbers diminishing, or whether the coasts of France proved more attractive for raids, or whether they found in Alfred too great a soldier, we know not ; but, though there were a few isolated raids and even outbreaks of the settled Danes during the rest of the reign, they were put down with ease. No doubt Alfred learned military lessons from the Danes ; the use of the axe and the coat of mail and the fortress stockaded with timber ; an English fleet was built, armed, and manned. It patrolled our Southern coasts, and in the succeeding reigns was so much improved that, under Edgar, it is said to have sailed right round the island. And this "naval touch" was never wholly lost, and so we may thank the Danish invasions and King Alfred for having started us as a sea power.

In his brief intervals of peace Alfred set to work to rebuild and recolonise in the part of England he had rescued. Foreign scholars were imported to teach in English schools, for "hardly a priest even in Wessex could read Latin," said the king sadly ; translations of good books from Latin into Saxon were made under his direct supervision ; to these in many cases he dictated quaint prefaces ; the Chronicle began to be kept at Winchester in the Saxon language from 887 onwards ; a code of laws, or rather of customs, common to the

Anglo-Saxon race was drawn up. Upon what principle the king's reorganisation of the fighting force was made we do not know, but probably it was upon a system by which each " hundred " supplied a definite number of men ; at any rate, it was a strong enough weapon to enable Alfred's three immediate successors to subdue frequent revolts of all the Danes settled in England, and to keep fresh pirates, as well as Scots and Welsh, at bay. Quaint old English inventions, such as the candle-clock and the horn lantern, show Alfred on his homely side. The king's life was written by his friend Asser, Bishop of Sherborne, who was a Welshman "imported " by the king. And so in 901, full of days—as age went then, for he was not sixty—and honour, but not of riches, Alfred died, and was buried in the old Minster of Winchester, the germ of that grand cathedral in which the wicked Rufus still lies in lonely state.[1]

The first, and indeed the only, task of Alfred's successors was to rescue the rest of England from the Danes ; not, we may well suppose, to disturb the settled Danes, who made excellent colonists of the land they had ravaged, and who probably did not now wish for fresh pirates from their native country to come disturbing their lands ; but to destroy the independence of the Danish " kingdoms " in the North and East. These included a somewhat shadowy confederation of towns known as the " Five Boroughs "—Lincoln, Leicester, Derby, Stamford, and Nottingham ; a more shadowy kingdom of Guthrum and his successors somewhere in Norfolk ; and a still more shadowy kingdom at York. From reducing these the kings of Wessex gradually went on to make themselves supreme over all "kings" in Great Britain. There were, indeed, at intervals revolts in the

---

[1] Alfred's bones were moved more than once, and finally rested in Hyde Abbey.

North, until Canute finally conquered all England; but Alfred's first four successors, Edward (901–924), Athelstan (924–940), Edmund (940–946), Edred (946–955), always put them down, and often with ease. These four reigns and (after a brief interval of civil war under Edwy, 955–959) that of Edgar (959–975) have always been considered the golden age of the old Saxon monarchy. Fine names, such as the "Magnificent" and the "Pacific," are given to these kings by the post-conquest chroniclers: the Anglo-Saxon Chronicle is more modest. But they give themselves on their charters fine titles also—"Totius Britanniae Monarchus," "Basileus of Britain," and the like; and they are said to have copied many of the fashions of the Byzantine Court: but whether it was this unaccustomed splendour or the hard work they had to do, almost all died young. The average age reached by Alfred's six successors was thirty-four years.

In the process of subduing their Danish and Welsh dependencies we must always remember that our kings were often obliged to recognise as viceroys or "aldermen" a good many of the descendants of the older lines. Edward "the Elder" (901–924) and his masculine sister Ethelfleda, who was married to a descendant of the old Mercian royal house, steadily fought their way through North-East Mercia up to the Peak country; and wherever they went they built or fortified the towns of central England, or, in the quaint language of the Chronicle, they "wrought and timbered the boroughs," which probably means that they built a great mound with a wooden fortress on the top of it and a fortified "base-court" surrounded by a water-ditch below; possibly also a wooden wall with a ditch round the whole town. In a rude state of society the town is generally the symbol of civilisation; in a settled one it is often the reverse. The division of Mercia into shires, as we now have them, probably dates from this reign also, and, as you will notice that all the Mercian shires are called after the towns, there is some reason to believe that to each of Edward's fortifications there was a district or " shire " assigned, from which supplies were to be sent to the garrison. Edward perhaps endowed a thegn, Edric, with five " hides " in the county of Warwick, and in return Edric had to defend the walls of Warwick against a siege. By the eleventh century we fear that Edric, though he kept the hides, had got exemption from the duty; otherwise England would never have been conquered by Swein, Canute, or William.

Athelstan's reign (924–940) is marked by the glorious battle of Brunanburh, fought at Bourne in Lincolnshire, where for a long summer's day he and his brother Edmund performed prodigies of valour against a mixed host of insurgent Danes, aided by the King of Scots and by Irish Danes, Picts, Welsh, and Cumbrians. It was perhaps the first great victory of South over North, and precursor of Northallerton, Towton, and Flodden. From that day perhaps begin the shadowy claims to supremacy over Scotland, which were never really made good save for a brief interval in the reign of Henry II., but upon which Edward I. founded many of his absurd pretensions, when

> " Long afterwards did Scotland know
> Fell Edward was her deadliest foe."

We certainly find princes from all countries within the four seas of Britain sitting in King Athelstan's assembly of " wise men," called " Witan " or " Witana-gemot," which begins to look more and more like a feudal gathering than what it had perhaps originally been—an assembly of the freemen of the tribe. But we also begin to hear of viceroyalties within Southern

Britain itself.   Athelstan, or Edmund, or Edgar, still more Ethelred or Canute, will group half-a-dozen of our counties together, and call it the "aldermanry of Central Mercia," or of "West Wessex," or the like.   Mind, all that means disunion and weak central government.   In the same connection we may notice that when Edmund (940-946) conquered "Cumbria," *i.e.* Lancashire and Cumberland, in 943, he gave it, instead of governing it himself, to the King of Scots, upon what would soon come to be called "feudal tenure," with the natural result that Cumbria had to be conquered all over again by William Rufus, who did *not* let go his grip of it or of anything else.

The splendid foreign marriages made by these West Saxon kings for their children are an undoubted proof of the estimation in which they were held abroad : no less than four of Athelstan's sisters married into royal houses; the Emperor Otto getting one, the King of the West Franks another.   Alfred began our close connection with Flanders by marrying his daughter to the count of that important country, and from their union there descended that good Matilda who became the wife of the terrible Conqueror.   When one of the last descendants of Charlemagne was driven from the throne of the Franks, it was to the court of Athelstan that he fled, and Athelstan restored him to that throne a little later, possibly by a Saxon army.

Like Athelstan and Edmund, Edred had to put down Danish risings during his short reign (946-955), and once penetrated far into Yorkshire in doing so.   With Edwy, who came to the throne at thirteen, there was a temporary slip backwards, as the boy had an unfortunate quarrel with his powerful Archbishop Odo, which led to a revolt and to a division of England between him and his brother Edgar.   The latter took Mercia and the North under his nominal rule, but united them again with Wessex on Edwy's death in 959. Edgar's coronation service seems to have been performed with unusual splendour, and to have been the pattern for all future coronation services, although it is curious that the ceremony did not take place until 973, within two years of the monarch's early death. This was also the year of the procession of boats on the Dee to which I have already referred, and as we hear of no Danish raids at all during his reign, we may judge that the fleet was really in a high state of efficiency. It is also interesting to see that when Edgar had imposed upon a Welsh prince a yearly tribute of three hundred wolves' heads, the Welsh prince complained, after a year or two, that the scarcity of wolves was making it impossible to pay. This was certainly a mark of progressive civilisation. Princely as this sovereign's assembly of wise men no doubt was, its numbers were not often more than thirty, of which the bishops and great abbots would be a " working majority," a fact which makes it difficult for us to distinguish the old English "Witan" from a clerical synod, and gives a preponderance to religious and clerical ordinances among our early laws. The shire courts would no doubt in peaceable times be kept in fair working order by the king's sheriffs, though even in them the power of the great aldermen and bishops was probably often used against justice ; but the hundred courts, though we have a law of Edgar ordering them to be held once a month, seem to have fallen largely into private hands. Justice as well as land tenure was being "feudalised" ; and though, as I have said above, that is not always an evil, yet it was so in the tenth and eleventh centuries, because it showed that the excellent principles of self-government which lay at the root of our institutions were not strong enough to maintain themselves without a strong king to watch over them.

Let us clearly understand what is meant by "feudalised." I mean that the right of holding law courts and exacting fines in them was falling into the grasp of the local landowners, instead of being worked by direct nominees of the Crown, accounting to the Crown for them ; and that, at the same time, these landlords were increasing their own acres and their own rents in labour and kind at the expense of the free peasants, who were consequently being depressed towards " serfdom," though seldom to actual slavery. Such laws as Athelstan's, that " every landless man must have a lord " ; such curious attempts as the " frithborh," or " frankpledge," by which every ten men were to be formed into a sort of mutual insurance company against theft and crime, point to a state of society in which the king " reigned but did not govern." If any one "governed " Higg and his kind, it was the neighbouring big landowner. And even he was by no means always a supporter of " law and order." The " wergild," paid by the slayer to the slain man's relations, and the "wite," paid by the murderer to the king or lord (paid, you understand, for the trouble the king or lord took of holding a court over him), were bad ; it really *paid* the king or the lord that his subjects should commit many crimes. And these fines were often so high as to mean slavery or ruin to the payer if he paid. But he did not pay ; the forests were vast, and he preferred to become an outlaw, and outlawry was a ridiculous punishment in such a wild age. It has been wittily said that a poor man would be only too glad to get his father killed by a solvent thegn, for it would set him up in cattle for life.

Edgar's reign is, however, rendered most memorable by the primacy of Archbishop Dunstan, that valiant

English saint who seized the devil with the tongs when his satanic majesty presumed to intrude upon his prayers. The power of archbishops and bishops became enormous, as more and more land was alienated to the Church by the piety—or the religious terror—of the kings, always with a view to the benefit of the souls of the said kings, but by no means without prejudice to their kingly duties ; sometimes, it is true, a rent is reserved, to be paid in soldiers, as in King Edgar's charter granting enormous lands to Saint Oswald of Worcester ; oftener, however, the rent was only paid in perpetual· prayers. Odo and Dunstan practically sway the state under Edred, Edwy, Edgar, Edward. And Dunstan specially strikes the imagination : after Alfred and Edward the Confessor he is probably the best known figure in English history before the Conquest, and he certainly was the most popular saint of the English Church until he was supplanted by Thomas Becket. His supremacy is marked by one of those " revivals " of monasticism which are to be so frequent in the Middle Ages ; revivals which are rendered necessary by the fact that the tendency of all communities like those of monks (who have no children to provide for), is to get lazy and fat and sensual, and therefore to need perpetual recalling to an older and higher ideal of work and devotion. And Dunstan seems to have gone about his work with great common sense, and not to have fostered, as later revivals too often did, the jealousy between the monks ("regulares," who live by " regula " or rule) and the parish priests ("saeculares," who live in the " saeculum " or world, though not of it). But it is as chief adviser to four successive kings that Dunstan most interests us ; and though he was once exiled for a brief space to Flanders, he returned at the accession of Edgar, and we may fairly assume that the prosperity of the reign of Edgar the Pacific is largely due to him. Remember, however, that the story is wholly told by churchmen; Edwy is perhaps the first king of England whose character has been handed down as radically bad, because he quarrelled with an archbishop; so perhaps there may be something to be said on the other side for Edwy, or even for Rufus or John, whose characters have suffered from the same cause.

Edgar's two sons were under age when he died in 975: the elder of them, known as Edward the Martyr (why?), was murdered, after a four years' reign, by a wicked stepmother; and the younger of them has been branded to all time as "Ethelred the Unready," or rather "Ethelred the Ill-advised" ("rede" means counsel or advice). In his reign, after an interval of over thirty years, the raids of the Danes began again; but this time upon a different scale, the scale of political conquest of one kingdom by another. The Guthrums and the Hubbas had, after all, been mere adventurous noblemen driven out from their own country for that country's good. But Swein Forkbeard, Canute, Olaf Trygvasson, and Harold Hardrada were kings or kings' sons at home, and powerful ones, before they tried to become kings of England. The first great invasion came in 991, and its chiefs were bought off by payment of "ten thousand pounds" in hard cash, a miserable expedient said to have been suggested by Archbishop Sigeric (Dunstan had died 988). This sum, stated in the Chronicle, is a ridiculous one; probably there were not ten thousand pounds in hard cash in England—the silver penny, of five to the shilling, being the only coin then minted, and all rents being paid in kind: the Chronicle probably only means "a lot of money." Anyhow, it was the surest way to whet the appetite of the

Danes for more silver pennies. From that time till 1014 the current coin of England was poured over and over again into the hands of the insatiable pirates, who stopped their ravages for a moment only when they were gorged with plunder. In order to pay, church treasures and plate were no doubt melted down, but the mass of the money was raised as a land tax of so much on each "hide"; one of the greatest objects of the landowners was to get their hides exempted from this tax, which was kept up after the Danes had gone; but though, in many cases, they were successful, enough remained to allow King William to regard his traditional right to raise this tax as one of the brightest jewels in his crown; and it was in order to see what hides still owed the tax, and what had got exemption, that he ordered the great Domesday survey to be held in 1086. When King Henry I. (whose figures we can trust) levied it for the last time, it brought him only a poor £2500.

Ethelred occasionally hit upon the still more curious expedient of buying one of the chief pirates, making him an English noble, and hiring him to fight against his own countrymen; indeed, one of them, Thurkill, fought very valiantly against his old master, Swein Forkbeard, for five years at the end of Ethelred's reign. To fight Swein with the whole force of England is the last thing that Ethelred seems to have been able to do. Good resistance was constantly being made in particular corners of the country, as by Alderman Brihtnoth at the battle of Maldon in Essex in 991, by Ulfketyl (his name shows him of Danish blood; probably descended from one of Guthrum's settlers) in Norfolk in 1004, but such resistance was always local, not national. Ethelred constantly assembled what the Chronicle calls immense armies, and even fleets, but they melted away without fighting, often owing to deliberate treachery on the part of individual aldermen. One feels pretty sure that all England north of the Thames was jealous of Wessex and profoundly disaffected towards the West-Saxon monarchy, and individual aldermen, like Elfric and Edric of Mercia, were more interested in making terms for their own provinces than in fighting.

The Witan, when it does meet—and it meets pretty often—has little better to recommend than more Dane-geld and a great deal more of prayer and fasting ; a fact which suggests that England was almost entirely governed by clerical influences. The Danes are regarded as a "punishment for the sins of the nation," more especially the sins of stealing Church lands and marrying nuns ; the sin of neglecting naval and military duties is not mentioned, but that was the real sin which the Danes came to punish.

The first two great pirate leaders, Olaf Trygvasson, King of Norway, and Swein Forkbeard, son of the King of Denmark, are interesting, for Olaf, evidently a savage heathen when he first appeared with Swein in 994, was baptized in the following year, during some temporary truce with Ethelred, and quitted the pirate trade in order to enforce Christianity at the sword's point on his reluctant Norwegian subjects ; while Swein, who had himself been baptized, and whose father had been quite a respectable man, relapsed to heathenism and remained a heathen till his death in 1014. Such a man could always command a following, if not of pure Scandinavian blood, yet of terrible Wends and Letts from the Eastern Baltic, a district which remained in a state of unrest for centuries after this time, whereas Denmark, Sweden, and Norway were more or less beginning to settle down.

Two other countries began about the same time to be of great importance as friends or foes to Wessex, the new Duchy of Normandy and the old County of Flanders. Normandy was the Lincolnshire of France ; the Danes had harried it into a desert, and the Frankish kings bought them off from further ravage by ceding the whole of that province to them, on condition that they should accept Christianity and swear allegiance to the Crown of France. The oath sat lightly on their souls, but they soon became, according to the lights of the time, the best and devoutest of Christians ; the faithful champions of the Pope without ever being his tools, the greatest church-builders and the greatest warriors of the Middle Ages. The cession of Normandy is in 913, and the West-Saxon kings at first seem afraid of their new neighbours, afraid especially that they may encourage their brethren from the North to sell English plunder in the ports of Normandy ; but towards the end of the century this attitude undergoes a change. Under pressure of the ravages of Swein, Ethelred married a Norman princess, Emma, and looked for help (which he did not get) to Normandy. When at last Swein was master of England it was to Normandy that Ethelred fled (1014), and his fatal son, Edward, was brought up in exile there.

Flanders, not yet conspicuously a land of merchants or manufacturers or gardeners, as it has been ever since the twelfth century, is from the ninth onwards conspicuously a land of hard fighters ; it has also some rough trade with England. It owns a more perfect blend of Teutonic and Celtic race than England itself, and its native stock is continually reinforced by pirates and outlaws, land thieves and sea thieves, for every one who has a strong hand is welcome at the court of the Baldwins. Under "Baldwin of the Iron Arm" (Bras-de-Fer) it begins to enter European politics as a first-class power ; we have seen how Alfred's daughter marries Baldwin II., and

E

the alliance of Flanders and Wessex is steady and conspicuous. But it is not a dynastic alliance. The Baldwin of the day is anxious to be friends with the King of England of the day, be he called Ethelred or Canute or William, just as his successor, Charles the Bold, in the fifteenth century, though he boasted that he was come of the noble "maison de Lanclastre," and that there was nothing in the world that he hated like "cette maison de Yorch," was compelled to keep friends with Edward IV. so long as the house of "Yorch" kept the English throne. If Baldwin lets Canute refit (after Swein's death) in Flemish harbours, it will be because he has a shrewd idea that Canute will soon be King of England.

And so he will. By 1012 Wessex has been ravaged from end to end, Exeter sacked, Canterbury sacked and its Archbishop (Alphege) murdered. London alone has held out, and, when Ethelred fled to Normandy in 1014, even London submitted to Swein ; and Swein, though never recognised as king in any formal assembly of the English Witan, was practically in possession of the sovereignty of England. A month later, Swein dropped down dead, and his ships sailed back to the North, under the lead of his son, Canute. Ethelred was recalled by the faithful Londoners, and blundered on for two years more till his death in 1016. But he left behind him a son by an English wife, Edmund Ironside, the last hero of the old royal line on the male side. A fresh invasion by Canute was certain, for Swein's elder son, Harold, was already in possession of Denmark, and Canute had to make a throne for himself. There were plenty of traitors in England to invite him, including the Alderman Edric of Mercia, and in 1016 he came.

CHAPTER VI

SHALL ENGLAND BE DANISH OR NORMAN?

FIVE great battles in one year young Edmund fought against the invader, enough and more than enough to show that the spirit of the nation only needed a leader. He relieved London, which Canute had closely besieged; he raised army after army with astonishing rapidity, now in Somerset, now in Kent, now in Essex. But he was fighting with a man who had a standing army to rely upon, while it seemed impossible even for an Ironside to keep the English militia together for above a month at most. After the last of these great battles at Ashington, in Essex, Canute agreed to divide the kingdom with Edmund (to whom he left Wessex only), being sure that he would soon be able to find a traitor who would rid him of his rival. And so it proved. Edmund "died suddenly" in 1017, and Canute the Dane became King of England.

He had waded through blood to the throne, but after a few politic murders (especially that of the traitor Edric) he became a reformed character, and the nineteen years of his reign were, strangely enough, a prosperous and happy period. The king was baptized, and really seems to have tried to live as a good Christian should— nay, to rule as a right English king. There were two sons of Ethelred, by Emma, in exile in Normandy, and two baby sons of Edmund Ironside who, after some vicissitudes, found a refuge in the distant kingdom of Hungary; but no one raised their claims nor disputed Canute's title by the sword. With great prudence, Canute kept up a small standing army of Danish warriors (finding the money for their pay by regular levies of " Danegeld "), whom we know as "house - carls," and who remained a bodyguard of the kings of England until the last of them fell beside Harold at Senlac. Equally prudent was Canute's marriage with the widowed Emma, a lady who must have been much older than himself (he was only twenty - one); and if we wonder at Emma's acceptance of his hand, we can only conjecture that she had so much enjoyed being Queen of England that she was not prepared to resign the position.

One cannot, however, say that Canute did anything to unify England; on the contrary, he still further stereotyped the existing political divisions : we hear no more of great "aldermanries," but (in Danish phrase) of great "jarldoms" or "earldoms." Godwin, Earl of Wessex, grandson of a cowherd they said; Leofric, Earl of Mercia, grandson of no one knows who; Siward, Earl of Northumbria, grandson of the Fairy Bear,—these are the viceroys by whom Canute and his successors govern England, and at last, under the pious and feeble Edward, their viceroyalties become mere feudal provinces. But something of this kind Canute was compelled to do if he was to govern at all, for he became King of Denmark in 1020, and King of Norway, elected in full "Thing" (Parliament) at Trondhjem, in 1028. He won back from the grasping German Emperor the real boundary of Denmark at the river Eider, which the Germans only recrossed in 1864. He made the greatest friends with the clergy both in England and abroad, went to see the Pope at Rome, and wrote from that city a "letter to his loving people" which we still possess. He showed especial devotion to English saints, and even had the astonishing effrontery to visit at Glastonbury the tomb of his murdered rival, Edmund Ironside : if we fancy that Canute did all these things with a secret smile, we shall, I think, be wrong ; his was a real conversion. But he is a strange character to find on the roll of the Vikings, a modern "Rex Politicus," adroit at managing men, hating warfare and preferring diplomacy. It was a knowledge of the limits of the possible, no doubt, which induced him to agree to the final cession of the Lothians to the kingdom of Scotland after the disastrous battle of Carham in 1017. Thenceforth the Tweed was the boundary, and Northumbria could be administered as one earldom instead of two.

When Canute died in 1035 there was some dispute in the Witan between the claims of his sons Harold (by an English wife) and Hardicanute (by Emma), and there was even talk of a partition. But the interesting point is that no one seems to have raised the claims of Ethelred's children, or to have attempted to upset the Danish dynasty. Both Canute's sons were worthless fellows, and quickly followed each other to the grave (1040, 1042) : then, as neither of them left heirs, the house of Ethelred was joyfully welcomed back in the person of Edward, the last male of the house of Egbert who reigned in England. It has seemed to many people, who are wise after the event, that a better candidate for the throne might have been found in Canute's nephew, Swein Estrithson, who was probably at the moment in England.

Edward was well over thirty years of age, had a red face and white hair (probably he was an albino) ; he had spent all his youth in Normandy, and cared for none but Normans, and for them only as far as they were churchmen or devoted to the Church. He is the very typical example of a bigot, in an age which has got hold of the unfortunate belief that a king's primary duty is to save his own soul by enormous gifts and favours to churchmen (which were called "gifts to God and His saints"), instead of ruling his people firmly and wisely. He was, therefore, certain to be swayed by Norman counsellors; the leaders of that mighty race were already looking for fresh fields for expansion, and Edward's court, Edward's bishoprics, abbeys, chaplaincies, and, still worse, Edward's civil and military service, such as they were, were at once open to them. His cousin, William the Bastard, was now fifteen years of age, and had been Duke of Normandy since he was eight. The Norman Conquest had begun.

But that conquest was not to be what is vulgarly called a "walk over." As William and his Norman friends begin to show more and more plainly what they expect to gain from the sympathies of Edward, so, in Wessex at least, a national party comes gradually into being, and groups itself round the figures of Earl Godwin and his son Harold. Godwin, who had risen to fame under Canute, had had a powerful voice in the last three elections to the crown, and soon contrived to marry his own daughter Edith to King Edward, and to provide for his sons with English earldoms. As Edward seemed never likely to have children, it is probable that Godwin early began to aim at the crown, if not for himself, at least for his descendants; he might well represent to his friends that he was at least a better alternative for England than Norman William. It is probable also that William knew this, and systematically set himself to work to checkmate Godwin. Every victory of William on the Continent, every diplomatic triumph in Flanders or elsewhere, was a blow at the family of Godwin. And remember that the struggle lasted twenty - four years, from William's sixteenth to his fortieth year. We cannot help being struck with the fact that Mercia and Northumbria had very little to say to this struggle : it is in the main Wessex *versus* Normandy. The family of Siward was almost independent in the North till the death of that old hero in 1055—if Siward crosses our vision at all, it is rather in Scottish than in English politics ; *e.g.* he restores Malcolm III. of Scotland to his father's throne, which had been usurped by the famous Macbeth (though I fear that Shakespeare's drama, in which he appears as " Old Siward," is not historically accurate enough to please modern critics). Similarly Leofric, the wise Earl of Mercia, seems to be comparatively uninterested or powerless to interfere in Wessex ; when on one occasion Leofric and Siward do interfere, they appear as decidedly hostile to Godwin.

It is probable, then, that from the middle of the century at least the north and centre of England would have preferred a king of the family of Canute, and from the point of view of the *independence* of England, they would have been right. It is impossible to doubt that Godwin and his sons were very grasping, that they carried " family politics " too far, showed their hands too openly, and that under their rule the once free peasants of Wessex were sinking more and more into a condition of serfdom—*i.e.* their rents, whether in kind or in service, were being increased, and their holdings perhaps curtailed. Even pieces of Leofric's earldom are at times shorn off to provide for Swein and Harold, sons of Godwin. On the death of Siward, Harold contrives to get the earldom of Northumbria, which should have gone to Siward's son Waltheof, given to his own brother Tostig. In the matter of Church preferment—a very important point when the Witan, which could decide the royal succession, consisted so largely of churchmen—the struggle is definitely between Godwin and Edward's Norman favourites. One can hardly doubt that the feeble king writhed in the grasp of Godwin. Still, we have no right, because the Norman Conquest proved a blessing in disguise, to disparage the men who resisted it.

At last, in 1050, Edward plucked up spirit to resist. The path of Godwin's eldest son, Swein, was marked by brutal murders and abductions of nuns from their convents, and still his father continued to shelter and plead for him. Suddenly Edward, taking advantage of these evil doings and of a quarrel between the citizens of Dover and some of the Norman favourites, called the northern earls to his standard, and outlawed the whole family of Godwin. It is significant that Godwin fled to Flanders, with which, to William's disgust, he had recently patched up a family connection by the marriage of his son Tostig to Judith, a daughter of the reigning Baldwin ; while at that very time William was trying in vain to get the hand of another Flemish princess, Matilda, for himself. Each, in fact, knew full well that he dared not grasp at the crown of England without the neutrality, if not the help, of Flanders. But William was prudent enough to take immediate advantage of Godwin's outlawry to pay a visit to his cousin Edward at Westminster (1051), and it was, no doubt, upon this occasion that a direct promise of the English succession was given to him, either by Edward's own mouth or by that of Robert of Jumièges, who had just been nominated, to the great wrath of the national party, to the Archbishopric of Canterbury. That Edward had no power to make such a promise without the consent of the Witan weighed nothing with William, who returned to Nor-

mandy to resume his wars and diplomatic intrigues.
Meanwhile Harold and his younger brothers had gone
to Ireland, and early in 1052 they returned, ravaging
the coasts in true Viking style. Godwin met his sons
in the Channel with a considerable fleet, which he
must have raised in Flanders, and the united fleets
sailed up the Thames almost unresisted. London welcomed them gladly (probably the rule of the Norman
favourites had been very unpopular), and there was
nothing for Edward to do but to accept the inevitable
with as good a grace as possible. Godwin and his family,
with the exception of Swein, were restored to estates,
honours, and earldoms. The Norman favourites fled in
a body, including the new archbishop, whose place was
taken by a creature of Godwin's named Stigand, while
Robert of Jumièges hastened to lay his cause before the
Pope.

We shall see presently what a powerful cause in the
eyes of Europe that of Robert became. In 1053 Earl
Godwin died, and Harold at once took his place as Earl
of Wessex and first counsellor of the crown. In internal
politics Harold's course was at first easy. Earl Siward
died in 1055, and, as I have said, Northumbria was given
to Tostig. Earl Leofric died in 1057, and his only son,
Algar, disgraced himself by a futile alliance with a Welsh
prince called Griffith ; Harold easily defeated him in
the field, and, after a temporary outlawry, allowed him
to return to a much-shorn earldom of Mercia, while
Harold's two younger brothers, Gurth and Leofwin,
were made Earls of East Anglia and Middlesex. It
must have been a blow to Harold when Edward sent
to Hungary for the heirs of Edmund Ironside, who, as
we saw, had taken refuge there forty years before ; but
their representative (also an Edward) died almost as
soon as he landed in England (1057), and left three

children, Edgar, Margaret, and Christina, mere infants. Harold, however, *professed* to look on Edgar "the Atheling"[1] as the heir to the crown. But whether Harold was more politic than his father had been or more kind to King Edward, he certainly seems to have irritated him less, and it is quite possible that Wessex at least was accustoming itself to look on Harold as the really "coming man."

But an unfortunate accident, which is probably to be dated 1064, gave William a great lever with which to overthrow the national party. The Bayeux tapestry, said to have been worked by the fingers of good Queen Matilda and her ladies, which pictorially gives the whole history of the Norman Conquest, begins with a scene under which is written—

"Haroldus et equites sui equitant ad Bosham,"

apparently with a view to hawking or some other sport. Bosham is on the coast of Sussex, and Harold, perhaps tired of hawking, proposed a yachting trip. In the course of this he was blown over to the French coast, and being seized, as shipwrecked persons then were, as lawful prize by a certain ogreish Count of Ponthieu, was rescued by Duke William, whose vassal the said ogre was. Harold went to William's court at Rouen, and evidently spent some time in a sort of honourable captivity there. He was the man of all others whom William most wished to get hold of, and he was not allowed to depart until he had sworn a solemn oath to help William to the crown of England. To have refused the oath would have meant not only lifelong captivity or death for himself—that would probably have been little to such a brave man as Harold

---

[1] An "Atheling" properly means a son born while his father wears the crown, and it is singular that the title should have stuck to poor Edgar alone in English history, for an "atheling" is just what he was not. Henry I. was a real "atheling."

—but it would have meant also the loss to England of the one arm which could defend her against the Norman. To take the oath and violate it, as he *must* do, would be to fight with the millstone of perjury round his neck. There is no doubt of the immense influence of this oath in the events of the next two years. The age believed that the saints, upon whose relics the oath had been sworn, would take a terrible revenge upon the perjured man.   Normandy believed it, and rejoiced ; England more than half believed it, and trembled. Harold returned to England, and evidently held his peace about the oath as much as possible ; but henceforth he appears to have taken every possible step to secure his own succession and to conciliate his enemies.

In 1065 his brother Tostig was driven from his earldom of Northumbria, because he had used great, but perhaps necessary, cruelty in endeavouring to stamp out the anarchy of that province. Harold made a bold bid for the friendship of the Mercian house by conferring the earldom upon one of Algar's sons, named Morcar ; while the other, Edwin, has just succeeded to his father's earldom of Mercia. "Edwin and Morcar" are always named together in the history of the Norman Conquest, because they were the two northern earls who failed to come (could they have come ?) to Harold's help at Senlac. No doubt they had profound and hereditary jealousy of the house of Godwin. Poor King Edward seems to have been vexed at this, as Tostig was rather a favourite of his. But King Edward's days were drawing to a close. His great new Abbey of Westminster was dedicated to St. Peter on Holy Innocents' Day, 1065, but the king was too ill to be present ; and on January 5th, with weird prophecies of evil on his lips, the last king of the male line of Alfred passed away.

Harold usurped the crown, and was crowned the next

day. I say " usurped," because it is impossible that a full Witan can have been called at such short notice ; but that the consent of all the national party in Wessex would have been given I do not doubt. Indeed, it is difficult to see what else Harold could have done. Edgar was a baby of ten. William was the national enemy. Swein Estrithson, the heir of Canute, was far away, and had over and over again shown himself too cautious in pushing his claims ; but for Swein Estrithson, Mercia and Northumbria would probably have declared could their mind have been known. Moreover, a fresh danger was threatening from the furthest North. Harold of Norway, called " Hardrada," the last of the great Viking monarchs, was fitting out a terrible fleet in Trondhjem, and its destination could hardly be doubtful. The exile Tostig, furious with his brother, was knocking at all doors, now at Baldwin's, now at William's, now at the Norwegian king's. England was the carcase, and the eagles were gathering. Indeed, it must in the course of the year have appeared doubtful to Duke William with which Harold he would have to fight. In the noble words of Mr. Kingsley : " What if two storm - clouds swept across England, each on its own path, and met in the midst to hurl their lightnings into each other ? A fight between William of Normandy and Harold of Norway on some moorland in Mercia— that would be a battle of giants ; a sight at which Odin and the gods of Valhalla would rise from their seats, and throw away the mead-horn, to stare down on the deeds of heroes scarcely less mighty than themselves."

Harold of England, however, was to prove more than a match for the mighty Viking and almost a match for the mighty duke. He at once took a further step to conciliate the Mercian house by marrying Aldyth, the sister of Edwin and Morcar ; he cleared out the remaining Norman counsellors of Edward, leaving only one Norman bishop (William of London). His chief counsellors appear to have been Stigand, Wulfstan (Bishop of Worcester), and Ethelwy (Abbot of Evesham). In March he and Wulfstan undertook a "royal progress" to the North, and were well received at York; in April he returned to London to concert measures against the double invasion which was now certain.

We must now retrace our steps some distance to understand the attitude of Duke William. The position which he had won among the feudal princes of France was a remarkable one. The new dynasty (of the Capets), which was to hold France for 800 years in the male line, had not yet been a century on the throne, and its power was hardly felt fifty miles from Paris. In the North four great houses completely overshadowed it. These were Normandy, Anjou, Flanders, Champagne. Though all were jealous of the King of France, they were even more jealous of each other, and there was in particular a lasting hatred between Normandy and Anjou, the battle-ground being the intervening county of Maine. Maine, it must be remembered, is a somewhat hilly region, lying at the head of the watershed between the rolling ground of Normandy and the rich little "pocket" of Anjou which occupies the valley of the Sarthe at and above its junction with the Loire.

In the history of William the Bastard, the conquest of Maine ranks as an achievement only second to the conquest of England. Even within his own duchy William had at first great difficulties; the descendants of the fierce Scandinavian pirates made the fiercest and most uncontrollable of barons, and were quite willing on occasion to call in the Angevin count or the French king against their own duke. Several of

William's guardians had been murdered during his minority; before he was twenty-one he had crushed a great combination of rebels at Val-es-Dunes (1047), and was twice again called to the same task (Mortemer 1054, Varaville 1058). From 1048–1063 he was engaged in the struggle for Maine, while, as we have seen, he was ever keeping an eye on England. From these struggles William had emerged the first captain and the first statesman of his age. Remember always that such a captain in such an age would be able to attract to his standard mercenaries and adventurers from every country in Western Europe provided he could pay them. And if he took England he would be able to pay them in the best of all wages—in rich food-bearing lands.

William had already succeeded in winning the friend-ship of Flanders, and marrying his beloved Matilda in spite of the objections of the Pope (there was some distant kindred between William and his wife which made the Pope hesitate to grant the required "dispensation"). The person whom he had employed to talk over the Pope was the Italian, Lanfranc, who was then Abbot of the famous Norman Abbey of Bec; and it was the same great ecclesiastical statesman who soon after secured for his master the Papal blessing upon the expedition to England. It is very easy to revile the Pope and his trusted counsellor, Hildebrand, for aiding and abetting such an enterprise as the Norman Conquest; but we have to remember that in the previous fifty years the Papacy had been reformed, but the English Church had not. Nay, the English Church was hardly aware that the Papacy had been reformed. William expressly made a bargain with the Pope that he would bring England into conformity with the rest of Western Christendom: the Normans, who had already grasped the temporal weapons of the horse-soldier and the arrow, which were the coming forces in warfare, were not slow to grasp the friendship of the Italian priest, which was to be the most potent force in politics for the next two centuries. The spirit which animated it and them was already the spirit of the Crusades, although the first Crusade was still thirty years off ; *i.e.* the spirit which will spread the religion of Christ with the sword, and which regards the Pope as the sole exponent of that religion. To put down the sale of bishoprics and livings in the Church (called the sin of Simony) was a noble and worthy object of the Pope ; to put down the marriage of the clergy was regarded by the Popes of that age as even more necessary. It was alleged, probably with truth, that England was full of married or quasi-married clergy, and that the sin of Simony was rampant. Moreover, the zeal for monasticism in England, which had needed requickening in Dunstan's time, had already gone to sleep again, whereas Italy and France were passing, and destined to pass in the near future, under wave after wave of fresh monastic and ascetic energy. And now England had recently, without any consciousness that she was doing anything unusual, actually driven out a lawfully consecrated Archbishop of Canterbury because he happened to be a Norman ; and a shudder of horror had run through Christendom at the deed. Robert's successor, Stigand, had not received proper Papal confirmation ; even Harold had tacitly admitted as much, when he got himself crowned by Aldred, Archbishop of York, instead of Stigand. Finally, there was Harold's "shameless perjury" to avenge. And so the Pope was induced to send William a "blessed banner," and to sanction the enormous enterprise of greed and slaughter as a sort of crusade.

Still the difficulties in William's path were enormous : such a man could have but few friends ; among his barons his one steady friend appears to have been William Fitz-Osbern, the son of his old seneschal and guardian. To him was entrusted the task of talking over the Norman barons. In the main this could only be by an appeal to their cupidity. The army and the ships to transport it were raised by what was called in Queen Elizabeth's time an "adventure" : *i.e.* you embarked or "adventured" so much capital (in the shape of men, horses, armour, ships) in the enterprise ; for which you would be rewarded, if it were successful, in so much English land. If it failed—well, you would probably be ruined.

On the whole the Norman barons did stake pretty nearly all they had got to stake on the success of the enterprise. But volunteers innumerable came from all parts of France, especially from Flanders, Anjou, Touraine, and Brittany. The summer, however, was far advanced before William's large fleet was brought together at the mouth of the little river Dive in Normandy (12th August), and meanwhile King Harold had not been idle. From May till 8th September a large fleet and army were keeping watch on our Southern coasts—no doubt every man that could be raised in Wessex and East Anglia was there. We are expressly told that it was provisioned without plundering, which speaks volumes for Harold's ability as a general and a king. But he could have no choice except to abandon to their own earls the defence of Mercia and Northumbria against Hardrada : for Wessex, and therefore for Harold, William's invasion was the more dangerous. But, as it happened, Hardrada came first. He landed at first in Orkney ; sailed to the Tyne, where he was joined by the traitor Tostig, and finally entered the

Humber in great force, driving before him the small fleet of Edwin and Morcar. The earls seem to have done their best; they collected a large army but were beaten by Hardrada outside York (Sept. 20th). Four days afterwards Hardrada entered York and was accepted as king.

One may fancy the feelings of King Harold when the news of Hardrada's landing reached him in London. William had just (Sept. 12th) transported his whole fleet to St. Valery, in the mouth of the river Somme, for his final spring upon England, for which he only waited for a favourable wind. Our own southern fleet and army had had to be disbanded (on Sept. 8th) for want of provisions; and here was this terrible Viking in the Humber! Harold flew to York and fought and slew Hardrada and Tostig at the great battle of Stamford Bridge (Sept. 25th), and then flew back on the news that William had crossed in one night (Sept. 27–28), had established himself at Hastings, and was ravaging Sussex with fire and sword. I have followed the received dates, but, considering the means of communication then existing in England, I am bound to say that they sound incredible. Harold is said to have reached London on October 5th, to have stayed there six days collecting his troops (Oct. 5–11), to have reached the hill of Senlac, seven miles north of Hastings, on the night of the 12th, to have spent 13th settling his position, and to have fought the battle on 14th. The great Duke of Marlborough on his famous march to Blenheim did not move at anything like the rate here attributed to Harold. Moreover, the very people who tell us of these incredibly rapid movements scold Edwin and Morcar for not being at Harold's side at Senlac; which, as Euclid used to say, is absurd.

F

. It would be rash to hazard a guess at the numbers of either army at the battle of Senlac. The chroniclers give William anything from 14,000 to 60,000; but Sir James Ramsay well points out that even 10,000 is beyond credibility, and that 5000 is the utmost number that could have crossed and been unshipped in the short time at William's disposal. Harold's force was by universal consent much smaller than William's; yet, from a military point of view, a few good troops, such as the house-carls undoubtedly were, should have been sufficient to hold such a position as the hill of Senlac. Whether the King of England did or did not fortify his position with a "palisade" is a point over which a furious controversy has recently raged; I prefer to believe that his closely-locked ranks of house-carls, with their shirts of mail and iron head-pieces and their heavy Danish axes, were its true fortification. How the rest of his troops were raised, what shires sent their levies, we know not; in fact, there is nothing of which we know so little as the old English army on the eve of its last battle. But from entries in Domesday of persons "occisi in bello de Hastings," we may guess that it was mainly Kent, Surrey, Sussex, Middlesex, Hants, and Berks that sent troops; and there may have been a few from the nearer Eastern counties. There is a story that Harold's brother Gurth begged to be allowed to conduct the defence at Senlac, while Harold should fall back upon London to collect troops and to ravage the country in order to starve out William. But, on the whole, Harold was right to choose his ground and fight at once.

The only difference in the armament of the two sides consisted in the use of the horse and the bow by the Normans, and the former must have been a doubtful advantage in charging uphill against such a position as Harold's. It is to the arrows of the archers then that we must principally ascribe the victory; for we must remember that the Danish axe needed two hands to wield it, and that while wielding it the Englishman could not use his shield to protect him from the arrows; the shields therefore were slung, as the Bayeux tapestry shows them, around the necks of the soldiers, and thus would protect the body from arrows in front, but not from arrows falling from above. It is to one of the latter shots that the Norman chroniclers ascribe the death-wound of Harold. As for "armour," the mail-shirt (of fine rings woven together and joined to the steel cap by a hauberk or "neck-piece" of the same ring-mail) appears to have been the universal wear of a heavy-armed man; but we must not forget that these were worn over thick quilted garments of leather. Such would form a defence against all but the very heaviest weapons; but it is surely probable that a blow from a two-handed axe would break bones, or utterly crush the man whatever defensive armour he might wear. It is certain that the battle was a desperately contested one; as long as the shield-wall was unbroken, nothing that William could bring or throw against the hill was of use; as at Waterloo,

> " dashed on every rocky square,
> Their surging charges foamed themselves away,"

and at last William was induced towards evening to try the hazardous experiment of a feigned flight. The temptation even to the disciplined house-carls to break their ranks was irresistible; they swept down in head-long pursuit, and were never able to re-form completely; or, if they re-formed, to keep the cavalry from getting inside the shield-wall. Their king, desperately wounded, was stayed up against the last charges and died beside his standard at evening, and with him fell the entire band of devoted followers who had fought nearest to him.

We do not hear of much pursuit of such as escaped, and the survivors probably retired as swiftly as possible upon London. William pitched his tent upon the spot where Harold had fallen, and ate and drank and gave thanks to God. Upon that very spot rose a few years afterwards the high altar of the "Abbey of Saint Martin of the Place of Battle," now known as Battle Abbey. Awful, indeed, to our ideas, is the conception of religion which could raise such an altar on such a place ; but it was the same conception which produced the Crusades. William had come to believe that he was fighting for the glory of God as well as for his own just rights.

William's movements immediately after the battle are interesting. He seems to have waited a few days at Senlac, expecting a general submission at least of Southern England. But there was no idea of submission yet. There must have been men alive who remembered the five pitched battles of Edmund and Canute in 1016; but, unfortunately, there was now no Edmund to organise resistance. Edwin, Morcar, Waltheof, and the two archbishops seem to have been at London on November 1st, when young Edgar Atheling was elected king, but not crowned. A worse choice than a boy of ten at such a juncture could hardly have been made, and William must have smiled when he heard of it. No steps, beyond that of holding London Bridge, were taken to check his advance ; but with great prudence William before advancing upon London set about the reduction of the Kentish seaports, which were of the utmost importance for keeping open his communication with Normandy. We can track him to Romney (Oct. 20th), by Dover to Canterbury (Oct. 29th) ; thence he sent a detachment to take Winchester, which was then in

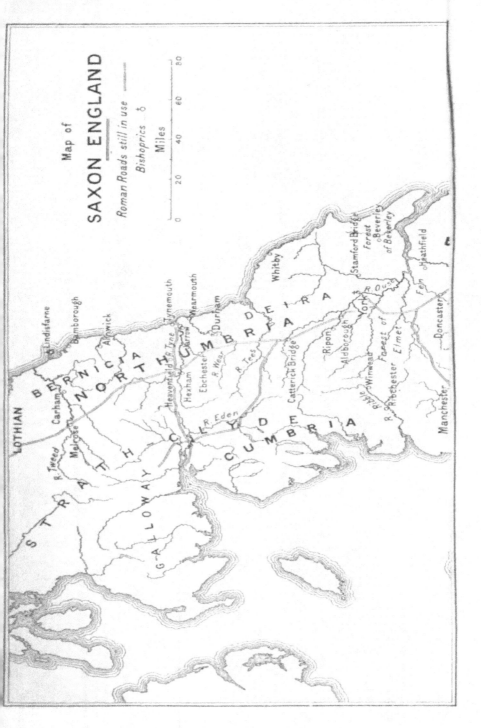

Map of

SAXON ENGLAND

Roman Roads still in use ⎯⎯⎯⎯
Bishoprics ☩

Miles

0   20   40   60   80

To face page 84

the possession of Edith, widow of the Confessor, who was believed to favour the cause of the Normans rather than that of her own brother Harold. Then by the old Roman road on the south bank of the Thames William advanced upon London, and on December 1st we find him glaring at the city across the river, but unable to risk any serious attempt to force the bridge ; we presume, therefore, that the remnants of the English host were in the capital. There was nothing for William but a march up stream until he could find a bridge or a ford ; and at last at Wallingford, nearly ninety miles above London by the river bank, he was able to cross ; after a long detour he arrived at Little Berkhamstead, fifteen miles north of London, a few days before Christmas. Edwin and Morcar had already fled to the North, but the two archbishops and their puppet king, Edgar, met William, and, making complete submission, conducted him to his crowning in Westminster Abbey on Christmas Day. During the whole of the long march his troops must have subsisted wholly upon plunder ; and it has been plausibly argued that we can actually trace the line of his march, in a track some ten miles wide, by the devastations in the villages on that track hinted at in the Domesday Book. The terror inspired must have been great, but we must not think of it as entirely new ; Swein Forkbeard had barely been dead fifty years, and his ravages were probably more terrible still. Everybody's farm was in those days burnt or eaten up occasionally, although not nearly so frequently in England as on the Continent, where private war was the rule. This terrible foreigner was coming, though no one knew it, to create a state of society in which such devastations should be of the rarest possible occurrence.

CHAPTER VII

THE REIGN OF WILLIAM THE CONQUEROR

THE moment he was crowned king William began to build the Tower of London, both to overawe the city and for his own safety. Dreadful and vast its stones must have loomed up on the little wooden London of that day; and more dreadful still as men began to hear that the Conqueror's path was to be strewn with new fortifications from the Channel to the Scots border. Castles at Hastings, Winchester, Bramber, Lewes, Carisbroke, Canterbury, Wallingford, Windsor, Norwich, seem to have been begun at once (Dover and Arundel had stone castles before the Conquest). It is not easy to say what number of these new castles were stone and what mere wooden fortifications of the older type. In Normandy, before the end of the tenth century the stone "keep" of rectangular shape had begun to supersede the earthwork raised on a mound; but the great rapidity with which William's castles were thrown up during the years 1067–70 indicates that they were probably wood-work defences of a temporary nature, to be superseded by stone keeps as soon as possible; and these last were probably begun at once. Domesday enumerates forty-nine castles altogether, and careful researches have disclosed over 600 as having existed at one time or another in England; of the Domesday castles two-thirds were built on the sites of old Saxon wooden strongholds. For the immediate future such fortresses must have been necessary to the safety of what was, after all, but a small French garrison in England; but they soon ceased to be a necessity, and even became a danger to the kings, which is a proof of the good peace these Norman kings made. " He who fears his people," said the great Italian, Macchiavelli, "will build fortresses, he who trusts them will destroy fortresses."

The importance of his coronation to William was great; it gave him a legal position as the successor of King Edward: Harold's reign was altogether ignored, and his acts treated as those of a mere usurper, who had for almost a year kept the lawful king "from his own." Consequently all who had not fought at Hastings, or taken any open step against William before or since that event, might reckon on retaining their lands in peace, especially if they made the new king a peace-offering in money. But — and here came in the iniquitous side of the business — it was just all the true-hearted Englishmen of the South-East who had resisted William: their lands therefore were forfeited. Had he been alone, William might perhaps have taken a different view, but to his Norman barons he was merely the head of an expedition for the exploiting of England: their heavy investments in that expedition must now be repaid with interest. So there followed at once the confiscation of all the good lands of Kent, Sussex, Surrey, Berks, Hants, and of much of the Eastern Counties, *i.e.* of the richest part of England. Again, however, remember that there was nothing new in such confiscation; it was the legal result of outlawry, and every real gentleman in the eleventh century expected to be outlawed at least once in his life. Possibly also many of those who had actually resisted redeemed their lands by solid cash payments. For William was avaricious; there's no denying that. Even abbots and bishops were obliged to buy his protection for themselves and for their lands with gifts of plate and jewels.   The Norman saints who had, doubtless, watched over the expedition, upon whose relics Harold's perjury had been made, had to be rewarded with gifts to their shrines—naturally at the expense of the English saints, some of whom, however, *e.g.* Saint Cuthbert, it would not do to offend too much.   William's gifts to foreign churches after Hastings were enormous, and give one a good idea of the quantity of wealth which had been stored in the Saxon churches.

Early in March 1067, before the North of England had been touched at all, William felt himself sufficiently firm on his new throne to leave England for a while and to go to Normandy.   Edwin, Morcar, Waltheof and most of the English leaders had come and made some sort of submission to William; they had been well received, and promised all manner of protection if they remained good.   Even Stigand had not yet been deposed, and was fairly well treated at first.   Most of these men were now taken in the king's train to Normandy.   The journey was no doubt prompted by a natural desire to show himself in his native land as a crowned king, and also by the desire to pay his devotion to his native saints.   But it was a mistake for all that.   The over-cautious Swein of Denmark was believed to be moving at last, and now indeed was the time for him to come, before a single Norman knight had crossed the Humber; there would be abundance of welcome for the Danes in East Anglia if not elsewhere.   The new Norman landowners were not likely to treat their English tenants well, and they did not; and in the summer of 1067 three centres of revolt began to show themselves, Kent, Cheshire, and Devonshire. William did not hurry back on the receipt of the news;

it would not do to show panic; but when he did come he struck hard and struck home (Dec. 1067). The Western revolt was the most dangerous. Harold's brothers had all fallen beside him at Senlac, but his mother and two of his sons, of whom there is no other mention in history, were holding the old Roman city of Exeter. But this and all subsequent insurrections followed but one law, that of the old disunion of England. William's marches also followed but one law, devastation, castle-building, confiscation; and so Dorset, Somerset, Devon, and Cornwall came to be added to the spoils. From a signal triumph at Exeter, which stood a severe siege (Feb. 1068), William turned upwards through Gloucestershire and Worcestershire, and then came back to London, while the Kentish and Cheshire risings sputtered and subsided again.

But the game of disunited insurrection had begun; the English leaders fled one by one from William's court, and put themselves from time to time at the head of serious movements. Most serious of all would be the North. In May 1068, and again in January and July 1069, York was the centre of rebellion. Young Edgar had been to Scotland and had obtained help from Malcolm Canmore. That wild Celtic barbarian obtained as a pledge of his help the hand of Edgar's sister Margaret—"Saint Margaret of Scotland"—who to some extent tamed her wild husband and began to introduce civilised practices and ideas into his wild realm. But if Malcolm helped Edgar, and Waltheof rose for Edgar, Edwin and Morcar, who probably had visions of a kingdom of Mercia and a kingdom of Northumbria for themselves, would be lukewarm; and we know that the Yorkshire and Lincolnshire Danes, the descendants of Swein Forkbeard's terrible Vikings, were looking not to a Saxon boy, but to their natural lord, Swein Estrithson, beyond the sea. And so in the clash of parties and armies King William "divisit et imperavit."

Swiftly he moved in the summer of 1068; from Oxford (Castle) we can trace him to Warwick (Castle), where Edwin and Morcar met him and submitted again; by Coventry and Leicester to Nottingham (Castle), to the Peak (Castle) and so to York (Castle No. 1, on the left bank of the Ouse, in charge of which he left the trustiest of his lieutenants, William Malet, with a large garrison). Then back through Lincoln (Castle), Cambridge (Castle), and Huntingdon (Castle). He has not touched Northumbria much as yet; but he appoints an earl of French descent to rule it, who is murdered of course; William calmly appoints another. Edgar flies again to Scotland, and still the Danes delay their coming. In the spring of 1069 Edgar is back again in Yorkshire with Scottish help; William flies back to York and builds Castle No. 2 on the right bank of the Ouse to shut the navigation against the coming of the Danes. At last in the summer Swein's fleet, commanded by his brother Osborn, entered the Humber; all Northumbria rose joyfully to receive it, and York and its castles fell, Archbishop Aldred (who was in York with Malet) dying during the siege. William was loth to send help, because he would not believe that Malet could be beaten out of York; but at last in the autumn he came, and the Danes thought it prudent to retreat to their ships (possibly William bribed them to do so); this time King William would make a full end of Northern insurrections, and he did. His devastation of Yorkshire up to the gates of Durham lives in history as one of those terrible crimes which it would be folly to seek to palliate. The results of it were felt far into the later

Middle Ages, some say till the eighteenth century.   In Domesday Yorkshire is returned practically as waste (vastata).   The survivors fled to Scotland.   William kept his Christmas of 1069 amid the ashes of York, and then by terrible forced marches, in which he was always foremost in every peril and hardship, crossed the Pennines into the plains of Cheshire, where a fresh revolt (of one "Edric the Wild") had to be stamped out in blood and fire.

The Danes meanwhile had to feed their sailors: their English allies were broken and dispersed and their land swept bare; they could therefore only move southwards and plunder their Lincolnshire kinsmen. Chance or design led them to the sack of the rich Abbey of Peterborough, and the havoc they committed there was not likely to endear them to the English.   Swein Estrithson should have come himself if he had meant to succeed; his brother was either incompetent or treacherous, and the great Viking invasion rolled back to Denmark heavy with dishonour and the spoils of Peterborough.

After the harrying of the North and of Cheshire but one last stronghold was left to English hearts, the impregnable fen-island of Ely, where a great outlaw captain called Hereward the Wake held out in the name of Swein till the autumn of 1071.   The story of that defence has been so finely told by Kingsley that I will not give it here; Ely cost William four weary months and countless lives, and was at last only taken owing to the faint-heartedness of its monks, who were shut up with the defenders.   The only other serious trouble to William came from sundry raids of Malcolm of Scotland, who completed the destruction of the North of England, which had been so terribly begun by William.   Malcolm indeed could hardly ever venture into Yorkshire, and occupied himself mainly with the county of Northumberland.

William avenged one of these raids in 1072 by a march as far North as the Tay, whither no ruler of civilised Britain had penetrated since the fall of the Roman Empire. At Abernethy Malcolm met the Conqueror and "put his hands between his hands" as the token of submission : which doubtless William interpreted to mean feudal vassalage ; but Malcolm thought otherwise. The castles built by William in the ruined North were few—Richmond 1069, Durham 1072, Newcastle 1080; but the monasteries like Jarrow and Whitby (in ruins since the Danish invasions) began to be rebuilt, and St. Mary's, York, was founded before the end of the reign. We shall find in the twelfth century that the recolonisation of the North is wholly due to ecclesiastical foundations. Edgar the Atheling found an abiding refuge at his brother-in-law's court along with many expatriated Saxon families, and these doubtless contributed much towards the comparative civilisation of Southern Scotland. We shall find Edgar reconciled to the new dynasty in the next reign, and he died at a great age, in the enjoyment of broad lands in England, after the close of the reign of Henry I. Apparently he never married, and with him the male line of Alfred came to an end. Revolts in plenty William had to deal with after this, but they were all with one exception in his French dominions —he had also struggles to retain the ever-rebellious Maine, or to make good his claim to another border land, the county of the Vexin, lying on the Seine midway between Paris and Rouen. After 1076 William spent most of his time in Normandy occupied with these troubles, which were much aggravated by the dis-affection of his eldest son Robert, a good-natured, hot-

tempered soldier, who was always clamouring to be
endowed with governments and counties, and always
proving himself unfit to govern.   In many of these
later wars William was unlucky, and the French king
was not slow to take advantage of him.   The Saxon
chroniclers were naturally apt to see in the king's ill
luck the hand of God avenging his ruthlessness in
England.   The corpulence which was hereditary in
William's family developed in his case into a "most
unwieldy belly," and it was amid the ashes of the
burning city of Mantes in 1087 that he received in
this part of his person the injury that caused his
death.

Before, however, we let the greatest figure of the
Middle Ages sink into his tomb we must pause to
consider what sort of an England it was that he left
behind him.   He has tried to tell us something of this
himself.   In 1085 "King William caused all England
to be described," and the Domesday Survey, in which
the "description" is recorded, is the most interesting
memorial of the period.   We must beware, even in
this, of reading into William's government an ideal
which he was far from reaching.   He did not order
all England to be described, for the reason for which
the British Raj orders surveys of India, namely, in
order to become acquainted with the needs of the
people and to legislate for them accordingly.   He
ordered it that he might see how he could get the
greatest amount of taxation (Danegeld he called it)
out of them.   "You are to inquire," he says to his
commissioners in each village, "who holds the manor
now, who held it in the time of King Edward," and a
whole string of other questions, but principally "what
it is worth and whether it can be made worth more!"
That it would be "made worth more" by the new

Norman landowners there was little doubt. They came of a race accustomed to make things pay ; to give but only one instance, there are in the heart of the great Sussex forest by the time of Domesday seventeen or eighteen villages which had no existence before the Conquest ; the true colonisation or breaking up of waste land of England was already beginning.

Shall we look back for a few minutes by the light of Domesday at our old friends in the village of Tubney, in the hundred of Rotherey, in the county of Sussex (see above, page 32). We may guess that it has changed hands several times since Higg the first caught the eels in the Rother which he sent some-what unwillingly to the early Saxon king. With Higg and his equals the changes have principally come in a reasonable (not a great) increase of population, which, together with the rising power of the feudal thegns or bishops who have successively held the lordship of the village since that time, has had the effect of diminishing the holdings of each free peasant very considerably. The last cause has also increased the labour rents of such of the villagers as pay them. As a general rule these rents will be harder and higher if paid to a present thegn or bishop than to an absent and distant king. A time, however, will come, or will perhaps have already come, when these rents and services tend to "crystallise" — *i.e.* to get fixed by custom. The average holding of such men as Higg will be a "vir-gate" (shall we say 30 acres ?). Such a holding may possibly still be entirely free of all rent except military service to the king ; it may on the contrary pay a heavy labour-rent and a heavy rent in kind, such as two days a week ploughing, five days a week in harvest, one hundred eggs in Lent. Then there will be the once prosperous Pigg now represented by a cottager cotarius) holding only 5 acres and paying an exorbitant labour-rent of three days a week all the year round for them ("three days" is exceptional in England). There is absolutely no rule. Domesday shows us all manner of names for the peasants, such as "villeins," "sokemen," "freeholders," "cottagers," "borders," "geneats," "boors," "roadknights," "serfs"; a mere wilderness of tenures; it also shows us all manner of gradations of rents (most people pay some sort of rent to somebody above them) and all manner of gradations of freedom, but with a *general tendency downwards, i.e.* towards serfdom. I take it that the liberty of even such men as Higg was trembling in the balance when King William came to England. The feudalisation of justice was also pretty complete. One might almost say that the king farmed out the hundred courts to great men to hold, though not often the county courts; these would still be held by the sheriff, who would account to the king for the fines in them. The bishops were usually large holders of courts as well as feudal landlords. The temptation of the kings to give away lands and courts "for the good of their souls" had been the cause of this. Very probably the smaller thegns had actually taken to holding small courts in the villages themselves, getting exemption or not, as the case might be, from the hundred courts. Such a court is now, on the eve of the Conquest, being held at Tubney by Wippo, a thegn, the steersman of Harold's ship, to whom Harold has given the labour-rents of the villagers there, together with the right to get what he can out of them in the way of fines. The Bishop of Selsey, who holds the hundred court of Rotherey, grumbles a good deal at this, which is a distinct pecuniary loss to him: probably he manages to insist that two villagers from Tubney shall be sent to that hundred court to represent it there; say Wamba the son of Witless, and Elfric the miller; when they appear at that court it is found that Elfric has ground short weight; therefore he is "in mercy" (misericordia), and the fourpence of his fine will go to the bishop's pocket, not to Wippo's; Wamba has struck the bishop's reeve—fine sixpence and penance at the church door four Sundays running.

Wippo is killed at Hastings, as becomes a valiant follower of King Harold, and three or four other villagers of Tubney as well; and one fine morning in the spring of 1067 there appear riding across the open fields five men in armour on big horses and a clerk on a palfrey, armed with parchments, the meaning of which is that Roger de Something-or-other, great-great-grandson of a Scandinavian pirate, has come to be lord of the manor of Tubney. He can speak no English, and is proud of the fact; he ought, of course, to be resisted in the name of the liberties of Englishmen. But—there is no doubt that King Harold and Wippo are dead and King William lawfully crowned. Tubney has changed hands several times during the preceding century, has heard terrible tales of Norman cruelty, and is disposed to accept Roger quietly. After all, Tubney is many and Roger is few, and, if he prove too gory a tyrant, it may get a secret opportunity of cutting Roger's throat in the near future. Roger is possibly inclined to treat all the villagers as slaves, and to add to their yoke; he is no doubt in a position to disregard custom and to make exceptionally favourable bargains of rent and service with his new tenants, to increase their services and fines, and to diminish their holdings. But, after all, what has he come to England for? To get rich;

and for that purpose he must get his "demesne" cultivated, or how will Tubney pay him? He has undertaken to supply the king with one fully armed knight
besides himself ; that will mean four war-horses and
certainly four attendants and lesser fighting men of some
sort, to be called out whenever the king goes to war.

Perhaps he will keep one of these French fellows who
accompany him, and get the king to give him lands out
of the forfeited holdings of those who fell at Hastings,
make him a "military tenant" under himself ; but the
others he is obliged to send off to garrison the king's
new castle at Lewes. The families of those who fell
at Hastings don't trouble Roger's compassion, if he has
any, a whit. For the rest there will be what we may
call an "economic limit," above which it will not pay
Roger to increase the services of his villeins ; they must
not be skin and bone, or his ploughs will not be kept
going ; Higg, the substantial and the prudent, may even
have his holding increased in return for a substantia
rent in hard cash, just the thing most difficult to come
by in the eleventh century ; if so, Higg will remain a
"freeholder of the manor," the ancestor of the yeomen
"whose limbs were made in England," as Henry V.
told them at the siege of Harfleur, and whose long-bows
won Crecy and Agincourt. The rest of the villagers
Roger, in his own mind, lumps together as "villeins" ;
and in his grandson's time the law will come to recognise but these two classes among the agricultural population—the freeholders and the villeins. These will no
doubt perform various kinds of hard agricultural service
on Roger's demesne (very much as they did on the
same land when it was Wippo's) under the eye of
Roger's bailiff. Custom will rapidly fix these services
and rents ; after two or three generations they will never
be able to be altered for the worse.

G

Roger will, of course, succeed to the little "manor court" of Tubney, which Wippo had begun to hold, and at first he will rejoice at the prospect of the fines ; perhaps even will make an attempt to hang his own thieves. But before very long he will find that this is not in the least likely to be permitted to him ; that there is now, what there never was before, a GOVERNMENT in the country which intends to save him that trouble ; and by the end of the twelfth century his rights of "sac and soc, toll and theam, infangenethef and outfangenethef" (barbarous Saxon jingle he calls it) have come to mean the right to fine Bessy the alewife twopence for brewing bad beer.

The right of presenting a parson to the church of Tubney will also come to Roger ; his Norman sense of decorum in religious matters is genuinely offended by the drunkenness and ignorance of the Saxon priest whom he finds there, and who actually brings to church a person whom he calls his wife. Before many years are past the bishop, whose see has been moved from Selsey to Chichester, will probably have got this man dismissed, and a respectable priest, who has perhaps been trained in Earl William's new Cluniac Priory at Lewes, will be presented. The new man will confine his drink to a modest three gallons a day, and will certainly not be married. But even before this Roger will have begun to build a stone church in place of the old wooden one, and the services will be more frequent and more splendid than before.

I don't suppose Roger will introduce new methods of cultivation ; that would be too much to expect of him, but he will certainly break up waste land, will plant and build, and clear and drain ; he is so restless, he makes such intelligent haste to be rich. His son will probably marry an Englishwoman, let us hope an heiress

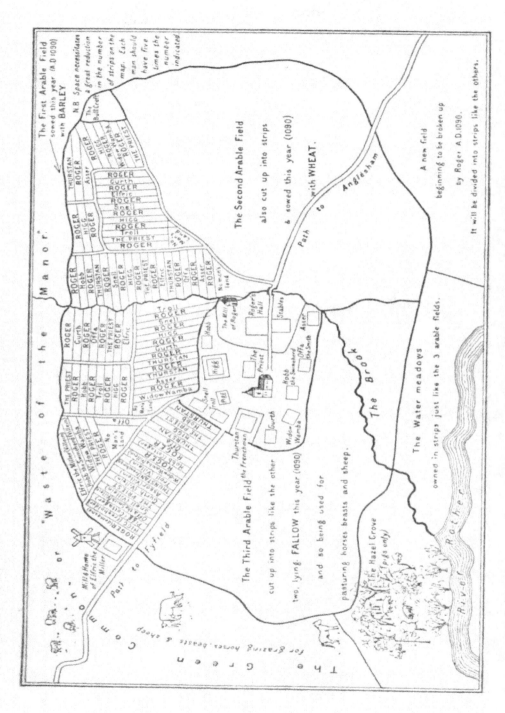

(though probably he will have to pay a very heavy fine to the king for leave to do so), and his grandson will speak English; one of the greatest boasts of Roger's remote descendants will be the double one that they "came over with the Conqueror" and "can't speak a word of any language but English."

Of course this is a favourable picture and must have been far from universal. Roger is a small man, a mere knight or squire. On one of the 150 manors of some Earl William or Earl John the Saxon peasant must have been far worse off. For such landowners will be usually absentees, who collect their rents by bailiffs, and seldom see their tenants except to fine them at the hundred court; they surround themselves with foreign underlings, rebel against the king once every five years, and try to get their tenants to follow them in that extremely unprofitable job. Even Roger would have had a much more pleasant, and his tenants a much more unpleasant time if the Norman kings (with the exception of Stephen) had not been mighty strong and terrible men. And this leads me to try to explain something of the System of Government established by the Conqueror. This system takes much from old England and much from old Normandy; it invents little that is actually new, but every institution undergoes some change.

The "Government" suggests to a modern Englishman certain amiable gentlemen meeting in frock-coats in Downing Street, mainly occupied with the task of defending themselves in Parliament and feverishly anxious to conciliate the newspapers and the mass of the ignorant voters. We are, however, apt to forget that these amiable gentlemen are at the same time heroically struggling to fulfil the *real* functions of government also (though, of course, sorely hampered

in this by the said Parliament, newspapers, and voters),
viz., the defence of the country and the maintenance
of order.   The other function of government (see above,
p. 30), that of doing justice between man and man, we
have long ago relegated to a special body of judges, who
perform it quite admirably.   Now a Norman king had
to perform all these functions of government, and,
though he was free from ignorant criticism and worry,
he was unassisted to any large extent by persons of
special knowledge, or by any habitual reverence of his
people for law and order.   The fact that he was obliged
to allot the greatest part of English lands to his French
followers, whose natural instincts were for rebellion
pure and simple, made the task infinitely more difficult
to William than it would have been to (say) Harold.
From the day of the fall of Ely in 1071 the danger to
order came not from the English but from this new
French garrison in England, *i.e.* the barons and their
followers.   For instance, in 1075-6, two of these barons,
Ralph Guader, Earl of Norfolk, and Roger Fitz-Osbern,
Earl of Hereford, enticed Waltheof, one of the few
great Englishmen who had been left in possession of
broad lands, to rise with them against William.   This
was the first "feudal revolt" in our history ; it was put
down with ease ; the earls were tried by the Witan,
and Waltheof, probably the least guilty of the three, was
executed.   But for exactly a century from that time
"feudal revolts" were constant, the last big one being
in 1174.   If I can succeed in showing you the causes
of these revolts, I may also succeed in showing what
the government of the Norman kings was like.

Now in Normandy the duke had little power, the
barons garrisoned their own castles, coined money,
hung thieves, and exercised the widest rights of private
justice.   In the case of private war all a baron's

tenants and vassals were bound to follow him, even against his overlord, just as Duke William's vassals were bound to follow him against the King of France. Private war was the most cherished of all these baronial rights, and was indeed, except hunting, the only known amusement of the eleventh century. Life in England must have appeared intolerably dull without it. Nothing but considerations of personal interest interfered in France to check the tyranny of landlords over their tenants. England would possibly have become just like that if a few more kings like Edward the Confessor had reigned. But King William was a soaring genius, far ahead of his age, and he determined from the very first to tolerate nothing of the kind in England. In the execution of this determination he was greatly favoured by circumstances.

First, by his enormous private riches from the confiscated lands—the 1400 manors which he kept in his own hands, including all the old royal domain of the kings of Wessex; and by the power of raising the direct and heavy tax called the Danegeld. Gold would buy faithful soldiers, and it did buy them. Next we must notice that he was able to scatter the estates of his new barons all over the country; except on the borders of Wales or Scotland he would never give much land in the same county to one man, but if he had to reward any man largely he would scatter his manors in fifteen or twenty different counties; so that Earl William could not make a feudal principality in Surrey, nor Earl Hugh in Warwick. Thirdly, though occasionally obliged to allow Earl Hugh or Earl William to build a castle, the king kept in his own hands all the more important castles of the kingdom, and trusted the captaincies of them to professional soldiers of lesser rank. Fourthly, there were still in memory, if not in existence, elements of old English life and old English royal powers which William at once set to work to polish up for immediate use. There was the sturdy, still partially free, peasantry, which, though it had always neglected its military duties, could be made and was made by a strong king to perform them; there was still a more or less free county court held three times a year in every county, and some (though few) free hundred courts held every month—and both these courts were attended by many English freeholders; even the greatest Norman barons should be made to attend them in person or by deputy; above all, there was still in every county a royal official called the SHERIFF.

It would be impossible to exaggerate the importance to King William of this last " discovery," as one might almost call it. We are perhaps used to think of the sheriff as the rather fat and pursy individual of whom Robin Hood so constantly made fun; but the Sheriff of Nottingham (whom Robin occasionally even hanged *pour encourager les autres*) must have been an exception to his class, as Robin was to his. Rather was the sheriff the concrete embodiment of the law; entirely dependent on the king, who appointed him annually, but towards every one but the king almost absolute. His duties were to watch and check the least movement of feudal rebellion, to preside in the county court and, by his deputies, in the hundred courts (wherever these were not in private hands), and there do justice in the king's name; to collect the king's enormous rents, and to lead to battle the old militia of his county. But were not the soldiers of this militia mostly tenants of some new Norman baron, and so would they not be bound to follow *his* banner to battle even against the king? So no doubt thought Earl Ralph or Earl Robert; but they found themselves very grievously mistaken. Perhaps on the very day in which they had planned a grand insurrection against the king, the sheriff suddenly appeared and called upon all their tenants to follow him in arms to the king's castle.   And, to the intense surprise and disgust of the earl, the tenants, who had been accustomed in a grudging kind of way to do the same for King Edward or King Harold, actually walked after the sheriff in a body.

In order to make this new right quite clear in the eyes of all men, King William, to whom the results of the Domesday inquiry had just been submitted, assembled in 1086 all the landowners in England at Salisbury, and there compelled them, great and small alike, to swear fealty to him against all men, *i.e.* against their own immediate overlords.   This was the mightiest blow ever directed against feudal anarchy by any king in Europe.   By itself it lifts William at once to the first place among mediæval statesmen.   It creates a new form of sovereignty unknown since the fall of the Roman Empire.   Edgar may have been King of the West-Saxons, head of their tribe ; may have called himself " Basileus of Britain," and so feudal overlord over the princes of Wales and Northumbria ; but William was supreme lord of every rood of land in England and of every man dwelling thereon.   We must not forget that the state of things thus established would soon become equally pleasing to the small Norman landowner and to the native Englishman ; the great barons alone would continue to kick against it.   The large majority of the 5000 knights who formed William's feudal army, as opposed to the national militia, and who were principally supplied to him by the great barons as their military " rent " or service for their new lands, were by nature and by settlement " small " men who would soon find their account in the new state of things.   Some of them were like our friend Roger of Tubney, who, you remember, supplies the king with two knights (himself and another).   But Earl William owes the king fifty knights ; the Abbot of Gloucester owes him twenty-five knights.   These great landowners are not obliged to enfeoff (*i.e.* endow with lands) fifty and twenty-five gentlemen respectively in order to get this service performed ; they may if they please keep this number of armed men on their own premises ; but the former will be infinitely the more convenient method for the earl and the abbot, and in time will become universal.   " A knight's fee " or fief, that is, a sufficient holding to enable a man to serve as a knight, will come to be reckoned as "land worth £20 a year," and at the end of the thirteenth century it will be the rule that a man possessed of so much land will be reckoned *ipso facto* a knight, and made to serve in the cavalry.   Once you settle such a man on land of his own (remember that he has to take the oath to the king even against the earl or the abbot who enfeoffed him) you give him a "stake in the country," which he will not willingly forfeit by encouraging the earl in rebellion.   Moreover the "feudal army" is very seldom called out by the king, who will soon prefer to take a tax called "scutage" or shield-money instead of such service.

William is obliged to keep up the meetings of his "wise men," now called his "Great Council of Tenants in Chief," which is really a feudalised and larger Saxon Witan, to which all bishops and greater barons are obliged to come three times a year.   Possibly he would like to have dispensed with even this check upon the royal power, but no feudal monarch in Europe could do that ; and this body is of course the true germ of the "Most High Court of Parliament," the supreme legislative and judicial body of the land. Little business, however, seems to have been really transacted therein, and very small check imposed upon the power of the Crown thereby before the reign of Henry III. All the real work was done by a small body of permanent officials, lay and clerical, who formed the king's actual court and household, and this body in the thirteenth and fourteenth centuries began to take shape as the King's "Ordinary," "Permanent," or "Privy" Council.

Finally, besides all these old or constitutional checks upon rebellions, William established, and his successors perfected, a grinding system of payments for all great barons. They must pay for leave to inherit their property (relief), pay for leave to marry their daughters (marriage), hand over their heirs, if minors, to the king's guardianship (wardship), while if they died without heirs their lands lapsed to the Crown (escheat). It was against all these things that the barons rose again and again, and (except in the wretched reign of Stephen) each time more fruitlessly than before.

One cannot help being struck by the extraordinary clemency even of the fiercest kings towards these feudal rebels. From the time of Waltheof to the close of the thirteenth century no great baron is put openly to death for rebellion ; occasionally one is imprisoned for life and perhaps starved to death ; minor rebels occasionally suffer death or mutilation, but it seems to be a recognised principle not to execute barons for treason before the age of the Edwards ; and even the garrison of a baronial castle is often allowed to march out, after surrender, with the honours of war. It almost looks as if the kings recognised certain "rules of the game" of feudal warfare.

There can be no doubt that the churchmen, whether Norman or English, did on the whole stand by the

Crown in all strictly feudal struggles. We do meet instances of rebellious bishops of baronial descent; and the Church herself soon entered upon a set of struggles of her own against the Crown, though not in the Conqueror's reign. But on the whole the Church was loyal as against feudalism. The monstrous pretensions of the twelfth and thirteenth century Papacy, which were directed to making national church government impossible, had not yet fully developed, and, though the Pope demanded from William homage for his new kingdom, he probably expected an even less courteous answer than he got. William refused all homage save to God alone, and further refused to allow any papal letters or "bulls" to be brought to England without his leave; but he published an "edict" which forbade the clergy to sit in temporal courts and allowed the bishops to set up special courts to try both civil and criminal cases in which clergymen were concerned—a concession which led to trouble in the reign of Henry II. He made almost a clean sweep of the English bishops, though he left the abbeys mostly in native hands, and he appointed foreigners of learning and distinction to all the sees except Worcester (where Harold's old friend Wulfstan lived on till the reign of Rufus). He pushed on energetically the papal crusade against Simony and marriage of priests (see above, p. 79), and he placed at the head of the Church one of the greatest men of the age, the Italian Lanfranc, late Abbot of Bec. The bishoprics began to move into the larger towns, perhaps in order to be under the shadow of the king's castles: the genius of the Norman race for building showed itself in almost every diocese, and there are few cathedrals which do not show substantial traces of Norman work, whereas, except in the crypts, none contain any serious Saxon work. Monks from the great continental foundation of Cluny began to come in, and "Cluniac" priories to be founded in England; a higher standard of clerical learning and clerical life was the result.

And in 1087 the great Conqueror died. May God have mercy on his soul. He did great and awful wrong, much of which he was great and wise enough to know to be wrong. His whole enterprise against England, to which his whole early life was devoted, was rooted and grounded in wrong. In carrying it out he was utterly ruthless as to the means and as to the suffering inflicted. But once it was effected he set himself to rule in righteousness, to protect the weak against the strong, to discipline and to unite the nation. Like Alfred, he again started England on the paths of discipline and unity from which she has never wholly gone back; and this a century before any other king in feudal Europe had grasped the meaning of union or discipline.

CHAPTER VIII

WILLIAM RUFUS AND HENRY I

IN days in which the strength and character of the king means almost everything, the most important "constitutional" question is the succession to the crown; only two kings, however, Richard I. and Edward I., succeeded to the crown with an undisputed title before the end of the thirteenth century. William II. and Henry I. both usurped the crown in the lifetime of their elder brother, Robert: it is true that the Conqueror had designated William to be King of England and Robert to be Duke of Normandy; for William "Rufus" was his father's favourite and had been perfectly loyal to him, while Robert had been in open rebellion. In spite of this, had Robert been on the spot either in 1087 or in 1100, he would probably have been chosen by the Great Council of England. The legal theory, then and long afterwards, was that the king's peace died when the king died, and that until the new king was crowned there was no "peace," and every one might enjoy his natural liberty to spoil and slay. Any reasonable claimant of royal blood who could get hold of the concrete crown (kept at Winchester) and bring it to London would probably be accepted in order to re-create a "peace." So Lanfranc crowned Rufus with all the old rites in Westminster Abbey; the native English rejoiced at the separation of England from Normandy, and Rufus began his reign with all sorts of promises of good government.

In person William Rufus was a sort of caricature of his father, shorter, fatter, fiercer to look at. In his private character he was infinitely worse, a scoffer at religion, morality, and all honour except military honour. In his public character he was also much worse, because he was supremely indifferent to justice and to everything but his own will ; but it so happened that the execution of this will usually fell in with the good of the nation as a whole ; indeed the good of the nation demanded but one thing, the suppression of the great barons, who would be sure to have their fling now that the Conqueror was dead. Rufus' hand was to lie upon them quite as heavily as his father's had lain. Intellectually the new king was not far behind his father, and the whole theory and practice of his father's kingship was thoroughly familiar to him. No serious change was made in government ; only we begin to hear more of a chief minister, or "justiciar" as he came to be called, who will in time develop into the chief judge in the king's law courts. Ranulf Flambard was Rufus' justiciar, a strong, unscrupulous, bad man, who must, however, be forgiven much for having built the greater part of Durham Cathedral.

Before a year had passed, before Robert was well settled in his Duchy of Normandy (which he never made any serious attempt to rule), the barons of England were up in arms, offered the crown to Robert, and proceeded to fortify their castles for him. Their leaders were two half-brothers of the Conqueror, Robert of Mortain and Odo of Bayeux ; at their back were Belesmes, Mowbrays, Bigods, Grantmesnils. The Earls of Chester and Surrey were faithful to William. But the rebellion was put down with consummate ease ; the native troops, "every man armed in his county," led by the sheriffs, were called out ("I will brand you as a 'nithing,'" *i.e.* a worthless coward, "if you don't come out," said the king); the rebels were beaten off from all the royal castles they attempted to besiege, and one by one their strong holds were taken and surrendered. A Norman castle, whether a thick rectangular tower (or keep) or a "shell keep," would be difficult but not impossible to take: a full-blown "Edwardian" castle, with outer and inner wards and endless ditches and circumvallations, was a very different business, but castle-building did not reach its perfection till the fourteenth century.[1] So Robert, who had got together a fleet in Normandy for the relief of Pevensey Castle, was obliged to go home to his duchy empty-handed. Odo was banished, went upon the Crusade and died.

From this time William had two tasks to pursue; the reunion of Normandy and Maine to the English Crown and the rounding off of the kingdom at home. The former was not a national task and brought no particular good to England; the latter was all-important. In the middle of these tasks William was drawn into the inevitable quarrel with the Church, but at the moment it was largely his own fault that he was drawn into it.

The Norman business began in 1090. Prince Henry, the youngest of the Conqueror's three sons, to whom his father had left £5000 in cash, in-

---

[1] Two forms of Norman castles are distinguished by our antiquaries: (*a*) the solid rectangular tower, such as that of London, with walls of immense thickness and no windows or doors on the "ground floor," but approachable only by a wooden bridge and stair reaching up to the narrow slits that served for windows on the "first floor"; and (*b*) the shell keep, a mere substitution of a light stone wall for the old English wooden wall; this would often be raised on an artificial mound, such as would not be capable of bearing the weight of a solid keep. The latter sort evidently prevailed in England till the end of the twelfth century; and from it, and not from the solid keep, the "Edwardian" type is developed.

vested a portion of this sum in the purchase from Robert (who was always impecunious) of that strange arm of France called the Côtentin (roughly speaking the country between Cherbourg and Avranches), and had fortified many castles there. He was a prudent young man, just of age, and he probably foresaw that Robert would never be able to rule Normandy ; yet if William got hold of Normandy his own position would be undoubtedly worse ; for the time, therefore, his interests lay rather with Robert than with William. But William, with the riches of England in his pocket, began to follow his younger brother's example and to purchase from Robert's vassals castles in Eastern Normandy ; the burghers of Rouen once made a futile rising on his behalf, which Henry and Robert suppressed. By 1091 about one-third of the duchy was in William's hands, and he came over to take possession. Robert and William met and arranged a treaty to the prejudice of Henry, in fact to deprive him of Côtentin ; they besieged him in his Castle of St. Michael's Mount, and when thirst brought capitulation they left him in possession only of the great rock of Domfront, on the borders of Maine.

After three years of comparative peace, during which Henry lived very quietly, and Robert squandered the gold he had got from William, William began the same game again (1094); but without much success till 1096, when the prospects of the first Crusade, which was just starting, tempted Robert to pawn all he still held in Normandy for the sum of £6000. Robert was in his element as a Crusader, and performed mighty deeds of valour. Rufus was in his element as the prudent stay-at-home king, who profited by the noble folly of others. But Rufus could show the same reckless daring himself when there was an immediate end to gain. The pledge included the county of Maine, which had never really yielded to Robert, and which was defended by Elias of La Flèche, a descendant of the old Counts of Maine: it now cost William a two years' struggle to get hold of the county, and in 1099 its capital, Le Mans, rebelled again. William was hunting near Salisbury when the news of this was brought; he simply turned his horse's head and galloped to Southampton, flung himself on board the first boat he could find—probably one of that very old pattern called an "Itchen ferryboat"—and demanded to be put across the Channel. It was blowing hard, and the men said they dared not risk the voyage; "Who ever heard of a king being drowned?" said William: he was landed near Seine-mouth next morning, rode straight to Le Mans, picking up troops as he went, and recovered the city.

One can fancy with what jealous eyes his nominal overlord, the King of France, still a very small man compared to many of his great vassals, watched this terrible King of England swallowing castles and provinces at such a great rate, and apparently able to rely on an inexhaustible purse of gold from his island realm. Rufus frightened him even more by making a treaty with the Duke of Aquitaine for the partition of the whole kingdom of France. It came to nothing but it is from such incidents as these that our long enmity to France took its rise.

All this time the really national task of rounding off the kingdom of England had been going on. Even in the Conqueror's reign the great barons of Gloucestershire, Shropshire, and Cheshire, the "Lords Marchers" of Wales as they came to be called, had been pushing their arms along the northern and southern shores of the Principality; from Chester to Rhuddlan and

Rhuddlan to Conway; from Gloucester to Chepstow and to Cardiff. Early in Rufus' time we hear of settlements of Normans in Cardigan, Pembroke, and Carmarthen; equally steady was the progress in Mid Wales, *i.e.* in Brecon and Radnor. By 1094 the independent part of Wales was reduced to that " Snowdonia " which managed to hold its own down to the time of Edward I. Rufus himself made two expeditions to the foot of Snowdon, but nothing was so effectual as castle-building. Henry I. also made two expeditions to Wales, and planted Pembrokeshire with Flemish and English colonists, so that it got the name of the " Little England beyond Wales." Old King Malcolm of Scotland, laudably anxious not to do anything so mean as to die in his bed, recommenced in 1091 the series of Scottish raids upon Northumberland. Edgar Atheling, now a grown man, appears from time to time in this business, now stirring up Malcolm to a raid, now mediating a peace between him and Rufus; once we find Rufus at the Forth (the " Scots water," as Englishmen begin to call it); but, more important still, we find him in 1092 overrunning and completely reducing to subjection the counties of Cumberland and Westmorland and the northern part of Lancashire, which the Conqueror had not been able to touch. Carlisle was rebuilt and fortified, and became that terrible border fortress which the Scots knew only too well down to 1745. To a Scotchman it smells of blood to this day.

In 1093 Malcolm journeyed to the court of Rufus at Gloucester, but Rufus, in some fit of passion, refused to receive him, and the old warrior went back to avenge the slight in one more raid, during which he was killed at Alnwick. His sainted queen died of grief three days afterwards, and, after a few years of

H

disputed succession, her son Edgar was restored to the Scottish throne by Rufus' help in 1097. The modern " Border " had now been regularly established : three sons of Malcolm and Margaret reigned in turn, Edgar, Alexander I., and David I., and there was peace between Scotland and England till 1138.

Thus the reign of Rufus may be considered as completing the work of his father on both sides of the sea. The England that Henry I. began to rule in 1100 was a much more compact realm than the England that the Conqueror had left ; probably also a much more orderly one. But Rufus' taxation had been most grievous, and his personality most odious. To his contemporaries he was the terrible savage, who mocked at religion and quarrelled with the Church.

It was, however, the bounden duty of a good king of England to quarrel, not with the Church as a whole, but with the pretensions set up in the name of the Church by that vigorous series of Popes from Gregory VII. to Boniface VIII., whose favourite text was—

" Thou shalt tread upon the lion and the adder ; the young lion and the dragon shalt thou trample under feet."

The lions were nationalities and independent states, the adder and the dragon the kings who attempted to defend them. Only two kings of England between the Conqueror and Edward II. refused to take up this insolent challenge : Richard I., who was only in England six months, and never paid any attention to its government, and Henry III., who simply truckled to the Pope. It is, however, impossible to bring the great case of " Rufus *versus* Anselm " into line with the other cases of resistance to papal oppression. Rufus appears almost like an impious boy who deliberately stirs up a dangerous animal to see whether he is afraid of it or not.

Lanfranc died in 1089, and the brutal greed of
Rufus was aroused when he thought of the vast estates
of the See of Canterbury now vacant. What if he kept
it vacant ? He might keep a lay fief vacant if there
were no heirs. Was not Canterbury a fief of the
Crown, which performed feudal service and homage,
owed and paid the service of fifty knights, &c. ? At
any rate he would try it, and for four years he did
so, pocketing the rents of the lands all the time. "The
feelings of the country were profoundly shocked," as
we should say now ; what public opinion there was
could only be expressed by the Church and the great
council of barons ; and we gather that it was expressed
freely. To do Rufus justice, he laughed at public
opinion rather than repressed it. In a fit of penitence
during a bad illness he resolved to fill up the see, and
sent for Anselm, Abbot of Bec, the most saintly and
learned man of his time. Anselm was most unwilling
to face the task, but finally accepted, and then immediately demanded restitution of all the rents which
Rufus had swallowed during the vacancy. Rufus,
however, had now got well again, and refused to dis-
gorge a penny. Anselm's next move was a more
doubtful one ; he asked for leave to go to Rome to
get his " pallium "—the symbol of his archbishopric—
from the Pope. The ordinary practice in recent times
had been for the Pope to send over the pallium. There
happened to be an obscure person in the service of the
German king claiming to be Pope — the "antipope,"
all good churchmen called him—and Rufus (merely in
order to worry Anselm, and without any intention of
really adhering to the antipope), professed not to be
certain which Pope he would recognise. After a great
council of the realm had been held, in which none of
the bishops supported Anselm, the pallium was sent

over, and Anselm, who refused to accept it from the hands of the king, took it from the high altar at Canterbury and put it on himself with his own hands. The king had been defeated, and had behaved most brutally throughout the quarrel ; but it is difficult to avoid seeing that Anselm was initiating the idea that his allegiance to the Pope was superior to his allegiance to the king.

Next came at an inopportune moment the Welsh war ; and Rufus was very probably right when he complained that Anselm had not furnished his proper contingent for that war. He cited Anselm, as he had a perfect right to do, before the great council to answer for this neglect of his feudal duty. Anselm altogether denied the competence of the tribunal to judge him, and again appealed to Rome. To appeal to a spiritual tribunal on a question of horses and armour was utterly ridiculous, and here Anselm was manifestly in the wrong. He was, in fact, on the edge of raising the great papal claim of the thirteenth century that the clergy owed neither allegiance nor service to the State at all, a pretension which would have made civil government impossible. No one in England raised a voice on Anselm's behalf in this second part of the quarrel, and yet he was allowed to depart to seek counsel from the Pope ; to whom he wrote on his journey begging to be relieved of his office of archbishop ; and thus he showed himself prepared to shrink from his duty, and left his flock to the mercy of Rufus.

Anselm was received by Pope Urban II. with the highest honours—honours, indeed, that seem to have turned his not over-strong head. Urban refused to allow him to surrender his archbishopric, and proposed there and then to deliver the Red King over to Satan by "anathema and the greater excommunication." Anselm pleaded against this, but would probably not have been sorry if Urban had been deaf to his pleadings. Rufus averted the unpleasant prospect by sending an astute diplomatist to Rome ; he knew that gold would buy votes there as well as castles in Normandy. But meanwhile a council of the Church, held in 1099, displayed the whole of the papal hand, and declared that from henceforth no cleric of any sort should " be invested with " any bishopric or living by a lay hand. That would mean that no king might nominate a bishop, and that the chief members of the great council of the King of England would be elected by the monks who formed the chapters of their respective sees. It was a defiance against all the lay rulers of the Christian world.

Anselm was at Lyons, not over pleased with Pope Urban, but no doubt burning with zeal to refuse allegiance to some lay power or other, when the news was brought to him that the Red King had been shot by an unknown hand in the New Forest and buried at Winchester without the rites of the Church, 2nd August 1100. There William still lies in impious defiance in the centre of the great Cathedral. Three days later Anselm would hear that King Henry had been crowned in London (August 5th) by the bishop of that diocese ; that he had issued a charter promising to the barons redress of their feudal grievances, to the nation at large lighter taxes and better justice ; above all, promising that he would not keep sees and abbeys vacant for his own profit. This had been the real wickedness of Rufus towards the Church, and Anselm should have met such an advance with open arms. We hear, of course, no more of his wish to resign the archbishopric, and whatever quarrel he may afterwards have had with Henry was always conducted decorously, and without any personal breach between them. He now came straight to England, and, to the horror of the whole council, at once refused to do homage for his lands ; and promulgated the whole doctrine of "investiture" as he had learned it at Rome. Henry asked for a delay of six months to consider this complete subversion of all the customs of England, and allowed Anselm to enter upon his lands and duties, to hold synods, and even to marry him to his queen without having done homage. Meanwhile Henry was applying the usual arguments at the court of Rome. Delay followed delay ; appeal to Rome followed appeal. At last, in 1103, Anselm himself left England, ostensibly to consult the Pope. For three years he remained abroad, the King and Queen of England showing him constant personal attentions and honours. In this obstinate attitude he would no doubt have died, but that Henry's "arguments" — one had better not inquire too closely what they were—at last prevailed on the Pope to forsake his own cause, and to allow Anselm and all future bishops to do homage to the king for their lands, provided that the "spiritual symbols of the office," such as the pastoral staff (a weapon which some bishops still carry) were not conveyed to them by lay hands. Henry did not care about pastoral staves ; he retained the homage, and therewith the power to appoint to bishoprics. This was the famous "Compromise of Bec," 1106. That Anselm had been utterly in the wrong throughout there can hardly be a doubt ; but the attitude of the Papacy was largely responsible for this. He died in 1109, and was canonised as a saint at the end of the fifteenth century. He was really much more fitted to be a monk than a bishop.

Henry was thirty-two years old at the date of his usurpation ; he could hardly have anticipated such a stroke of luck as the sudden death of his brother, but it is evident that he had no hesitation in seizing the throne ; evident also, from the extreme haste of the proceeding, that it was a seizure and not a regular election. The new king had enjoyed the advantage of an excellent education ; to him is attributed the maxim that " Rex illiteratus est asinus coronatus." He evidently could understand, speak, and read English, and by the English people he was welcomed as being a real " Atheling," *i.e.* born while his father was on the throne. He does not appear to have shown much open favour to Englishmen of rank, and his chief adviser, the Earl of Leicester, was reputed to be decidedly hostile to them ; but, as one by one the great " Conquest barons " were uprooted and their properties regranted to smaller men, it is not surprising to find English names among Henry's counsellors and sheriffs. I take the tradition of the continued repression of the English race to rest very largely on the fact that during the twelfth century hardly any bishoprics were filled by men of English race. Henry was a much more peripatetic, as he was a much more industrious king than Rufus ; we find him perpetually on progress to all parts of his kingdom and often far beyond the borders of Wessex, out of which, except in time of war, the first two Norman kings never travelled. He was fond of staying in the monasteries and making friends with the monks, to whom he could talk as a scholar. Best of all, he hastened to marry the heiress of the old royal line, Edith, daughter of Malcolm and Margaret, who had been brought up by her aunt Christina, Abbess of Romsey. It seems to have been a love match, and Queen Edith, who, to please Norman prejudice, took the name of Matilda or Maud, was evidently a person of great importance and dignity. She seldom travelled with her husband, but held a magnificent court at Westminster, corresponded with the Pope, and enjoyed the friendship of Anselm.

The usual feudal rebellion heralded in the reign. Robert must have been a man of tough constitution ; we left him on the Crusade, where he performed prodigies of useless valour, but when he came back he was quite ready for a brotherly struggle for the English crown. Normandy was up in arms and anarchy within a week of Rufus' death, and Robert never really ruled there at all. He received homage from most of the Norman barons, and was then incited by the typical robber baron of the time to claim the crown of England (1101). This was Robert of Belesme, Lord of Shrewsbury, Arundel, and Tickhill in England, Montgomery in Wales, and Belesme on the frontier of Normandy and Maine. Duke Robert could fairly allege that Henry's assumption of the English crown had been a flagrant usurpation ; and three–fourths of the Anglo-Norman baronage were ready to back him. In July he came to Portsmouth with a large fleet ; but the politic Henry advanced to meet him with two powerful arguments—a large English army disciplined by Norman captains, and the offer of a pension of £2000 a year. These arguments were quite enough for Robert, who calmly threw over the friends who had risen for him, spent a couple of enjoyable months at free quarters with his rich young brother, and then returned to Normandy. As soon as he was gone Henry turned on the rebel barons and battered down their castles one by one. Belesme was banished, and thirty years of peace followed in England. The old Saxon chroniclers (who were still writing) called the king the " Lion of Justice " foretold by old bards of Celtic race. Justice, however, ought to mean even-handed justice between rich and poor, and it is tolerably clear that under the " Lion," the scale leant heavily against the rich. Not that Henry was neglectful of the poor when they committed crimes against the peace ; the first two Norman kings had chiefly made use of the mutilating knife, as the Church of the eleventh century deprecated capital punishment ; but Henry was strong and brave enough to restore to its proper place that noble old engine of civilisation, the county gallows. Very much surprised the good people of Hundhog (wherever that may be) must have been when " Ralph Basset and the king's thegns " appeared in their midst, and after fair trial " hanged in one day so many thieves as were never hanged before, to wit four and forty men." It evidently surprised the chronicler who recorded it ; but the forests were vast and teemed with outlaws, and we may be tolerably sure that even King Henry did not overtake one-half of the thieves who deserved hanging. What system of law Henry's courts administered, it is not easy to say ; but it was probably a kind of rough equity, and based both on old Saxon custom and old Norman custom. The shire courts and hundred courts of his day would contain men versed in both customs ; and we hear now for the first time of special commissions sent from the king's court to hold these local courts, and so to supersede for the moment the authority even of the sheriff. Such commissions were the parents of our quarterly assizes, and would bring with them the " custom of the king's court," *i.e.* the set of principles by which the lawyers decided cases *coram rege :* and so gradually before the end of the century the " custom of the king's court " will become the " custom of England," and the parent of our " common law."

No doubt another object of these commissions was

to increase the king's rents and taxes ; even your sheriff was occasionally liable to be bribed or to falsify his returns to the king. It is quite a mistake to contrast the feudal ages with modern times as regards greed for money ; nay, it is quite evident that money would buy allegiance or anything else then even more effectually than it will now. So Henry trusted nobody, not even his sheriffs, and established (or perhaps re-established) a regular system of account-keeping in his court : each sheriff had to appear twice a year at his "exchequer" and hand over bags of silver pennies, the sum of the king's dues which he had collected during his year of office. The officers of the exchequer weighed and tested the silver to see if it was of the requisite weight and fineness ; and probably the sheriff who "sat at account" had a very bad quarter of an hour while the process was going on. For the rents of crown lands and the ordinary fines in the courts the sheriff compounded at a fixed rate : for everything else he had to account to the last farthing. For the thirty-first year of Henry's reign we have an actual leaf out of his account-book called the "Pipe Roll," which shows us that we may guess his total revenue at something under £30,000 a year (say three-quarters of a million of our money).[1] The power of the justiciar is much increased under Henry : he is head both of the legal and financial system ; he is always an ecclesiastic, and never one of great feudal family : it is the same with Henry's diplomatists, they are nearly all low-born clerks who have risen by sheer ability, and who are

[1] I have estimated the purchasing power of Henry's money at a little over twenty-five times that of our own ; but all such calculations are complicated by the fact that the penny unit of the twelfth century was different from our own ; thus 240 of Henry's pennies are really equivalent to £3, 0s. 6½d. of our money.

provided with bishoprics, which, except in matter of cathedral building, they scrupulously neglect.

But while Roger of Salisbury and Alexander of Lincoln and Nigel of Ely administered Henry's state and finances ; and while Robert Bloet of Lincoln and William Warelwast of Exeter negotiated for him with popes and emperors, the more spiritual elements of the Church and laity alike were drawn into one of those great ascetic "revivals" which from time to time swept over Western Europe. The great "Cistercian" foundations of Waverley, Tintern, Rievaulx, Fountains, and Furness take their origin in Henry's reign ; and "Augustinian canons-regular" are established by good Queen Maud in Aldgate, and by Rahere (once Henry's court jester) in St. Bartholomew-the-Great at Smithfield ; and at one of these new homes of religion (at Merton in Surrey) Thomas Becket received his elementary education. Henry himself founded the great Benedictine Abbey of Reading, and was buried there ; he also established two new bishoprics, Ely (carved out of the vast diocese of Lincoln) and Carlisle. But the reign also witnessed a distinct revival of letters and learning, the first since the days of Alfred. William of Malmesbury, of mixed English and Norman parentage, is the first real historian of England ; he had seen, when a very little boy (perhaps at the great meeting on Salisbury Hill) the great Conqueror himself ; he describes for us, evidently from personal recollection, his ponderous bulk and his terrible voice ; he had travelled all over Southern England in search of material for his work, and many of his notes upon places must have been made on the spot. The first trace of lectures at Oxford, where Henry had a palace in what is now Beaumont Street, are discoverable before the end of the reign.

As for the peace in Normandy, that was quite another thing. In annexing the duchy to his own crown, a thing he was bound to do in time, Henry was not so uniformly successful as Rufus had been. Robert of Belesme, forth of England, was only transferred to a more congenial sphere of anarchy, with the result that the few orderly elements in the lower Seine valley quickly came to the conclusion that the King of England was the only possible sovereign for them. Before 1102 was out Henry had been invited over and had begun to make good his hold on various places. The details are utterly wearisome till we come to the great battle of Tenchebray, 1106, won by an English army fighting on foot in the old close order, with Henry and his knights on foot to lead it. We do not know with what weapons it was won ; possibly with the old Danish axe ; but it may be fairly claimed that Tenchebray reversed the verdict of Hastings in favour of that "astonishing infantry" which afterwards won Crecy and Waterloo. Duke Robert was taken prisoner, and spent the remaining twenty-eight years of his long life in honourable captivity in various English castles. His friend, Edgar Atheling, was taken with him, but was restored to his English estates and died, also at a great age, in 1138. Robert of Belesme escaped for a time, but only till 1112, when Henry caught him and shut him up at Wareham, not at all in honourable captivity, till his death, and no man knew the hour or the manner thereof.

The later wars of Henry on the Continent were not so successful ; King Louis VI. of France was a wiser and stronger man than his predecessors, and began to gnaw at that little county of the Vexin, which forms the boundary between the respective spheres of influence of Rouen and Paris : he had a useful weapon in his hands in the person of William, son of Duke Robert, who however died in 1128. Good Queen Maud died in 1118; Henry's only legitimate son, William, was drowned in 1120 in the wreck of the "White Ship," and his only daughter, Matilda, turned out a terrible virago. In her extreme youth she had been married to the German Emperor-King, but by 1125 she was a childless and widowed Empress. In 1121 Henry married Alice of Louvain, but by her he had no family, and was therefore driven into the awkward predicament of establishing Matilda as his heir. He arranged for her an extremely useful and politic remarriage with Geoffrey Plantagenet, heir of Anjou, Touraine, and Maine; but its advantages lay wholly in the future, for the old hatred between Normandy and Anjou rendered it for a time the most unpopular move. Moreover, no child was born to this couple (who quarrelled incessantly and embittered Henry's last years with their quarrels) till 1133, two years before the old King's death. That child was destined one day to put everything straight again under the glorious name of Henry II. But in the meantime there was a terrible trial awaiting this our land.

Before Henry's death (25th Nov. 1135) all the barons of England had sworn fealty to Matilda as heiress, or at least had sworn to Henry to maintain her cause: but Matilda and her hated Angevin husband were far away at the moment, and a popular and dangerous competitor was near at hand.

CHAPTER IX

STEPHEN AND ANARCHY

THE Conqueror's youngest daughter Adela, Countess of Blois and Champagne, had three sons, Theobald, Stephen, and Henry; of these the eldest, Theobald, a peaceable, prudent man, was content with ruling his paternal duchies well. The two younger boys had been high in favour with their uncle Henry; the youngest, Henry, was in holy orders, had been Abbot of Glastonbury, and had recently been made Bishop of Winchester. He was before all things a churchman, though equally far removed from the saintly (or Anselmian) type and from the purely business (or Roger of Salisbury) type; it is probable that from him came the first suggestion to his second brother, Stephen, to claim the crown of England. Stephen was at Boulogne (*i.e.* within a few hours of London), which county he held in right of his wife, a granddaughter of the Scottish King. He, however, seems to have hesitated, for it was not till three weeks after the death of Henry that he presented himself in London for election. It is a great proof of the growing influence of the Church that no one seems to have thought of crowning Robert, Earl of Gloucester, King Henry's eldest and ablest illegitimate son; a century before, the fact that the great William was a bastard was not deemed any serious bar to his coronation.

Both Stephen and this Robert had sworn to King

Henry to uphold Matilda's claim, and much of the subsequent contest turned upon the deliberate perjury now committed by Stephen in violating this oath. For the moment, however, the hatred felt for Matilda herself, as well as for the Angevin connection, overbore all scruples in England. Stephen was personally very popular, known to be one of the bravest and most accomplished knights in Europe, and therefore guessed to be an easy-going man, who would not be too hard on a poor baron who fortified his castle without royal leave. But above all his election was a clerical "job." Stephen was quite ready to promise anything to clerk and layman alike, and the Church was only lying in wait for such an opportunity to extend its privileges to the uttermost. Henry of Winchester knew how to interpret promises as well as the most skilful diplomatist of the papal court.

So we find that in his second charter King Stephen (he was crowned 22nd Dec. 1135) stoops to declare that his title to the crown is derived from his "election by the assent of the clergy and people of England, his consecration by the archbishop, who is also papal legate, and his confirmation by the Pope." Hardly even John, when in his uttermost need he surrendered his kingdom to the Pope, stooped lower than this. In vague words Stephen promises that he will "make the Church of England free": and his bishop-brother interprets it to mean that the Church of England renounces all allegiance to the crown of England. The crown reaped the due reward of such complaisance; for, during the nineteen years of feudal anarchy that desolated England, the Church alone stood upright and increased its power on every side. The court of the good and learned, but utterly un-English and un-Norman Archbishop Theobald (1138–1160) remained the only peaceful place in England, and therein were trained all the great ecclesiastics of the next generation. The famous Pope Eugenius III. and St. Bernard of Clairvaux, whose personal reputation for holiness, extreme asceticism, and fierce denunciation of temporal power elevated him, in the minds of churchmen, even above the Pope himself, both patronised and corresponded with Theobald and his courtiers without apparently giving a thought to the terrible forces of destruction that were at work in England. The result, as we shall see, was that Henry II. was called upon during his whole reign to face an opposition infinitely more dangerous to nationality than any mere combination of feudal barons.

The first two years of Stephen's reign, though not really quiet, were quiet in comparison with what was to come. The administration was left in the hands of Roger, Bishop of Salisbury, a thoroughly capable man ; and London certainly supported the king, although, in the oaths of allegiance sworn to him by London, as well as by some of the barons, there are expressions which show that such allegiance rested upon a definite compact—as if they said, " Sire, we and you know that you are not the rightful heir to this kingdom, but we hereby take you as a substitute for anarchy, and will obey you as long as you can protect us, but no longer." Perhaps this explains the ease with which London accepted Matilda in 1141, and again reverted to Stephen when Matilda had made herself impossible. Even the King of Scotland and Robert of Gloucester appear to have sworn some sort of allegiance to Stephen, but the former had to be bribed to do so with the cession of Cumberland (under the name of the earldom of Carlisle) as well as the confirmation of his hereditary earldom of Huntingdon.

Matilda at once appealed to the Pope on the simple ground of Stephen's perjury (1136), and Stephen (or his brother Henry, who probably "knew his Rome") accepted the arbitration. Though declining to absolve Stephen entirely, the Pope saw clearly that he was from the Papal point of view the right man, and made no difficulty about recognising him as King of England. Nothing daunted, Matilda prepared for war. Stephen had paid a hurried visit to Normandy soon after his coronation, and had done homage for that duchy to Louis VI. by the mouth of his son Eustace. Like the Pope, Louis felt that Stephen would be a safer man for him than the politic and grasping Angevin. But this recognition was the only hold on the duchy that Stephen ever got. Geoffrey of Anjou took little part in the ensuing civil war in England, and perhaps hoped that the dreadful woman whom he called wife would succeed in England and leave him to enjoy life on the Continent ; at any rate he found the Channel a blessed barrier between himself and her. So he devoted all his attention to swallowing Normandy, and by 1147 he had fairly got hold of it and received investiture for himself or for his son Henry from the hands of Louis VII., who was a weaker man than his predecessor.

The troubles in England were not long in beginning. Stephen's policy, if one can call it so, seems to have been unlimited conciliation to the great barons ; previous kings had created very few earldoms, and the estates of nearly all were widely scattered ; but Stephen created eight earldoms, and actually endowed them with crown lands, thus being the first king to dissipate the greatest source of the wealth of the monarchy. Matilda afterwards followed his example, and, in the part of the country that obeyed her, created six earldoms. Moreover these grants contained far larger privileges of

I

jurisdiction than any earls had had before.   A baron, so endowed and made sheriff and "justiciar" in his own county, was as good as an independent prince, and would have as small scruple in going over to Matilda, if he thought she was going to win, as Matilda would have in inviting him by the promise of more and more extensive privileges.   Geoffrey Mandeville, Earl of Essex, changed sides three times in six years, and each of his four charters of investiture gave him more and more power.   Such a baron would be able to hire mercenaries to his heart's content.   Stephen never seems to have been able to call on the English armed forces even of the counties that were nominally in his obedience, and so he could only rely upon the feudal levies of his temporary supporters or on mercenaries from Flanders and Brabant.   Although he never licensed private war, he did nothing to stop it ; and private war had begun before 1138, and would have gone on under Stephen even if there had been no Matilda to dispute his title.

The struggle for the crown, however, came most opportunely for the barons.   The first to draw the sword for Matilda was King David of Scotland in 1138.   He began by claiming the earldom of Northumberland, and invaded England with a wild army of Galloway men and Highlanders, who committed frightful ravages which he was quite unable to check. But in North Yorkshire he was met by the aged Archbishop Thurstan of York and all the Anglo-Norman barons of the North, and utterly defeated at Northallerton.   This so-called " Battle of the Standard " was the greatest victory of South over North since Brunanburh.   A Bruce and a Balliol fought side by side for England ; but we must not forget that many of these barons held lands in Scotland as well as in

England and Normandy.   The reign of David had seen a great influx of both Normans and Englishmen into the Lothians and even into Galloway.   In spite of this victory Stephen was obliged to grant David the coveted earldom of Northumberland, and as David already held Cumberland, the frontiers of the Northern kingdom were now actually brought down almost to Durham and Lancaster.

Before the end of that same year (1138) Robert of Gloucester had renounced his allegiance and declared war on Stephen.   The focus of the conflagration naturally lay in his vast Western estates, *i.e.* round his castles of Bristol, Gloucester, Castle-Cary, Dunster, Shrewsbury, Hereford, Ludlow, and Wareham.   The valley of the Thames, with the awkward exception of Wallingford, was for Stephen, so were Kent, East Anglia, London, Northampton, Derby, and York.   The Earl Palatine of Chester, the most powerful feudal baron of the kingdom, was at first neutral ; when he came at last to decide for Matilda in 1141, the King was beaten and captured at Lincoln ; when Matilda's cause had proved hollow and she herself had retired, the Earl of Chester continued a civil war with Stephen on his own account.

Long before this, however, Stephen had entered on his inevitable quarrel with the Church.   He was by no means without kingly instincts, though he generally employed them in a wrong direction.   In 1139 he suddenly suspected the loyalty of old Bishop Roger and of the Bishops Alexander of Lincoln and Nigel of Ely. The immense privileges granted to the Church had not prevented these astute persons from using their baronial position also, and fortifying their castles, perhaps merely as a precaution.   Anyhow Stephen pounced upon them, imprisoned Salisbury and Lincoln, and drove

Ely to fly to the enemy.   Henry of Winchester, brother though he was, could not overlook this attack on the persons of churchmen, and was up in excommunications at once.   No doubt he was also angry with Stephen for not supporting his recent candidature for the See of Canterbury.   So, when Matilda landed at Arundel in September 1139, Henry threw over Stephen and declared for the lady.

Thereon begins a great civil war all over the South of England.   Stephen's methods of warfare are peculiar.   He springs like a lion at every castle that defies him, but seldom has persistence to take it : he builds a " counterwork " before it, and then springs off to some other neighbouring castle and does the same there.   He has been well compared to a bull in a Spanish bull-fight, at whom all the bull-fighters are flourishing red cloaks ; he makes a dash head downwards at each in turn, but seldom succeeds in tossing any one. Occasionally he burns a town, but is dreadfully sorry for having done so ; his followers and his enemies burn and are not sorry.   Ludicrous traits of chivalry are also recorded of Stephen ; he could easily have captured Matilda on her first landing and sent her back to Normandy, but he " scorns to make war on ladies " (such a lady !), and so he gives her a safe-conduct to Robert of Gloucester at Bristol.   There was only one real pitched battle, that of Lincoln, where Stephen was taken prisoner (1141), and one big scuffle in and outside of Winchester where a similar fate befell Robert of Gloucester in the same year.   Stephen at Lincoln fought like a lion, fought on foot till his sword broke, and then laid about him with a great Danish axe, which a valiant burgher of Lincoln (who had perhaps inherited the axe from one of his viking forefathers) thrust into his hand.   Nor did he yield till he was knocked down by a great stone, such as Ajax used to hurl in the *Iliad*.

During the King's captivity Matilda got hold of Winchester, and therewith of the actual crown and the treasury (probably empty), and was saluted as "Domina Angliæ." Not "Regina Angliæ," however, could she ever become, for she delayed her advance upon London until she had made enemies of many who would gladly have crowned her. She was quite as ready as Stephen to promise anything to the Church, and Henry of Winchester exacted his full pound of flesh. He is said to have told her that the election to the crown belonged to the clergy, and she promised to consult him in all important matters. When she at last advanced to London and was received by the astute Geoffrey Mandeville, who was holding the Tower, she disgusted the citizens by her haughtiness and rapacity, and after a few days a frightful tumult in the city forced her to fly for her life. Stephen's queen advanced and recovered London: Matilda was driven from Winchester: its bishop changed sides again: Robert was taken prisoner and exchanged for Stephen. Stephen (who had by this time found that it is occasionally necessary to make war on ladies) began hunting his rival about the country, among other things driving her to escape from Oxford Castle to Abingdon and Wallingford in her night-gown on a snowy night.

And so on, and so on, and so on; there seems no end to the sieges and town-burnings and devastations. The most cheerful news is that Geoffrey of Mandeville dies in 1144, having earned, as a prize brigand, fame almost equal to that of Robert of Belesme. Robert of Gloucester dies in 1147. In that year the Second Crusade (St. Bernard's Crusade) draws away some of the best as well as some of the worst elements of society to the East ; but on the whole from 1144 the tide has been turning steadily in favour of Stephen, in spite of the fact that little Henry, Matilda's son, is in England "assisting his mother" from his ninth to his fourteenth year. Perhaps to the precocious boy it was a useful lesson in what anarchy meant. At last in February 1148 "Domina Angliæ" retired to Normandy, of which her husband was in safe possession. There she remained, and curiously enough lapsed into a staid and prudent matron, to whom her son was much indebted for good advice in the early years of his reign. But Matilda's departure did not mean peace for England : many of her partisans held out, and Ralph of Chester began intriguing with Scotland in a manner that looked as if he hoped to get the old kingdom of Strathclyde or " Cumbria " restored in his favour. Stephen was forced to outbid David's offers by a series of grants to Ralph which almost amounted to a restoration of the old earldom of Mercia. Again there is a fierce quarrel between Stephen and Archbishop Theobald, who is of course supported by the Pope. England is laid under its first (but not its last) interdict. During an interdict the services of the Church can only be performed with maimed rites, and religion suffers terribly ; nevertheless the Popes seldom scrupled to employ this weapon for political reasons. The poor King of England, who at the beginning of his reign had laid himself almost at the feet of the Church, drew near to the end of it in a state of open defiance of the Church. His authority, however, cannot have been strong, when Prince Henry was able to travel unmolested from Wareham to Scotland to be knighted by his uncle David in 1149.

In 1151 Stephen sent his son Eustace to the Continent to see if anything could be done in the way of disturbing Geoffrey and Matilda in Normandy, but the expedition proved utterly fruitless. Geoffrey died in 1152, and Henry was recognised as Duke of Normandy, Count of Maine, Anjou, and Touraine. It was perhaps as a set-off to this that Stephen attempted to get Eustace recognised by the barons as his heir in England. Some few barons did apparently swear fealty to Eustace, but no bishop could be found to do so, for the " Pope had forbidden it." Eustace, moreover, was a very unamiable savage, utterly unlike his father.

At last the end came suddenly. A remnant of Matilda's party, almost the last remnant, was holding out at Wallingford, and cried aloud to Henry for help. Henry, who had just made the match of the century with Eleanor of Aquitaine, heiress of all between the Loire and the Pyrenees, and divorced wife of Louis VII. of France, was now a man of nineteen. He hurried across the Channel and relieved the beleaguered castle. Stephen and he were actually talking of coming to an armistice, if not a peace, to which the main obstacle was the furious opposition of Eustace, when the arm of the blessed St. Edmund smote and slew that young man, who had been ravaging the crops of the monks of Bury St. Edmund's (Aug. 1153). Thereupon Stephen, a man of sixty-seven years, worn out with years of warfare, readily consented to the Treaty of Winchester.[1] Henry is to be " justiciar " for the rest of Stephen's reign, and to succeed Stephen on his death. He will not have to wait long, and he will do his " justicing " well.

It is impossible not to be sorry for Stephen. As Sir James Ramsay says, he was one of the " best fellows " that ever sat on our throne. He exaggerated bravery and generosity till they became extreme rashness and

[1] Or Wallingford ; the treaty was arranged at Wallingford, ratified at Winchester.

ludicrous simplicity.   Nothing mean or ungentlemanly is ever recorded of him, but he was surrounded with treachery more flagrant than that of the Wars of the Roses.   He could not bear to shed blood but in the heat of battle ; but he was destined to see England deluged in blood from one end of his reign to the other.

Pope Eugenius, St. Bernard, Stephen's Queen, King David, and Earl Ralph of Chester, all died about the same time as Eustace (1152–53) ; the stage is rapidly clearing for new actors. *Novus rerum nascitur ordo*, and, though there will be one more big feudal rebellion (1174), and plenty of rough " justicing " to do, King Henry will soon, in the language of the Treaty of Winchester, " destroy the unlicensed castles, terrify thieves and brigands with the gallows, fill the pastures with flocks, and decorate the mountains with sheep."   Every one who can read is busy devouring Geoffrey of Monmouth's wonderful new romance of " King Arthur," and believing it to be real history, when the bells ring on 19th December 1154 to say that Henry is crowned King of England.

" Arthur is come again, he cannot die."

CHAPTER X

HENRY II. AND LAW

THE rulers of Anjou, the house of "Plantagenet" as they were now to be called, were the most French of all Frenchmen : their origin is lost in myth and cannot really be traced behind the latter half of the ninth century. A series of Fulks and Geoffries then begins to appear holding a small territory on the middle Loire, defending it valiantly against Normans and Bretons, and generally acting as loyal allies of the French kings. The centre of their strength lies on that rock of Angers, which frowns down on the river Maine (whose tributaries drain the southern slopes of the province of Maine), a little before its junction with the Loire. To one of the early counts the prophecy had been made that the dominions of his descendants should extend from the rock of Angers to the ends of the earth—a prophecy that has been fulfilled beyond the wildest dreams of the nameless prophet. In order to set about its fulfilment in a business-like way the Fulks and Geoffries had swallowed Touraine and a little strip of Brittany, and, by the marriage of Henry's grandfather with the daughter of Count Elias, had recently acquired Maine. And Anjou, the kernel of these territories, is the most French of all French provinces, a pure strip of sunny France, one of the sunniest, merriest lands in the world. The " merry month of May " is *the* month of the year in Anjou ; to our cold island it is only a fiction which came in with the Plantagenets and their courtier-poets. We have bravely endeavoured to believe in it, not without shivering.

These Fulks and Geoffries had been great builders, but rather of castles and cities and aqueducts than of churches and abbeys; they had never knitted up a close alliance with the Roman Church and Pope such as that which had served the Normans so well. Crusaders they had been, but more for sheer love of adventure or to expiate terrible crimes than from any deep religious feeling. For they had been super-humanly wicked too, and their blood was supposed to be crossed with that of an unearthly ancestress. Richard I., when he had more than ordinarily forgotten himself, used to excuse his passions on that ground. Frightful outbreaks of rage followed by terrible remorse seem to have been characteristic of the race. But neither passion nor remorse interrupted their noble restlessness and their boundless thirst for knowledge and power. There were among our Angevin kings, as there are in every race, marked exceptions; John, in whom was the demon of passion without the ability; Edward II., the *rex illiteratus*, the crowned ass; Henry VI., who, in his virtues as well as his defects, seems wholly an alien; but if we take them all round no more remarkably virile line of kings ever lived.

The young man of twenty-one who now had to undertake the task of reducing the most important half of Western Europe to order was anything but kingly to look upon. Henry was tawny-haired, round-headed, and freckled, with large flashing grey eyes, thick-set and coarse of frame, of the bull-dog build, a plebeian type of man; utterly indifferent to dress, to food and drink, to all the conventionalities and shows of kingship; so restless and active that he seldom slept two nights

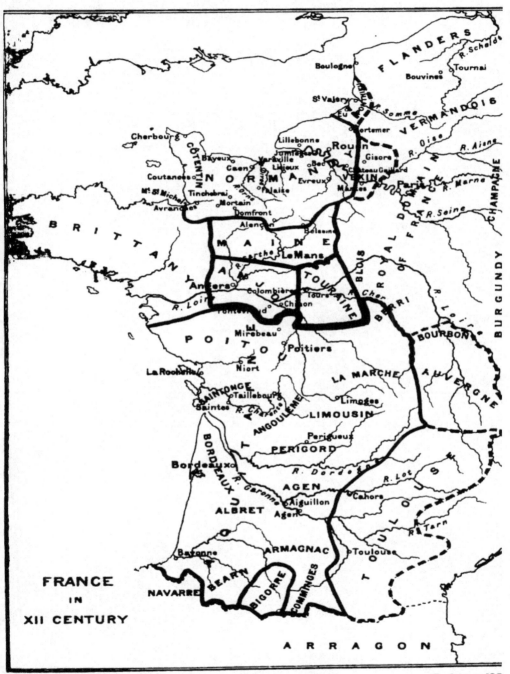

FRANCE
IN
XII CENTURY

FLANDERS
R.Scheldt
Boulogne
Bouvines
Tournai
St Valery
R.Somme
VERMANDOIS
Eu
Mortemer
R.Oise
R.Aisne
Cherbourg
Lillebonne
Rouen
Gisors
R.Eure
R.Marne
Bayeux
Jumièges
CÔTENTIN
Yarville
Bec
Château Gaillard
Paris
VEXIN
R.Seine
Caen
Lisieux
Evreux
Mantes
Coutances
NORMANDY
FRANCE
R.Marne
Mt St Michel
Tinchebrai
Falaise
R.Seine
Avranches
Mortain
Domfront
Alençon
Bélesme
MAINE
BRITTANY
Sarthe
Le Mans
BLOIS
ROYAL DOMAIN OF
R.Loire
Angers
Colombières
TOURAINE
R.Cher
BERRI
R.Loire
BURGUNDY
CHAMPAGNE
Fontevrault
Chinon
Tours
Mirebeau
BOURBON
POITOU
Poitiers
AUVERGNE
La Rochelle
Niort
LA MARCHE
SAINTONGE
Taillebourg
Limoges
Saintes
R.Charente
ANGOULÊME
LIMOUSIN
Périgueux
PÉRIGORD
BORDEAUX
R.Dordogne
R.Lot
Bordeaux
R.Garonne
AGEN
Cahors
ALBRET
Aiguillon
Agen
R.Tarn
Bayonne
ARMAGNAC
Toulouse
TOULOUSE
NAVARRE
BÉARN
BIGORRE
COMMINGES
ARRAGON

London: John Murray, Albemarle St.

To face p. 138

running in the same bed, a passionate sportsman but one who never let sport interfere with business; knowing something about almost everything, and much of law, philosophy, history, languages, and poetry; never ceasing to add to his stock of knowledge and experience, and never missing an opportunity to pick the brains of a learned man; a firm friend but a good hater, proud and unforgiving, and given to such frightful outbursts of passion that he would fling himself on the floor and gnaw the rushes which then did duty for a carpet.

A man of this extraordinary character naturally perplexed the grave and reticent Normans, especially the old ones who remembered the stately court and decorous ceremonial of his grandfather's time: it was no doubt annoying to be the minister of a king who expected you to do business of the most important kind as you rode with him to the meet, usually at a moderate gallop: still more annoying to find that he expected you to keep up with him throughout the run and resume the thread of your business at every check; you had perhaps "forgotten where you were"; he had not, he never forgot anything. Still more annoying must it have been to be the rebellious feudal baron of such a man, and to find that he, whom you knew to be in Rouen four days ago, suddenly appeared before your castle in Northamptonshire at 5 A.M., with an entire English army at his heels, long before you had been able to lay in your stock of lead for melting and lean salt beef. The only thing to be done was to let down the drawbridge and ask him to breakfast; perhaps his politic clemency was the hardest of all to bear. The existence of such a king made rebellion a more sacred duty for the barons than ever; but it made it infinitely more hopeless of success.

The extent of Henry's dominions, so enormously greater than those of any of his forerunners, rendered them much more vulnerable to rebellion. They stretched from the Pyrenees to the Tweed. To England was added after 1171 a considerable strip of Ireland, and after 1174 the overlordship of Scotland: to Anjou after 1169 the overlordship of Brittany, while to the whole the marriage with Eleanor had added the vast Duchy of Poitou or Aquitaine, with vague claims over Toulouse and Auvergne. The Southern portion of this inheritance, which we may roughly class as "Guienne and Gascony," had hitherto been a world practically apart from French life ; though it possessed a few rich Roman cities like Bordeaux, it was mainly a land of small and very turbulent barons with impregnable rock-perched castles.

Every one of these territories Henry held by a separate title, and the question from whom true homage or allegiance was due for each of them was often a hard one to solve ; when it was solved the homage was still harder to enforce. To have kept the whole dominion together until the eve of his death was a great feat ; to have accomplished this almost without bloodshed was a still greater. The task kept him much away from England, as their smaller tasks had so constantly kept his Norman predecessors, but so ably did Henry choose his ministers that his long absences were scarcely felt. He hardly ever took the English soldiers to serve abroad, and certainly did not overtax England for objects with which she had no concern. So strong indeed was the government that he maintained in his island realm, that the dangers ahead were all in the direction of despotism, not of feudal anarchy.

All the contemporary chroniclers (and they are

many and good, for it was a learned age) speak of the swiftness and sagacity with which Henry set on foot the old administrative and judicial systems of his grandfather *post bellicam tempestatem, i.e.* after the anarchy of Stephen's time. One of the old ministers, Nigel of Ely, was made treasurer, and the chancellorship was given by the advice of Archbishop Theobald to the famous Thomas Becket. Of mixed English and Norman parentage, the favourite scholar of Theobald's peaceful court, Becket was indeed a man, such as Shakespeare has described Wolsey as being, "of unbounded stomach." As passionate and unforgiving as Henry, he lacked altogether Henry's breadth of view and statesmanship. Single-hearted devotion to an idea he had, but it was only to the idea that was uppermost in his own brain at the time. The wisest of his contemporaries distrusted him and deplored the excessive confidence which Henry at first placed in him. As chancellor, Becket delighted in outshining every one in splendour and sumptuous living; when he went on an embassy to the King of France he took with him a train of attendants fit for a Roman emperor; when he afterwards became archbishop he went to the opposite extreme of fanatical austerity, and delighted to mark his utter severance from all worldly interests whatever. The result was an apparent inconsistency in Becket's career; as chancellor he was the first to suggest the enforcement of the new tax called "scutage" on the lands of the Church (1159); as archbishop one of his first acts was to declare that the Church should not pay a penny—*ne unum quidem denarium,* said he—to the State. These changes do not imply hypocrisy; Becket was no hypocrite, he was only an honest fanatic, incapable of seeing two sides of a question at the same time.

The justiciar's office was at first divided between Robert Earl of Leicester and Richard Lucy; on Robert's death (1168) it was held by Lucy alone till 1179; and afterwards, until the end of the reign, by Ralph Glanville, one of the greatest lawyers of the Middle Ages. Not to his ministers, however, but to his own intensely accurate and legal mind, are Henry's great reforms to be attributed. It is these, and not his quarrel with the Church or his vast continental dominions, that make Henry's reign one of such supreme importance. Let me therefore try briefly to sum them up.

(1) One of the first requisites for a civilised government is to have a known system of law, and a set of professional judges to whom people can go to get redress for their private or public wrongs; as we should say, the government must "specialise" its judicature. We have seen that Henry I.'s system was rather one of routine than of law, though the "custom of the King's court" was tending to become the custom of England; his servants went occasionally on circuits to the county courts and did judicial business there, but they did other business there also, and were in fact a sort of "royal commission" to look after all the king's rights. Now Henry II. "specialised" both the system of law and the men who administered it. He had studied Roman law himself, and many of his lawyers were deeply read in it. Though few principles of Roman law have filtered into English jurisprudence, Henry took all his ideas of unity and harmony, and of development of one legal idea out of another from that fertile source. In 1178 he created a definite court of five judges, to be the supreme tribunal in all legal questions, saving an appeal to the king and his great council; this court and this appeal became re-

spectively the parents of the Court of "King's Bench" and of the final appeal to our House of Lords. Further, we see that these judges, and many others also, are continually going on circuit for judicial business, and for that only. The sheriff will soon cease to be a judge in his county court; he will remain merely an administrative officer, who convokes the court to meet the judges, and who carries out their decision whether with the rope or the writ. Next we have

(2) The application to all forms of litigation of the idea of the sworn jury which lies at the bottom of so much of our "self government." The old Anglo-Saxon "compurgators" (*vide supra*, p. 36) were neither jurors nor witnesses; they were merely your friends who swore in a set form that they believed your oath. Henry's jurors are chosen by the sheriff from men who are likely to know the facts, and to have "no fear or favour" for either party. In several forms and to several ends Henry applied this principle: first to the settling of civil disputes about land. Before his time, if you claimed the manor of Tubney from me, the only way to make good your claim was to get a writ from the King to compel me to get on a horse and fight you for it. This was called "appealing to the judgment of God." Obviously it was more of the nature of an appeal to our respective physical strength and horsemanship. Henry now allows me (by the Great Assize, 1162) to get a writ, empowering the sheriff to "impanel" a jury of twelve men who will investigate the facts in the presence of regular trained judges, who will direct them as to what the law of the case is. You (being no doubt the stronger man and better rider) grind your teeth with rage at this unheard-of novelty, but between us we get justice. Again

Henry applies (by the Assize of Clarendon, 1166) the same principle of a jury to criminal matters; instead of allowing sheriff, or even justices, to come and "indict" men, or accuse them of crimes, upon perhaps vague rumour, he requires all accusations to be made by a "jury of presentment" (nowadays called the "grand jury") of twelve lawful men from each hundred every time the justices come round. These jurors will present all known or suspected criminals in their districts, and, though these criminals will then be liable to go to the ordeal of hot iron or hot water (another appeal to the so-called "judgment of God"), they will have a fair preliminary trial. Henry would no doubt later on have felt strong enough to abolish the ordeal altogether but for the fatal result of his quarrel with the Church in 1170. The ordeal was abolished in 1216 all over Christendom, and the "common jury" of to-day, a body distinct from the sworn witnesses, gradually grew up to take its place and to give the final "verdict" (*vere-dictum*, a "true speech"). Moreover, Henry applied the jury system to the assessment of taxes on his subjects. It has been said that there are three methods by which a king can assess his taxes, and that they have very different results. The method of the King of France was to go to the man and say, "You shall give me so much"; and the man had to give it— result, despotism; the method of the King of Germany was to go to the man and say, "How much will you give me?" and the man replied, "Nothing; go away, I don't know you"—result, anarchy; the method of King Henry and his successors was not to go to the man at all, but to a sworn jury of his neighbours, and say, "How much can he afford to give me?" and the jury, knowing that each of them would be assessed in the same way, gave a fair assessment. Of course this is putting it crudely; what Henry asked the juries to do was to value each man's property in the presence of his commissioners, and then rate him at such or such a proportion of it. This method was first employed for the "Assize of Arms," 1181, and the " Saladin tithe," 1188.

(3) Henry also introduced by these same enactments the principle of taxing other interests in the state beside the landed interest. Danegeld, scutage, &c., had fallen wholly on the land, because, till towards the end of the twelfth century, land was the sole source of wealth. But now there were considerable riches (in the towns, of course) in the hands of traders and merchants who never owned land at all, and these Henry taxed freely: and we shall soon see a curious result of this new taxation, namely that, when an "interest" in the state comes to be taxed, it will come to have, or at least to claim, a voice not merely in the assessment of taxes, but also in the granting of them. Theoretically, no feudal monarch could take any land-tax without the consent of his great council —who were, of course, all land-owners (" tenants-in-chief " or " barons "); when he wanted to get a tax from other sources he would find it convenient to get some sort of consent from the payers. Now, though all tenants-in-chief could, perhaps still did, occasionally attend a great council, it was obviously impossible for all merchants to do so; and if you wanted their opinion or their consent you could only get it by summoning *elected representatives* from their class. Henry II. did not go as far as this, but Henry III. repeatedly did; and finally Edward I. said, " Let there be a model parliament, to which all interests which I tax shall send representatives." So, as Bishop Stubbs has said, out of taxation is born a parliament. But

K

both Henry II. and Edward I. would have been very much astonished if they had been told that the ship, of which they laid the keel, would come in the twentieth century to be filled by a crew elected largely by men who contributed no direct taxes to the State, and had no interests of property in it.

(4) Henry established an uniform coinage and endeavoured to establish an uniform system of weights and measures. During the anarchy the barons had exercised private rights of coinage, with very serious results to buyers and sellers, as most of the baronial coin was full of alloy. There had been also many lawful mints in different towns, but Henry now established (1180) one mint and one standard coinage, a great blessing to the rising mercantile classes.

(5) Another great aim of his was to protect titles to landed property ; what with rebellions, confiscations, and crusades from which men never returned, there was a general uncertainty about titles to land. Powerful men were very apt to seize the manors of their neighbours, or to claim them in virtue of some older and perhaps fictitious title or charter. Henry will protect the " man in possession " until he is found by inquest of jury in the King's court not to have a good title ; hence the great principle of English law that no man may be turned out of his freehold without a lawful judgment in court against him.

(6) Before the end of the reign we find that the whole criminal law has undergone a complete change, and this without any definite enactment. Though Henry I. began and carried out as far as he could a system of punishment for crimes, crime was still supposed in his time to be more of an offence against the person wronged than against the State or the " King's peace." So the old Anglo-Saxon

practice of fixed and enormously high "wergilds" and "wites," for great and small crimes alike, lingered on, with considerable benefit no doubt to the King's exchequer, but not to the peace of the country. Before 1189 all that has disappeared; a few big crimes stand out, and life or limb are paid for them; for all smaller crimes the judge will fix a suitable and reasonable fine, and let you out of prison when you pay it; for there are now prisons in every county. Outlawry, as a punishment, has also ceased. So the crimes of Henry's subjects, instead of being a source of profit, have become a source of expense to him, and we may be sure that he will repress them valiantly. And in this matter his courts make no distinction between a freeman and a villein. It is obvious that great barons, if they ever did possess the right of hanging their own villeins, would be slow to exercise it, if those villeins were sturdy, useful fellows, whatever crimes they committed: and the majority of crimes of violence were probably committed by the villein class. And it is humorous, but it is all for the good of the villein, that the first notice the King takes of him is to allow no one to hang him but himself. But when a system of law takes notice of a class in criminal matters, it will soon take notice of it in civil matters also: in the next reign we shall find villeins serving on assessment juries; in Henry III.'s reign they will be sworn to bear arms for the defence of the State just as if they were freemen.

(7) This brings me to the last and greatest of Henry's acts, his Assize of Arms, in 1181, by which every freeman, irrespective of any exemption, irrespective of his tenure, but simply because he was the King's subject, was bound to serve in war, and to provide himself with arms of different kinds according

to his wealth. Though often altered to meet the changing requirements of warfare, this edict has never been repealed, and ought to be considered as still binding on us all ; indeed I think it quite possible that before long we may have to put it in force.

It is most interesting to see that no amount of foreign complications and rebellions, not even the fierce six-year-long quarrel with Becket, interrupted the steady march of Henry's reforms and enactments in England, and the steady assertion of the *Rule of Law*. That the King should be uniformly successful was not to be expected, and the unfortunate end of the quarrel just referred to robbed Henry of the fruits of one of his greatest works, and bequeathed a host of difficulties to his successors. But we must proceed to look at some of the leading political events of the reign.

To knock down the remaining unlicensed castles of the barons was the proverbial " work of a moment " (it is probable that most of these castles, hastily run up during the period of anarchy, were very slight affairs). No distinction was made between the partisans of Matilda and those of Stephen, and there was little resistance (1154–1156). Then Northumberland, Cumberland, and Westmorland, which for seventeen years had been in Scottish hands, were finally and for ever regrasped by the King of England ; Malcolm IV. withdrawing his garrisons from Newcastle, Bamborough, and Carlisle (1157).

A grab at the county of Toulouse, to which Eleanor had shadowy claims, was not so successful, and brought Henry for the first time (1159) into direct though not very violent hostility to his overlord, the weak but cunning Louis VII. of France. Henry hated open war, and always, where possible, acted by means of gold and diplomacy in preference.   He never really got acknowledged in Toulouse, though he held much of that county for some time.   But he had already secured a better object nearer home—the Vexin (see above, p. 124) ; by a treaty in 1158 he had arranged a marriage for his infant son Henry (whom we will call " Young Henry ") with Louis' infant daughter, Margaret, who was to bring the oft-disputed Vexin as her dowry : by an adroit trick he had the babies married at once, and occupied in their name the principal castles of that territory, of which the most important was Gisors.   It was perhaps hardly fair on young Henry when he grew up that his father should retain his wife's dowry.   But Henry, though passionately, and often foolishly, fond of his children, had no intention of " taking off his clothes before going to bed," or stripping himself of power for their benefit. The children naturally thought otherwise, and were afterwards often encouraged to rebel by their mother, a woman of unscrupulous and violent temper, whose love of her husband soon turned to hatred.

And so, while by the marriage of his daughters the King secured a series of brilliant and useful alliances with Germany, Castile, and Sicily, when it came to be a question of providing for his sons, quarrels inevitably arose.   Richard was betrothed to Adela of France and created Count of Poitou ; but his father would never let him carry out the marriage, and, though he employed him as his lieutenant to put down disorder in Aquitaine, he never allowed him any independent power there.   Geoffrey, the third son, was married to the heiress of Brittany, but his father administered that province in his name.   Young Henry was called Duke of Normandy, and, in 1170, was even crowned joint-King of England (in order to secure his succession in the event of Henry's sudden death) ; but, as his father-in-law, Louis, kept on reminding the boy, it was an empty title that he got in each case. When John, the youngest and favourite son, was betrothed to an Alpine lady, Henry proposed to endow him with Norman and Poitevin lands at the expense of his elder brothers, and this produced more than friction in the family. Henry in fact did either too much or too little for his sons, and can hardly have been blind to the fact that at his own death the eldest of them would claim the whole paternal and maternal inheritance. But it is a very difficult thing to know what to do with royal male babies : if you marry them, as Edward III. did, to English heiresses, they begin to fight in the next generation for English earldoms ; if you keep them unmarried and hanging about court, as George III. did, they get idle and dissipated. The Turks have invented a plan which, though shocking, has its conveniences ; a wise Sultan begins his reign by bowstringing his (usually numerous) brothers.

With a wife like Eleanor, with two successive French kings——the second of them, Philip Augustus (1180—1220), the most subtle politician of the Middle Ages——ready to whisper rebellion into the ears of four stalwart sons, who had the demon blood of Anjou boiling in their veins, and with hundreds of rebellious barons on both sides of the sea ready to take advantage of any mistakes, King Henry's task was not likely to be an easy one.

Perhaps he might have triumphed all along the line but for his fatal mistake in making Thomas Becket Archbishop of Canterbury. When Theobald died, in 1160, Gilbert Foliot of London, the most learned and prudent churchman of his time, was the natural and obvious candidate for the primacy. But Theobald had recommended Thomas, and Henry was bent on carrying out one grand reform, namely, to make the clergy amenable to the ordinary law of the land. Thomas had hitherto cordially espoused this idea ; who could foresee that his elevation to Canterbury would drive him in precisely the opposite direction ? Not his fellow-churchmen certainly ; it is evident that most of them mistrusted him and thought him likely to "give them away" to the State. Indeed, few even of his own immediate followers ever believed in the sincerity of Becket's conversion during his lifetime, and most men regarded the ostentatious asceticism which he adopted as mere hypocrisy ; it was not until the monks of Canterbury, on stripping his martyred body, found a hair-shirt beneath his costly vestments, and the vermin dropping in crowds from his unwashed skin, that they exclaimed with rapture, "See, see, what a true monk he was, and we knew it not ! "

Anyhow, from the very first moment of his election to the archbishopric (1161) Thomas set himself against the King ; he surrendered his chancellorship and all his secular offices, laid claim to all the lands and privileges of his see alienated since the time of William I. ; declared against the taxation of Church lands (1162) ; and finally, when, in 1164, Henry promulgated his "Constitutions of Clarendon," the Archbishop, after swearing in a moment of vacillation to accept them, utterly repudiated the royal authority, and declared that he must go to Rome to get absolution from his oath.

By these "Constitutions" Henry, who professed merely to be reviving the law of his grandfather's time, was really seeking to undo the mischief of William the Conqueror's edict (see above, p. 107). Nowadays when a clergyman commits a murder or other felony he is hanged or imprisoned like any other felon, but this has only been the case since the Reformation. In the twelfth century he was merely subject to "spiritual penalties," *e.g.* suspended from saying mass, degraded from priest to deacon, &c., and could only be tried by a bishop. More than a hundred murders committed by clerks since Stephen's death had gone unpunished, and Henry was resolved to put an end to this. There were other points in the "Constitutions" by which the rights of the State over the Church were made equally clear, *e.g.* the prohibition of appeal to Rome without the King's leave ; the right of the layman to appeal to a jury in disputes between a clerk and a layman ; the full right of the Crown to nominate bishops. To all such claims of the State the Church had, by her appointed leaders, for nearly a century been giving a more or less qualified "No." Henry, though distinctly an irreligious man, was far too good a statesman to underrate the force of this "No," or to provoke an open quarrel with the Church ; and had Foliot been in Becket's place a moderate measure of reform would no doubt have been agreed upon, which would have preserved the sanctity without the independence of the Church. It was good that the sanctity of the Church should be respected utterly, good that in a rude age she should give shelter to the weak and oppressed, admit the poor and the unfree to holy orders, enforce pure living and preach righteousness without fear of secular vengeance ; but it was not good that her sons should commit murder and robbery and then take refuge under her cassock ; not good that she should refer questions relating to English lands to an Italian priest ; not good that her rulers should be elected by monks and should regard the State merely as the executioner of her sentences. But Becket was resolved upon nothing short of this complete independence, and in seeking to compass it he was prepared to go much further than even the Pope himself.

The King's surprise at Thomas' early behaviour in his archbishopric grew into rage at this defiant attitude, and when Henry was in a rage he was not a pleasant person to do business with. In fact he stooped to many petty and unworthy acts of vengeance against his enemy. Becket fled to France and appealed to Pope Alexander III., who was living in exile during one of the frequent twelfth-century quarrels between the Papacy and the Empire. There was now a very strong Emperor, called Frederick Barbarossa, who had occupied Rome and set up the usual antipope. The real fear for England was that Henry might be tempted to throw in his lot with the Emperor, for the natural alliance between England and Germany pointed in the same direction. One could hardly represent it as a religious question, and, when his first anger was over, it became to Henry more and more a question of expediency. And, in answer to this question, Henry decided that England and he had more to gain from adhering to the Pope acknowledged by three-fourths of Western Christendom, even though that Pope should interdict and excommunicate them.

But Alexander never did go that length : he condemned the " Constitutions," of course, and with Italian suppleness, flattered and endeavoured to soothe Becket ; but he was not going to throw away an adherent who ruled from the Pyrenees to the Tweed if he could help it. Like Rufus, Henry " knew his Rome," and English guineas——or shall we say Saxon pennies ?—— did their usual work. More papal than the Pope, because a more honest fanatic, Becket raved and chafed against the light rein with which Alexander tried to check him, and at last went to the court of Louis VII., who was delighted to get hold of such a weapon against his terrible Angevin vassal.

So for six miserable years the quarrel dragged on: the details of it are unnecessary, and would be wearisome. Several attempts at reconciliation were made, but it was not till 1170 that Becket was allowed conditionally to return to England. The English bishops, though none of them liked the Constitutions, had felt it their duty to make the best of them, and thoroughly respected King Henry's honesty of purpose ; they were very angry at Becket's obstinacy and defiance, and not unprepared to be excommunicated by him. This, in fact, happened, in 1169, and it was only on an express promise of revoking this sentence that Becket was allowed to return in the following year. But once in England the haughty man forgot his promise, and passed sentence of excommunication on all who had accepted the Constitutions. Some people have said that he was posing as a candidate for martyrdom as a necessary preliminary to saintship. I do not think this is true : I think he was so inordinately proud, and knew so well the terrors that the Church could wield, that he believed no one would dare to touch him. But the news of this fresh defiance was brought by the Archbishop of York to the King, in Normandy ; and in a fury Henry ground out between his teeth the fatal words crying for vengeance on "this upstart priest."

Then followed a wholly unlooked-for tragedy. Every one knew King Henry and his passions ; he lived in the open light of day, and was not given to mincing his words ; he was utterly incapable of planning a murder, and he had often used words almost equally strong against Becket. But four knights of his court, who had their private grudges, were glad enough to take the words as warrant for anything and everything. They crossed the sea, and simply murdered their enemy (who met his death with splendid courage) at the foot of God's altar, in his own cathedral (Dec. 29, 1170).

Thus and thus only was King Henry's work for the union of Church and State undone. All Christendom rang with horror at the deed, and the most horrified man in it was the King of England. Alexander laid the kingdom under interdict, but did not venture to excommunicate Henry, who promised instant submission and the surrender of his "Constitutions." Becket became a canonised saint (1174), and for 300 years was the most popular saint of the Church of England; "by Becket's bones" became the most popular oath in England. A shrine of marvellous cost and beauty rose above those bones, and Chaucer's "pilgrims," who

> " From every schires ende
> Of Engelond to Canterbury wende,
> The holy blisful martir for to seeke,"

are a household word even now. But Henry VIII. broke the shrine and plundered its jewels, and with grim humour had the memory of the holy, blissful martyr attainted of high treason.

A penitent of less active mind than King Henry II. would have hidden himself at once in a cloister, and perhaps resigned his kingdom; to hide himself for a time was indeed an absolute necessity, and fortunately Henry now bethought him that he had long had in his pocket a bull from a deceased Pope authorising him to undertake the conquest of Ireland. It was not in the nature of things that the Norman barons of South Wales, when they had pushed their arms down to the farthest limit of Pembrokeshire, should not glare across the strait that separated Waterford from Milford Haven by only a few hours' sail.   Wild Irish "kings" beyond that strait were tearing each other and each other's tribes to pieces much in the same way, and perhaps with the same bronze or even stone weapons, as their relations had used in Britain before Cæsar's time.   The few Norse settlements on the Eastern coast were dying of atrophy now that the Viking age was over.   It seemed that a few hundred stout Anglo-Normans in ring-mail could have a "walk-over" if they landed in Ireland. One of these Irish "kings," Dermot by name, had come to Normandy, in 1168, to implore Henry's aid in some tribal quarrel, and Henry had bade him try his luck in recruiting in South Wales.   Nothing loth were the De Clares and Fitzgeralds and Fitzstephens of that district for the goodly game.   They went, and where they went they conquered (1168–1171).   Henry felt with justice that the new powers acquired by these baronial subjects of his were a matter that required looking into ; here too was his opportunity of escape, and here was work to do ; so on October 17, 1171, he landed at Waterford, and for five months was safe from papal interdicts, legates, penances, and the like.

As was the Irish State so was the Irish Church—in anarchy.   Not till 1152 had a real synod been held and a real division of dioceses made : parish churches as yet there were none, or hardly any.   Unwarrantable as papal "bulls authorising conquest" usually are, there was something to be said for a Pope who wanted to organise the Church of Ireland, and one result of Henry's mission was that the island was once for all completely brought into reunion with Rome as regards diocesan organisation, ritual, and the like.   In secular matters Henry was equally successful up to a certain point : he made peaceable progresses through Leinster and Munster, he colonised Dublin with Bristol merchants, he set up the skeleton of county and central government, he confirmed the Norman adventurers in their new fiefs, and he was acknowledged by all existing "kings" as overlord of all Ireland. But he never crossed the Shannon or visited Ulster ; the conquest was an incomplete one, or, rather, it was not a conquest at all ; the barons left behind became, as all who have subsequently made their home beyond St. George's Channel have become, *Hibernis ipsis Hiberniores*. Wave after wave of the best blood of England has since then flowed over that green island, but Erin has taken all her conquerors captive and made them all her own—

> "The tear and the smile in her eye
> Blends with the rainbow that shines in her sky,"

and has bred poets and wits and soldiers and ardent patriots, but not that sober "political animal" which, according to Aristotle, builds up states. As Browning said of Italy, Ireland has been to us "the woman-country, wooed not won."

Henry returned, in May 1172, to find a terrible state of things brewing in the more solid parts of his dominions. Perhaps he had too often in the course of the Becket quarrel appealed to the old baronial spirit to help him against the Church ; but more probably the regular system of justice and the regular circuits of the justices, inaugurated by the Assize of Clarendon (1166), galled the barons too sharply and made them feel that they must strike now or never. The dangerous position in which Becket's murder had placed the King gave them the best of opportunities. At Avranches, in May 1172, Henry was solemnly absolved by the papal legate from all share in the murder of the Archbishop, and again solemnly renounced the Constitutions of Clarendon. But Louis VII. was knitting up a widespread conspiracy which was to shake the Angevin throne to its foundation : Eleanor was working upon her two elder sons, young Henry and Richard, to the same end ; they were now nineteen and seventeen respectively. Young Henry had, as we have seen, been crowned joint-King of England, in 1170, at the very crisis of the Becket quarrel ; he was already titular Duke of Normandy as Richard was of Poitou : they now proposed to make their claims good. Practically all Normandy rose to support them, and as much of the English baronage as still held lands on both sides of the sea. Besides Montforts, Mowbrays, Tancarvilles, Morvilles, there were the Earls of Chester, Norfolk, Derby, and Leicester ; there was the last baron-bishop, Hugh Puiset of Durham ; and worst of all, that most gallant knight, William the Lion, King of Scotland. Anjou and Maine were on the whole loyal ; but Brittany (recently acquired by the marriage of Geoffrey with its heiress) was seething on Henry's left flank, while young Richard could call out any number of Gascons and Poitevins in his rear.

For loyalty in England King Henry could, of course, always look to the freeholders of the shires, and to the lesser nobles whether of mixed or Norman blood— Glanvilles, Lucys, Stutevilles, Bohuns, and Mandevilles (the son of the archbrigand Geoffrey de Mandeville was quite loyal). Richard Lucy, the justiciar, had to be left for nearly a year to deal as best he could with the rebellion in England, though Henry did pay one wonderful flying visit to strengthen his hands. Like all twelfth-century wars, it was mostly a war of sieges and raids, in which the valour of the English soldiers led by Norman captains did the King's work effectually. The rebel castles fell, the royal ones resisted ; even William of Scotland vainly besieged both Wark and Carlisle.

But, in France, Flemish and Brabantine mercenaries were the King's only effective weapon, and Henry was often hard put to it to pay these gentry. Yet wherever he came in person he was victorious, and, by the summer of 1174, his foes were mostly prisoners in his hands. Then he ventured to cross to England, where the North was in imminent danger; and it was on the very day on which he went as a barefoot fasting pilgrim to Becket's tomb at Canterbury, and there underwent a severe scourging at the hands of the monks (who no doubt laid it on with a will), that the faithful Ralph Glanville took the King of Scots prisoner at Alnwick in Northumberland.

After that the rebellion fizzled out rapidly, and Henry returned to France and delivered Rouen, which the King of France and young Henry were besieging. The final peace was made at Falaise, and the King's extreme clemency proves how complete his victory had been. The rebellious princes were forgiven; the earls were set free and soon afterwards restored to their lands; the Bishop of Durham was let off with a fine; but the King of Scots had to do homage for his whole kingdom (mind, this is the solitary instance, unless you count the Balliols as real Kings of Scotland, which I totally decline to do), and to place his chief castles in Henry's hands as securities. Only Eleanor was unforgiven and banished from her husband's court for the rest of her life.

Prosperity is less interesting to the historian than struggle, and the next eight years (1175–1183), busy as they were, were comparatively uneventful; Henry's legislation and reforms went on apace and unchecked, and, with the exception of the growing independence of the Church, which Henry could not venture again to curb, the Government was far stronger in 1183 than before the rebellion.   But in that year the troubles began again in Aquitaine, and, after slowly growing serious till 1186, culminated in a general outbreak, which was to continue with little interruption till John lost Normandy, Maine, and Anjou in 1205.   The real mover in this business was the new King of France, Philip Augustus (1180–1220).

Louis VII. had been always ready to prove himself hostile, but he was rather a feckless man of little persistence.   Philip was one of the great founders, perhaps the greatest, of the mighty monarchy of France.   Though at first a friend of Henry, who had contributed much to his peaceful succession, he was soon unable to resist the temptation of stirring up the vassals of his vassal for the benefit of his own crown.   Young Henry was the most easily stirred of these vassals, but happily he died in 1183 ; yet he died childless, and so the Vexin (his wife's dowry, remember) ought to have reverted to France.   Geoffrey, the third son, now twenty-four years of age, felt that it was his turn to graduate in rebellion, for which he had been too young on the previous occasion ; but Geoffrey also died, in 1186, and left a posthumous son, Arthur, Duke of Brittany ; and Philip, as overlord of all, at once claimed the wardship of this baby.   Henry could afford to let go neither the Vexin nor the baby.   But, above all, Aquitaine was the worst danger.   Richard, a child of the North, was always a foreigner in that duchy, and, though he ruled with great sternness and almost succeeded in keeping order, he could not quite succeed, and the Aquitanian barons were always ready to appeal to Philip against him. Henry perhaps gave Richard too little assistance, and it is easy to see that Richard (after 1183 the heir of all) was kept perpetually anxious as to his succession owing to his father's absurd fondness for his youngest son John.

Still, Richard would naturally have supported his father against Philip but for Philip's ceaseless efforts to sow strife between them. Thus, while England remained in profound peace, the break-up of the Angevin dominions on the Continent was at hand.

For a moment all strife was interrupted, in 1187, by the terrible news from the East. The Christian kingdom of Jerusalem, that noble but vain dream of the Middle Ages, had tottered on since 1099, but was now once more in imminent danger. The second crusade, in 1147, had failed to give it any real access of strength, and, on the death of one of its kings (Baldwin IV., 1185), envoys arrived in England to offer to Henry, as to the greatest sovereign of Christendom, the crown of the Holy City. A great council of English barons, held at Clerkenwell, unanimously begged him to refuse, and he refused. The new king, of the house of Lusignan, fought on valiantly for two more years, and was then routed by the Saracens with terrible slaughter in a great battle in Galilee. The true cross fell into the hands of Saladin, and three months later Jerusalem fell. It was this event that first made a crusader of Prince Richard, whom we shall henceforth know as " Cœur-de-Lion." Philip, Richard, and Henry at once followed the example of the aged Emperor Frederick and "took the cross," _i.e._ vowed to go on crusade.

But Henry, though only fifty-six years of age, was worn out with hard work and domestic trouble ; and neither of these three princes dared to go alone and leave his dominions at the mercy of the other two : the mere prospect of Richard's departure caused all Aquitaine to rise in one jubilant squeal of rebellion, which Richard was mad enough to believe that his father had provoked. So at last Richard went wholly over to the side of Philip ; they gathered large forces

L

and suddenly fell upon Henry's favourite city of Le Mans, where he lay ill and almost alone; they drove him from place to place, and at last to a meeting with them at Colombières, where he was obliged to acknowledge himself vanquished and to grant all their requests—Richard should succeed him in all his dominions, the Vexin and Arthur should be given up.   Two days later, on learning that his favourite, John, had been playing into the hands of Richard, the King of England turned his face to the wall and died of a broken heart, July 7, 1189.   His deathbed was tended only by his faithful illegitimate son, Geoffrey.   He was buried, with little pomp, at Fontevraud.

The end had come with fearful swiftness, and, if we seem surprised at such a pitch from such a summit of power, we must acknowledge that the effort to hold the vast and scattered domain together was too great an achievement even for a man of the force and genius of Henry II.; when once one of the supports broke the whole edifice tottered, and Henry's health and vigour had been the main pillar of the whole.   No one among our rulers has impressed the stamp of his own personality so deeply upon English history as this typical Frenchman; a less awful figure than William I., a lesser lawyer than Edward I., a lesser warrior than Henry V., with a hundred bad faults that were patent to all his subjects, he yet seems to us the most human, the most intelligible, the most modern of our mediæval kings. His reign closes with shame and defeat to himself, and with the first steps in the dissolution of the empire of his house, but yet to the eye of history he seems to persist and to triumph over it all.   Nothing can take away the fact that he gave us once and for all the Rule of Law.

CHAPTER XI

RICHARD I. AND JOHN

THAT rule was to withstand severe shocks during the next two reigns, those of Richard I. (1189-1199) and John (1199-1216), but was to grow stronger all the time. Foreign politics, striking as is the part played in them by these kings, are of little direct interest to England. Richard is wholly busy either with the crusade or with the desperate effort to resist the growing force of France ; John is on the defensive, so far as his Continental dominions are concerned, from the very first. Both are continually draining England of money, as no kings before them have drained her, and for objects which are becoming more and more alien to her. England, however, is rich and can bear it ; she does not grumble much at the heavy taxation for the crusade ; that is a plain duty to bear, and (as in the eighteenth century) she helps Europe rather with subsidies than with men. Still, a great many distinguished Englishmen, including the old justiciar Glanville, go upon the crusade. The country is proud of its splendid King, the foremost captain of Christendom, and even bears the enormous taxes necessary for his ransom. But when he returns, and England finds that he regards her merely as a farm out of which to squeeze rents in order to defend Normandy and Anjou, and, worse still, Aquitaine and Brittany, against Philip, she begins to grumble a good deal ; when John succeeds Richard and continues the grinding taxation, nay, increases it very much, without any results in the way of military success, when he shows himself not only a gory tyrant but an idler and a poltroon, then

"The grumbling grew to a mighty rumbling."

The swing that Henry II. had given to the government of England was so great, and the machine worked so smoothly, that it took Englishmen some time to realise that in worse hands the machine might be used as an agent of extortion or tyranny ; when they did realise it, they began to realise also that they had voices to express their feeling, and that the barons were no longer their natural enemies, but something not unlike natural leaders. And, as the Angevin house came to stand more and more on the defensive for its foreign possessions, barons and bishops in Normandy and England began to ask what service they owed to the King for Aquitaine, where none of them had lands; for Anjou, where very few of them had lands. If Normandy should ever (Heaven forbid) be lost, all question of service beyond the sea would be at an end. Two things then stand out in this period as foreshadowing a great change in English history : the great increase in direct taxation, and the alteration in the whole question of foreign service owing to the loss of Normandy, &c., in 1205 ; and in tackling both these questions the barons had the nation at their back ; and the results were the rising of 1215 and the Great Charter.

On the canvas, if we take a preliminary peep at the period, Richard stands out with his noble knightly figure, his generous and forgiving nature, his kingcraft and warcraft, but also his entire devotion to objects alien to England ; John, alternately cringing and blustering, stands a little way back, watching his brother furtively ;

he only longs to see Richard off to the East that he may indulge unchecked every selfish passion that his cruel and rapacious nature suggests. Attempts have been made by historians to whitewash almost every evil character in history, but no one has ever yet, to my knowledge, said a good word for John. Eleanor, now quite a dear old lady, who has learned wisdom from adversity (for indeed she is practically only just released from fifteen years of captivity), stands between her two sons, and would fain keep the peace between them ; above all, she is determined to keep the whole Angevin inheritance together safe from the clutches of Philip of France, who lurks behind the three with the smile of coming triumph on his evil face. Resolved he is to march to his rightful end, the unity of the realm of France, by any road, fair or foul, that presents itself. In the background of the picture we see a crowd of distinguished ministers, barons, and bishops, some of them crusaders, all of them loyal to Richard while he lives, but none of them liking too openly to quarrel with John, in case Richard should not return from Palestine. There stands Hugh Puiset of Durham, once in rebellion, but now quite loyal and the bulwark of the North against the Scot ; he has royal blood in his veins and does not forget it. There Geoffrey, the one loyal (but illegitimate) son of the great Henry, glancing disdainfully at Hugh, for he has just been elevated to the See of York ; scowling at the little crooked figure of William Longchamp, Bishop of Ely, Richard's faithful friend and chancellor, who has but now succeeded to Glanville's position of justiciar. Every one hates Longchamp; he is a foreigner of the lowest extraction, but he will prove nearly a match for them all. There is Walter of Coutances, the stately Archbishop of Rouen, the type of the cosmopolitan

churchman ; there Hubert Walter, soon to be Archbishop of Canterbury, the favourite pupil and kinsman
of Glanville, who is to lead the English host back from
crusade after Richard's hasty departure, and who, as
chancellor and justiciar in one, shall rule England
loyally and wisely from 1194-98.   Last we see the
figure of St. Hugh of Lincoln, to whom alone of
churchmen of the Anselmian type King Henry had
listened ; he seems, amid the worldly and busy throng
of statesmen and ministers, like a ghost from the early
ages of the Church.

Richard bought his peaceful accession from Philip
by giving up of a lot of small outlying claims ; but he
did not give up the Vexin or the wardship of Arthur,
and, in fact, give up what he would, he had, in inheriting
his father's various crowns, stepped at once into the
position of natural enemy to the King of France.   In
Britain he averted all danger from the North by re-
leasing William the Lion from the homage due from
Scotland since the treaty of Falaise, and he made ten
thousand marks by the transaction.   He went on to sell
every office under the Crown to the highest bidder—
the wonder is that the buyers afterwards administered
their offices as well as they did.   Then, leaving old
Hugh Puiset and Longchamp as justiciars, he sailed
away, in company with his rival Philip, to Sicily and
so to the East.   His adventures there do not concern
us, but it is worthy of notice that it was on the crusade
that all his best qualities came to be recognised—his
masterly strategy, his great personal daring, his complete honesty of purpose, and his boundless generosity
to friend and foe alike.

Richard and Philip quarrelled at Messina, and again
in Palestine—it was, in fact, Philip's great object to pick
a quarrel—and soon after the fall of Acre, in November

1191, the astute Frenchman slipped away home to begin the game of grab on Richard's continental dominions. In this game he rightly expected to find a useful tool in Prince John. By the end of 1192, the news of their intrigues having reached the East, Richard resolved to hasten home, although he was obliged to leave Jerusalem untaken. On his way through Germany he was caught by an Austrian duke, imprisoned, and then sold as a captive to the new Emperor, Henry VI. Henry was no natural friend of the King of France, still less of John, both of whom implored him to keep Richard safely in prison; but he had differences with Richard's Sicilian relations, and for a poor man the opportunity of extortion was irresistible. He therefore valued Richard at about twenty-seven times his own weight in solid gold (Richard was a heavy man), or £100,000; it took a long year to raise three-fourths of this ransom even in rich England, and, when three-fourths had been paid, Richard was released and made his way home in February 1194.

One great mistake the King had made, in 1189, and that was not to take John with him on crusade; instead of doing so, he had sought to quiet his ambition by endowing him with four great English earldoms, Devon, Cornwall, Dorset, and Somerset, with the county of Mortain in Normandy, and with a whole string of "honours" (large manorial estates) and castles on both sides of the sea. That the prudence of Eleanor and the growing prospect of the succession would have some effect in checking John, he may also fairly have thought. This last prospect was much nearer in 1194 than it had been when Richard left England; the King's marriage with his first betrothed, Adela of France, had never come off, and on his way to the crusade he had married a princess of Navarre, to whom he was tenderly attached, but by whom he had no children. He had always avoided recognising Arthur as his heir; if Normans and Angevins had once hated each other badly, in 1194 they all hated Bretons much worse, and Englishmen hated Bretons worst of all. Arthur, moreover, was only seven years old.

The appointment of Longchamp as chancellor and co-justiciar was also a mistake. Richard knew him to be an able financier and a devoted servant, who would account to his master for the uttermost farthing; but Longchamp had from the very first, by his insolence and his exactions, made himself impossible, and before two years were out Richard had been compelled, at the urgent requests of all the barons and bishops of England, with Prince John at their head, to send Walter of Coutances to inquire into the administration of England. Walter found John and the chancellor almost at open war. The latter had dispossessed Hugh of Durham of his co-regency, and was perhaps scheming for the succession of Arthur; when he proceeded further to fall upon Geoffrey of York, he gave a chance to all his enemies to attack him. At a great meeting in London, at which John craftily represented himself as acting entirely in Richard's interests, the chancellor was deposed from all his offices and compelled to fly the realm. Walter of Coutances took the justiciarship, and held it until the return of Hubert Walter from the crusade early in 1193.

Thus John had made a great stride in power; yet there was no disloyalty to Richard in any one's breast except his, and Richard on his return afterwards acknowledged as much. When, however, Philip arrived in France, at the end of 1191, and began to intrigue with John, it was difficult for the Prince to conceal his treasonable intentions longer. The two entered into a regular treaty by which Philip agreed to invest John with all Richard's fiefs, and John in return ceded to France all the right bank of the Seine except Rouen, and considerable territory on the left bank also ; when the news of Richard's capture arrived a year later, John proposed to put this treaty into execution.   But the lesson of 1174 had been well learned even in Normandy, and John could never get a foothold there at all except on his own estates.   He could do, and did homage to Philip for the rest of Richard's French dominions ; he could, and did fortify a few castles on both sides of the sea ; but he could never have held them for long against the King's able ministers and the universal loyalty of his subjects.   But while Richard's fate was uncertain (for the most conflicting rumours had reached the West concerning him), the barons and ministers were unwilling to proceed to extremities against a man who might to-morrow be their king.   Early, therefore, in the summer of 1193 the justiciar patched up a six months' truce with John, without mention of Philip, who not unnaturally railed at John for deserting him.   On the news of his brother's release John made a frantic attempt at open rebellion ; but he had not a partisan worth the name either in England or France ; one by one his castles surrendered to the King's officers, the last of them, Nottingham, to Richard himself a few days after his landing.

Of course Richard pardoned John ; of all his race he was the most forgiving.   But, unfortunately, he was also the least grateful, and now, in return for all that England had done and suffered on his behalf, he only stayed two months in the island, and only thought of squeezing fresh riches out of it.   In May 1194 he went off to settle accounts in a grimmer fashion with King Philip.   He had had enough of divided authority in England, and he left Hubert Walter behind him practically supreme in Church and State ; John, though pardoned, was restored to few of his lands and none of his castles.   For four years more the great minister toiled on, years to which we owe several important legal enactments—increased power of the justices on circuit, increased regularity of their circuits, election instead of nomination of the grand jury, the new office of coroner to make a preliminary examination into crimes and to report to the justices, a great increase of the class of cases reserved for the King's Court under the name of "pleas of the Crown," and the germ of our once admirable system of county government by the "justices of the peace."   But the great accumulation of offices, secular and spiritual, in one hand was offensive to the papal churchmen. Hubert was unpopular with the monks of Canterbury, who had the ear of the Pope, and, in 1198, he was compelled by the advent of a new and vigorous Pope (Innocent III.) to lay down his justiciarship.   He was succeeded by Geoffrey Fitz-Peter, one of Henry II.'s old servants.

Philip had been profoundly disgusted at the weakness of John, and he therefore turned all his attention to getting possession of Arthur and using him as an agent against Richard.   In this he succeeded in 1196 ; but for the remainder of Richard's life the fortunes of the two were fairly evenly balanced.   Though Philip had succeeded (by marriage) to the greater part of Picardy and so completely cut off Flanders from his Norman rival, though he had set up a focus of insurrection in Richard's rear by the possession of Arthur and so of Brittany, Richard had gained the friendship of Toulouse, and succeeded in getting his nephew, Otto of Saxony, elected to the imperial crown in Germany.   English gold was flung heavily into the scale against Philip, and was busy buying back friendships and castles on which Philip had laid hands during his rival's captivity. The crowning point of Richard's career was the building, in 1197–98, of Château-Gaillard, the "Saucy Castle," as the southern defence of Normandy in its most vulnerable part. It utterly blocked the Seine half-way between Rouen and Paris.

Yet, after all, no amount of English gold, no fortress-building, no military genius, could stem the flowing tide of nationality which Philip had in his favour. Richard's territories were but a group of feudal provinces, without common tie save allegiance to his person, and each looking to a different capital and a different administration for its orders. Philip's kingdom from its centre at Paris was fulfilling a historic mission, a mission which his successors steadily kept before their eyes down to the latest hour of the monarchy : the Rhine, the Alps, the Pyrenees, and the Ocean were the limits of old Gaul ; they should one day be again the limits of new France. Would it not soon dawn upon Angevins and Normans, and even upon Aquitanians, that they were all after all mainly Frenchmen, as English barons were daily discovering that, of whatever descent, they were after all mainly Englishmen ?

Richard was badly wounded in besieging a small castle in the province of Limoges, and died of the wound, April 6, 1199. John had no difficulty in making good his claims, first on Normandy and then on England ; but Maine, Anjou, and Touraine fell away almost at once, while only Eleanor's presence kept the Aquitanians quiet for a moment. John left Richard's ministers in office in England, and Hubert Walter, still archbishop, was his best adviser. But in Normandy war began almost at once, for Philip claimed the execution of the treaty of 1192, whereby John had ceded all the right bank of the Seine, and much on the left bank. As long as Philip had possession of Arthur, now twelve years of age, he was obliged to walk warily, and there were truces from time to time. But John was his own worst enemy: he would dawdle away whole months at Rouen, safe behind the screen of Château-Gaillard, while Philip was conquering right and left upon the Loire; or he would wander aimlessly about Normandy, now gathering forces and now dispersing them. He would dash over to England, and levy enormous taxes for expeditions which never came off, or he would gather an English army and fleet, and then dismiss them without putting to sea. He repudiated his wife, the heiress of the earldom of Gloucester, but stuck to her inheritance, and thus alienated the English barons; and then seized and married a princess of Angoulême, who had already been betrothed to a member of the great house of Lusignan, and thus equally irritated the lords of Aquitaine, who made a fierce appeal for help to Philip. Finally, that which John no doubt counted his own greatest stroke of luck, the capture of Arthur, in August 1202, was really to prove his ruin.

That he would murder Arthur might have been safely predicted by any one who knew John. None of his ancestors would have committed the blunder, few of them the crime, for a parallel to which we must look back to Danish times or forward to the horrible feuds of the fifteenth century. When and how Arthur disappeared we don't know, but he was dead by Easter 1203. Philip jumped at his opportunity, proclaimed John a forfeited traitor and murderer, and got the conscience of all Frenchmen on his side. Moreover, the disappearance of the boy left the French vassals of John no choice but that between him and Philip.

From that moment John could rely only on a few faithful Norman families (like the Gournays) and on the general turbulence of Aquitaine, which was averse from all government.   Philip had only one difficulty to contend with, but it was a great one—he had to take Château-Gaillard.   The siege was one of the greatest feats, both of attack and defence, in the annals of the Middle Ages.   For nine months Roger de Lacy, Constable of Chester, held out on the rock against blockade and sap and storm; against line after line of fortified entrenchment; against "mangonels" and "per-rières," which flung huge masses of rock and vessels full of burning pitch; against scaling ladders and movable wooden towers filled with crossbow-men; against "cats," sheathed with boiled hides, which clawed their way into the walls.   He saw a relieving fleet of seventy vessels repulsed and shattered on the river beneath him; he got a letter from John explicitly saying that he must expect no relief from him; he saw his outer-guard taken and his inner-guard fired, but till March 1204 the citadel itself resisted everything that mediæval siege-craft could do.   At last the great walls of this also yielded to a mine, and 156 starving men were disarmed after making a desperate resistance to the whole French army, which poured in at the breach.

Then Normandy was at Philip's feet, and he swept it from end to end.   Rouen was almost the last place to surrender; Anjou, Maine, and Touraine were already gone, and Philip followed up his success by taking everything in Poitou up to the gates of La Rochelle. Normandy was on the whole ripe for the change of allegiance; few of its great barons still held possessions on both sides of the sea, and of these fewer still elected to remain French subjects.   It rapidly settled down into

the most peaceable of French provinces.   But it was
otherwise with Aquitaine, even after the death of Eleanor
(April 1205) had removed the last legal obstacle in
Philip's way.   The Southerners soon discovered that their
normal pastime, rebellion, had been much more easy and
could be played with much safer rules under a distant
English sovereign than under a near French one ; and,
though the northern half of Aquitaine (*i.e.* the duchy of
Poitou) never really got back into English hands except
for a brief moment during Edward III.'s reign, the
southern half, the land of rich Roman cities as well
as of adventurous Gascon squires, clung tightly to the
nominal overlordship of the English kings almost to
the end of the fourteenth century.   Indeed, the last
fragment of Eleanor's inheritance was not finally torn
from us until 1453.

It was, therefore, not without instinct that John,
whenever he did rouse himself for a bang at Philip,
usually started from La Rochelle rather than from
Cherbourg or Caen ; but the English barons rightly
said that, whatever service they might have owed for
Normandy, they owed none for Poitou, and so refused
to follow him.   In 1206 and 1214 the King raided northwards from La Rochelle as far as Angers ; but it was with
an army of mercenaries only.   In 1213 an English fleet
burned a few Norman coast towns ; but every one rapidly
became aware that the old connection between England
and Normandy was gone for ever.   John's last hope was
crushed when a great combination of Philip's enemies,
headed by the Emperor Otto and the Count of Flanders,
was defeated by an inferior French force at the battle
of Bouvines (July 1214).   On the whole, John was
obliged to be content with occasional truces, which
allowed him to retain and transmit to his son a pre-
carious hold on Guienne.

There is no greater testimony to the good government of England, since 1154, than the fact that the country did not at once rise, in 1205, against the defeated and discredited poltroon who wore its crown. The barons were, of course, the greatest losers, and their personal grievances were multiplied every day. We have only to run through a list of the taxes recorded in the numerous chronicles to realise how very heavily they must have pressed upon the landed classes. But they fell upon the non-landed as well, upon the British merchant, the sort of John Bull whom you see in *Punch's* cartoons jingling his guineas in his pocket, who was already beginning to be a power in the country. But on merchant and baron alike the majesty of the law lay heavy. John had to sink much lower before any one would move, and, even when he did, men moved very tentatively.

His quarrel with the Church partakes of the sordid and brutal character of everything to which he put his hand, though its origin is such as to enlist some of our sympathy for him. Hubert Walter died three months after Eleanor (July 1205)—the King, by the way, received the news with horrid glee, and swore with horrid oaths that "now, for the first time, he was King of England," and a disputed election to the archbishopric followed. The royal right to nominate bishops was among the most ancient rights of the Crown, and the abrogation of the Constitutions of Clarendon, which had reasserted that right, made no difference to it. But the monks of Canterbury thought that this might be a favourable opportunity to assert themselves, and some of them met and made a hasty election of an incompetent monk. John ignored it, and nominated an equally incompetent and very worldly bishop. Innocent III., the greatest and one of the best men who ever ruled Rome, had no wish to quarrel with England, and tried hard to show the King what an unfit candidate he had selected, and to persuade him to accept a very able and honest man, Stephen Langton. The King rightly stood on the ancient rights of his crown, and utterly refused to accept a papal nominee; but it is difficult to avoid seeing that a general attack on the clergy (which might end in the confiscation of a good deal of clerical property) had its charms for a man like John. Every papal wile, every diplomatic resource was for three years exhausted by Innocent before he launched an interdict against England (1208); he then intrusted the publication of it to three bishops, who promptly fled after publishing it. But whereas, in 1164–70, the majority of the bishops had stood by the King, in the five years that followed Innocent's interdict the Church, as a whole, espoused the cause of the Pope. This was not only owing to the repulsive character and evil life of John, but was also the natural result of the failure of Henry II. to nationalise the Church of England. Probably the interdict was not very strictly observed; but John did confiscate the lands of all the clergy except those of the Cistercian monks. The lesser clergy were gradually allowed to redeem their lands by payment; but the property of the bishops was either kept in the hands of the King, who simply rioted on the proceeds, or given to unworthy favourites, of whom John always had a crowd at his court.

But if the clergy were necessarily inclined to the side of the Pope, it was otherwise with the laity; though they feared the Pope much, they hated him more —even more perhaps at first than they hated the King. Indeed, it is from this time onward that we may date that deep distrust of sacerdotal pretensions which is such a remarkable factor in the history of such a deeply religious people as ourselves. The confiscation of the clerical lands seemed to many pious laymen a regrettable but righteous retribution for the enormous wealth and greed of all orders in the Church. Thus although one cannot say that the sober part of the laity gave John an enthusiastic support against Innocent, at all events it gave Innocent none against John. So, when Innocent launched, in 1209, a bull of excommunication, John was able successfully to watch the ports and keep the outrageous bit of sheepskin out of the country. When, in 1213, this was followed by a bull of deposition, the execution of which was committed to Philip, the nation rose in wrath and mustered a great fleet and army to resist invasion. Thus the worst King was on the whole preferable, in the eyes of England, to the best Pope who ever reigned.

But John forsook himself; though grossly irreligious, he was profoundly superstitious, and, after vainly trying to amuse himself during the interdict with a raid in Ireland and with attempts to bully the King of Scots, he began, in 1213, to have tremors on the subject of his soul. Sated as he was with the spoils of the bishops, the difficulty of compensating them became daily greater; but the Pope was quite politic and ready for a reconciliation, for he probably found Philip a very unsatisfactory ally—Philip, indeed, had had his "bellyful of interdicts" in his time. Suddenly, therefore, the whole position was reversed. John flung himself at Innocent's feet and promised to receive Langton, to pay 40,000 marks compensation to the bishops, to hold England and Ireland as fiefs of the Pope, and to pay tribute for them.

It is needless to say that no English king had ever

M

stooped, or was ever to stoop, as low as this ; and equally needless to say that no great council of English barons had been called to sanction such a grovelling transaction. Barons and people and the better half of the clergy were alike furious ; the removal of the interdict, glad as every one was at that, counted for nothing against such a humiliation. The nation as a whole suddenly seemed to wake to the consciousness that it was a nation, an entity capable of suffering a grievous wrong, a "corporation capable of being sued and suing" against kings and popes alike before the arbitrament of high Heaven.

Luckily the man whom Innocent, in defiance of King and Canterbury alike, had selected for the archbishopric was a thorough patriot. Of Langton's origin we know nothing ; he is believed to have been a Lincolnshire man, and to have studied at Paris ; it illustrates the cosmopolitan character of the mediæval Church that he had been both prebendary of York and of Notre Dame in Paris ; in character and learning he was not unlike Foliot, and he certainly resented the vassalage of England to the Papal See. But he must have been a man of high courage, for he at once began to bind the nation to a united resistance to a tyranny which had now become unendurable.

Philip was naturally furious when Innocent, who had been urging him to attack John *vi et armis*, suddenly turned round and said, " hands off my new vassal," and he fell upon John's allies in Flanders with right good will. But the English fleet, which had been watching against a French invasion, now sailed over and thoroughly defeated the French fleet off the Flemish coast. Further than this, however, the barons were not prepared to go ; they utterly refused to accompany John to Poitou, and also refused to pay the scutage which he demanded for his expedition thither. Langton had already convened a great meeting of them at St. Paul's (25th August 1213), at which he appealed not only to their new national, but also, in a guarded manner, to their old feudal instincts; rightly judging that, now Normandy was gone, all serious chance of a purely feudal rebellion was gone with it. "Here," said the Archbishop, who had perhaps been rummaging among the old parchments in the Tower, "is the charter of King Henry I.; make this the basis of reform; the Church has suffered, you have suffered, the whole community of the land has suffered; you should arm in the name of Church and nation, and get the King to sign an expressly worded series of promises to behave better in future." Even then the barons hesitated; the majesty of the law was upon the King's side, every important castle was in his hands, he was rich, and could command hosts of mercenaries; but one by one they at last came forward and swore to do something of the kind suggested by Langton. Then for over a year, while John was exhibiting his tyranny and military incapacity in Poitou and Anjou, they brooded over the matter without taking any overt steps. At last, in November 1214, they held a fresh meeting at Bury St. Edmunds, in Suffolk, and there was produced the document which was to serve as a basis for the Great Charter. It is called the "Petition of the Barons." Who drew it up? We have no means of knowing, but we may fairly guess that Langton's hand was in it. As at St. Paul's so now, one by one, the barons came forward and swore that they would withdraw their fealty from John if he did not agree to all their demands. Robert Fitzwalter, a comparatively obscure Northern baron, was elected commander of the "Army of God and Holy Church"—remember, to their honour, that they were enlisted against the self-styled head of that Holy Church, the Pope, and his vassal—and they dispersed to prepare for war.

Even so, some 2000 knights was the utmost force that they were able to muster in the following April ; to take the paltriest royal castle was a task utterly beyond them.   If John had collected his mercenaries quickly, instead of moving restlessly about the island, quartering himself upon unwilling abbots, and using frighful language ("by God's teeth" seems to have been his favourite oath), he could have dispersed the barons as his father dispersed the rebels in 1174.   But when London threw open its gates to the baronial army, on 24th May, the affair began to look different.   London, as we have seen, had put, and almost kept the crown, on the head of Stephen ; in wealth and importance it was probably even more out of proportion to the rest of the kingdom than it is to-day ; and so John, to the surprise of every one, executed one of his sudden changes of front and professed himself ready to agree to everything and sign anything.   The Great Charter was signed at Runnymede on 15th June 1215.

This signature, which we have sometimes been taught to regard as the close of a great epoch, was in truth but the beginning of a struggle.   The ink was hardly dry before John sent to Rome to get absolution from his oath.   Innocent was of course ready with absolution, and at once summoned Langton to Rome to explain his extremely antipapal conduct.   The Great Charter of England had the supreme honour and good fortune to get itself cancelled by the Pope, at a dirty little town in Southern Italy called Anagni, where the "Chief Pontiff proceeded further to excommunicate the barons by name and in the lump."   Then, fortified by these distant thunders of Rome, the King in September struck hard and struck home at the little army of the barons. Falkes de Breauté, a famous mercenary captain, brought him strong reinforcements from Flanders, and he gathered all his other mercenaries from his different castles. He drove one party of the barons in headlong flight into Scotland, and followed them up to the Scots Water (the Forth). Langton, not daring to disobey Innocent's summons, went to Rome, was suspended from his priestly and episcopal functions, and kept as a sort of prisoner till 1218. Deprived of their wisest counsellor, another party of the barons took a very foolish step, and offered the crown of England to a French prince (afterwards Louis VIII. of France), who accepted it joyfully. Louis landed, and was well received in London ; but a good third of the baronial party had refused to subscribe to this project, and his whole time was taken up in fruitless sieges. The shire levies of the country either refused to stir or were called out to serve the King as usual, and the whole rising was apparently following the course of an ordinary abortive feudal rebellion, when John, on his southward march, was overtaken by a tragic disaster as he tried to cross an arm of the Wash at low tide. There he lost in the waves all his baggage and a portion of his army, and a few days later he died suddenly at Newark (Oct. 19, 1216).

CHAPTER XII

HENRY III. AND THE GERM OF PARLIAMENT

THE Great Charter of 1215 is in form a treaty between King John and his barons, who act or claim to act on behalf of the "whole community of the realm." No other body of barons before this time had made such a claim, and therefore it is a new departure in English history. "If you will keep certain specific promises contained herein," they say, "we will obey you; *si non, non*. We provide a regular means of disobeying you if you break these promises, for we provide a committee of twenty-five barons to watch you." This then is the foundation of the doctrine that the monarchy of England is a "limited monarchy." A long struggle is inevitable before (1) the kings are willing to recognise this limitation, (2) the machinery by which the limits are imposed is perfected. But the idea was started, and the name of "constitutional government" gradually came to be attached to it, and to imply that the monarchy was controlled by some sort of parliamentary assembly. When in later years we have talked big about the immortal "British Constitution," we have always meant the British system of parliamentary government, and always regarded the barons of 1215 as its founders and fathers. We have asked this Constitution to give during the last eighty years the strongest proof of its immortality by altering it every day, until its founders and fathers would not recognise it; so much so that a witty French writer has said that it "does not exist," by which he means that King and Parliament can make in it from hour to hour any change which they please. Most people have considered this to be a great virtue in our Constitution, which can thus adapt itself to the changing needs of changing times; others think that such a virtue may be carried too far.

But the point for us now to grasp is, that the barons of 1215 had one or two notions of a real "constitutional" kind; the principal one, in the 12th and 14th articles of the Charter, being that the King shall take no direct taxes without a grant made by an assembly; an assembly, however, of the old kind to which they are, or ought to be accustomed—the natural feudal court of all tenants-in-chief. They made a distinction within this body: archbishops, bishops, abbots, earls, and "greater barons," are each to receive a special writ summoning them by name to this assembly; lesser tenants-in-chief are to be summoned by the sheriff of the county in which they live. Our old friend Roger of Tubney, who held that manor of the King by the service of two knights, was originally a "baron" just as much as Earl William with his 150 manors. But the name "baron" was clearly going to stick only to the "greater barons," and where the line was drawn it is impossible to say. In the thirteenth century it was mainly a question of wealth, and wealth then meant only broad lands; some 100 or some 90 great families had come, by the accidents of history, to stand out above the other tenants-in-chief (whose numbers had multiplied rapidly); and of these 100 or 90, those that remained into the fourteenth century gradually made good a customary right to receive the special writ. When made good for several generations, this right could be no longer denied, and it passed from eldest son to eldest son, and so constituted "peerage." In the fifteenth century we shall call these men no longer the barons, but the peers, the "most high court of Parliament." By that time their number will have very much diminished.

Probably this 14th article was to the barons of the time the most essential point of the Charter ; next to it would come the earlier articles, which limited the grinding and arbitrary exactions of the Crown in the way of reliefs, wardships, and feudal dues generally. Reliefs are fixed ; heiresses are not to be sold ; widows are not to be compelled to marry ; land shall not be seized for debt as long as chattels will suffice to pay the debt ; services shall not be demanded which are not owed by custom. The Crown had founded its necessary and useful power of crushing feudal anarchy largely upon its arbitrary exactions in these matters, and the nation, so far as it had any voice at all, had applauded ; but John had overstepped all reasonable limits, and the exactions were becoming intolerable. When, however, the barons go on to say that suits relating to land shall not be summoned to the King's court by writ, they go too far ; Henry II. would have turned in his grave at this (the 34th) article of the Charter, for it was a claim to reassert the feudal jurisdictions, for which he had provided such an excellent substitute in his regular system of judges. It cost the Crown lawyers endless trouble to circumvent this article.

The rest of the Charter is a curious jumble of legal reforms, vague principles of justice, and articles of temporary application. Side by side with the disastrous 34th article we find it stated that the justices, and they only, are to try the pleas of the Crown ; that regular circuits of them are to go round ; that a court of "Common Pleas," *i.e.* suits between private individuals not involving Crown rights, is to be held in some fixed place (Westminster obviously intended) ; that fines shall not be excessive ; that the abuses of the forest laws shall be redressed ; that no one shall be tried by his inferiors in social station ; that no freeman can be dispossessed of his freehold without a judgment at law ; that justice be not denied or sold to any man.

It would obviously be difficult to enforce many of these legal principles, but the history of the thirteenth century threw the very words of the Charter into great prominence, and the lawyers glossed and commented on them, and in many cases built on them doctrines of common law which have remained to this day. If you look at the Charter as a whole, you will see that it is in the main a series of particular remedies against particular wrongs, likely to be committed by the King or his officers. That is an essential idea in our Constitution, and this is why the Charter is the first of all constitutional documents. For instance, parliamentary government was instituted, not in deference to a "sacred principle" that every man has a right to be consulted, but as the simplest method of providing against arbitrary taxation ; so also the doctrine of "habeas corpus" grew out of the 39th article to provide against arbitrary imprisonment. No article in the British Constitution (supposing you could get a written text of it) would say : "It is the right of every man to do this or that, to meet, to spout on a tub in Hyde Park, to print anything he likes, to elect any one he likes." It would only say : "The Crown cannot restrain you, A. B., from doing this or any particular act, but you must take the legal consequences of your act ; if the Crown, by the rude hand of Policeman X., pulls you down from your tub and interrupts your eloquence, you can bring an action against the said policeman, or even the Crown itself ; but to win your action you will have to prove that you were not inciting to robbery or murder or any other felony ; you will have a perfectly fair trial."

So we may conclude by saying that Magna Carta indicates the direction in which our Constitution will march ; in the next reign it is a watchword, almost a fetish, to those who would further restrain the Crown ; by the end of the fourteenth century it has been systematised into law, and legal principles have been built on it.   It has been re-enacted nearly forty times in the course of English history.

Yet its worshippers must at first have been profoundly disappointed.   Henry III. was nine years old when the happy event of John's death put him on the throne.   A few barons, as we have seen, had rallied to John rather than follow the French prince, and more and more rallied to little Henry during the next year, so that by 1217 Louis was glad to conclude a treaty and to clear out of England.   Meanwhile the government of the country fell into the hands of a few great barons and the legates of the Pope, who was now, in strict feudal law, guardian of a vassal king during his minority. The boy was crowned, and you would have expected that the barons would at once have called the great council to give its consent to taxation, in accordance with the 14th article of the Charter.   Not a bit of it. Some sort of baronial assembly evidently was called, and William Marshall, Earl of Pembroke, was chosen regent; and then the Charter was reissued, but *without articles* 12 *and* 14, and with several other omissions.   Perhaps the barons, being now the "government," found that these restrictions fettered them too much ; if so, they were only like the leaders of modern parties, who make beautiful promises when they are in opposition, but evade fulfilment of them when they are in power.   Perhaps it had already dawned on some of their leaders that a great council of *all* tenants-in-chief, now not far short of 1000 souls, would be a totally unworkable assembly, that the idea had been an antiquated one, and that tenure-in-chief was not a good basis for parliamentary government. Perhaps the old lawyers of Glanville's and Hubert Walter's school kicked against conferring so much power on a feudal assembly—we cannot say for certain.

The Charter was reissued again in 1217, and this time the "forest articles" were put in a separate charter of great length and importance, really abolishing all the most vexatious of the game laws; and again in 1225, and this was the last time the text was (very slightly) changed.

The odd thing, however, is that Henry III.'s barons, who, very early after the King's majority, entered upon a real constitutional struggle with him, always act and speak as if article 14 was still in force. Several times they refuse the King money, "because they, 'the greater barons,' have not been summoned according to Magna Carta." They don't complain that the lesser tenants-in-chief have not been summoned, and these apparently don't complain of it themselves. The reign contains a regular national rising of national barons, national churchmen, and the upper classes generally, against Henry, who is submissive to the Pope and fond of greedy foreign favourites. Every one shouts "Magna Carta! Magna Carta! Confirm! Confirm!" For seven years (1258–1265) the King's government is practically in abeyance while this cry lasts; there is civil war, and men are killed for it. But all the while the shouters hardly realise what they are shouting about. The reinsertion and punctual observance of article 14 would have satisfied nobody, for, as in all prolonged struggles in a prosperous country, the causes of struggle undergo a sensible change as the struggle goes on. By 1258 we shall find that the barons habitually call themselves "parliament," but that both King and barons realise that they have other classes to reckon with, to conciliate, and perhaps to admit to a share in parliament. The barons are always a little bit behind the time. If we are to tabulate the other "cries" put forward during the struggle, they will appear somewhat thus—(1) England for the English, "down with foreigners in Church and State;" (2) Parliament to control not only taxation, but the King's private council and the three great officers of State (justiciar, chancellor, treasurer); (3) the King to keep some sort of accounts, or his ministers to keep them for him. The last two cries are, of course, new; to some extent all are new. The victory of the parliamentary party is only very partial; in the actual civil war Henry wins; the control of Parliament even over taxation is very partial till the time of Edward III.; and as for control over council, ministers, and accounts, that is a thing for which Parliament struggles intermittently till 1688 and even after. But the great thing is that Parliament gets itself recognised as a factor in government, a thing from which no subsequent king can ever quite shake himself loose. The shape that it assumes does not at present concern us; by a series of flukes, one might almost say, it assumes eventually a very fortunate and successful shape, and all the serious interests of the country get themselves represented in it.

Henry III. was not at all a bad fellow, but he was rather a bad king : he was impatient, restless, and hot-tempered, as became an Angevin, but fussy rather than business-like, learned rather than clever; pious after his lights, which unfortunately led him to look to Rome for guidance. Two really bad qualities he had inherited from his father, untruthfulness and extravagance; he did not mean consciously to lie, as John did, but he forgot his promises as soon as made, or explained them away, or got the Pope to absolve him from them ; as for his extravagance, it was boundless. On the whole he was a spirited, active, untrustworthy man, who rebuilt Westminster Abbey.

The Church should by rights have been in clover under such a king ; Henry was devoted to the memory of Becket and enriched his shrine greatly ; an article of Magna Carta had declared the absolute freedom of Church from Crown, *i.e.* the right of the chapters to elect bishops uncontrolled by the Crown ; England was the vassal kingdom of the Pope, and it was the age of great Popes—Honorius III., Gregory IX., Innocent IV., Alexander IV. But the churchmen were Englishmen too, and some of them very great and learned Englishmen, who had no idea of letting John's foolish concession to Innocent III. be interpreted into a license to the Pope to treat England as a farm, out of which he could squeeze rents at pleasure. This, however, was exactly what the Popes tried to do, and bade Henry help them to do.

We have an excellent contemporary historian of the reign down to 1259 in Matthew Paris, a monk of St. Albans, who knew the King well, and who was evidently more man of the world than monk. The reign opens with one of our first great naval victories over the French fleet, fought off Sandwich by the Justiciar Hubert de Burgh. Naval battles of those days were very like land battles, and by no means so unlike Nelson's battles as one would suppose. The great object is to board your enemy, and for this purpose you begin with a shower of arrows and missiles till you have cleared the deck sufficiently to allow you to let down a sort of gangway and rush over it. The " royal navy " of the Saxon and Danish kings had been replaced by the quasi-feudal navy of the

"Cinque Ports," *i.e.* the five chief Kentish ports—Dover, Sandwich, Hythe, Romney, and Hastings, to which Rye and Winchelsea, called the "two ancient towns," were afterwards added. These towns undertook, in return for considerable privileges, to furnish a definite quota of ships. Dover appears in Domesday as "owing the King twenty ships"; as England became more and more a maritime nation all the ports on the east and south coast, from the Wash to Cornwall, were made to contribute in the same manner. But the situation of the original five, almost on the Straits of Dover, shows that the danger to our coasts came mainly (after the period of Viking raids was over) from our gallant French foes, and from them it continued to come from the time of Henry II. to the early years of the nineteenth century.

> " Littora littoribus contraria, fluctibus undas
> Imprecor, arma armis ; pugnent ipsique nepotesque ! "

said Edmund Burke, in 1793, quoting Dido's magnificent defiance of Rome. In the thirteenth, fourteenth, and fifteenth centuries the Governments of France and England might often be at peace with each other ; the sailors never were. And though perhaps on the whole we won more of the pitched battles, in the game of piracy, reprisals and raids it is hard to say who had the best of it ; we burnt each other's coast towns with great steadiness. Anyhow, it is pleasant to record that Hubert de Burgh was one of our first naval heroes.

At Henry's council board also Hubert had it pretty much his own way until the King came of age in 1227. John's mercenary captains were gradually got rid of. Langton came back and ruled the Church wisely and well till his death in 1228; and the papal legates were expelled. But from the date of the King's marriage with

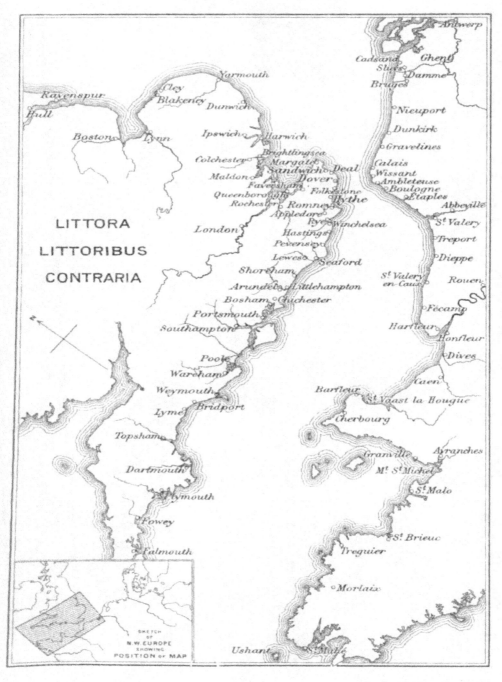

LITTORA
LITTORIBUS
CONTRARIA

Antwerp
Cadsand
Sluis
Ghent
Bruges
Damme
Ravenspur
Cley
Blakeney
Dunwich
Yarmouth
Nieuport
Hull
Boston
Lynn
Ipswich
Harwich
Dunkirk
Gravelines
Colchester
Brightlingsea
Margate
Calais
Maldon
Sandwich
Deal
Wissant
Queenborough
Faversham
Dover
Ambleteuse
Boulogne
Rochester
Folkestone
Etaples
Appledore
Romney
Hythe
Abbeville
London
Rye
Winchelsea
St Valery
Hastings
Treport
Pevensey
Dieppe
Lewes
Seaford
St Valery
en-Caux
Rouen
Shoreham
Arundel
Littlehampton
Bosham
Chichester
Fécamp
Portsmouth
Harfleur
Southampton
Honfleur
Dives
Poole
Wareham
Caen
Weymouth
Barfleur
St Vaast la Hougue
Lyme
Bridport
Cherbourg
Topsham
Granville
Avranches
Dartmouth
Mt St Michel
St Malo
Plymouth
Fowey
St Brieuc
Falmouth
Treguier
Morlaix
Ushant
St Malo

SKETCH
OF
N.W. EUROPE
SHOWING
POSITION OF MAP

To face page 190

Eleanor of Provence we can trace the incoming of a new swarm of foreigners—Valences, Lusignans, Montforts and Plessis; some of them were endowed with English earldoms, and settled down after a generation or two into respectable national barons. But it was time that this infusion of foreign blood should cease; it had been going on pretty continuously since the reign of the Confessor. One of the Queen's relations, Boniface of Savoy, was in 1237 made Archbishop of Canterbury, and did not prove a good one; the impatient King dismissed Justiciar Hubert in 1232, and then blundered on without any wise advisers or any real officers of State for twenty-four years, until he provoked a civil war. He made an attempt to recover Poitou in 1241, but his truly royal neighbour, Louis IX. (known as St. Louis), beat him at the battle of Taillebourg, and might have stripped him there and then of the last remains of the old duchy of Aquitaine, but, after years of negotiation, allowed the northern boundary of our French possessions to be fixed at the river Charente (1259). These possessions are henceforth usually called " Gascony " or " English Aquitaine." Henry had misgoverned them considerably, and it is in connection with them that we first hear the name of Simon de Montfort.

This able adventurer of Norman-French stock had inherited from his mother's side the Earldom of Leicester; a great soldier, he was also a man of learning, and the friend of learned men, especially of Robert Grosseteste, Bishop of Lincoln, who was the champion of the national party in the Church against papal exactions and foreign-born bishops. Simon had tried his fortune round Europe, and even in Palestine, before he played a leading part in English politics. In 1248 he was made Governor of Gascony, and constant complaints were made to the King of his severity in that office, whether rightly or wrongly it is hard to say ; the Gascons, as we have seen, were a turbulent race, and a strong hand was no doubt necessary. Anyhow, Simon came back very sore against the King who had listened to these complaints, and retired to sulk on his Leicester estates, and nurse his grievances ; probably he was already prepared to head a rebellion if necessary.

And by 1257 we may perhaps agree that something of the kind was necessary. The great Popes of the period had, one after the other, exploited for their own benefit Henry's devotion to the Church ; we begin to hear of endless payments demanded by Rome from the English clergy, "annates," "first-fruits," "tenths." We hear of demands that one canonry in every cathedral should be reserved for the Pope, who would thereon present it to some Italian favourite who never came to England but merely took the money ; similarly one or two livings in every diocese were to be "reserved." Then the laity were being galled by incessant demands of the Crown, which had to pay the Pope the "tribute of John" ; both clergy and laity were incessantly asked for "tenths for a crusade," and by this time every private quarrel of the Pope was called a crusade. One fierce quarrel the Pope always had on hand, that with the imperial house of Hohenstaufen, now drawing to its tragic close and dragging down Germany in its fall. This house was also reigning in Naples and Sicily, and as the "Empire" nominally included North Italy as well as Germany, the Pope was apt to be like a nut in the grip of a pair of nutcrackers if the Emperor chose to give an extra squeeze. When the great Emperor Frederick II. died, the Pope was resolved to extirpate his descendants from Southern Italy and Sicily at least. Who would be more ready to help him than his English vassal ? the Angevins and the Hohenstaufen had been foes ever since Richard I. had been held in captivity by the Emperor : it was in alliance with the Hohenstaufen that Philip had beaten John's troops at Bouvines.

And so one fine day in Lent 1257 King Henry, who had consulted no one but a few of his foreign counsellors, brought before a "great Parliament" his second son, Edmund, dressed in a Sicilian dress, and said : "See, my faithful people, here is my son, whom God has been pleased to endow with royal dignity," and then added, quite as an after-thought, that he had pledged the Kingdom of England to the Pope to pay 140,000 marks towards the acquisition of the Sicilian crown. "When they heard these things," says Matthew Paris, "the ears of all men tingled, and their hearts stood still with amazement" (*vehementer obstupuerunt*). Where was the money to come from ? The Church made a feeble promise of one-third of the sum ; the lay barons would not hear of it. The Pope had already begun to spend money in Sicily, and was getting handsomely beaten. Henry's brother Richard had already been elected by a papal party in Germany to the vacant imperial throne, and so is known in English history as "Richard, King of the Romans," or "Richard of Allemagne" (Germany), though he never got hold of a rood of German soil. It seemed, then, to the English barons as if their royal family was squandering its strength upon enterprises far more foreign to England than Henry II.'s had been ; such was indeed the truth, and England declined to pay the bill.

The barons were, perhaps, not great men individually ; perhaps they had not at their back such great men as they had in 1215, but they undoubtedly had at their back the whole nation, in a sense far other than in 1215 —a nation richer by forty years of peace and union, and beginning to be very conscious of its own strength and

N

of the King's misgovernment. The result was that, at a Parliament held at Oxford, in 1258, Henry had to draw in his horns entirely, and consent to a sweeping measure of reform dictated to him by the barons, who had found a mouthpiece in Simon de Montfort. It is hard to say whether personal grudges against the King did not play a large part in stimulating Simon to take the lead. He seems to have been a difficult man to get on with, and he quarrelled during the next few years with nearly every one of his own leading supporters. Popular legend called him "Sir Simon the Righteous," and treated him almost as a saint, but this was because he led the opposition to the Pope and to an extravagant King. Later historians have loaded him with praise, because during his rule the form in which the House of Commons took permanent shape was first used. He had probably little to do with preparing the first scheme of reform, which is called the "Provisions of Oxford," beyond lending his influence to force it on the King. By this scheme the Crown was for a time virtually "put in commission," *i.e.* its powers were to be superseded for a time by sundry baronial committees. But, further, all Henry's acts were to be controlled by a permanent council of fifteen, half chosen by himself and half by the barons; the three great officers of State, the justiciar, chancellor, and treasurer, were to be elected by and responsible to a baronial Parliament; and there was to be something (very ill defined) of the nature of a Parliament three times a year. No foreigners were to hold any office in the realm; the temporary baronial committees were to see to the payment of the King's debts and to investigate grievances.

On the whole it was a clumsy scheme, and was worked by clumsy though probably honest hands; its main interest for us lies in the fact that the King published his adhesion to it in English as 'well as in French, and this is the first legal document in the language which has come down to us since the Conqueror's charter to London.   Queer English it is too.   The King sends "igretinge to alle hise holde (faithful men), iloerde and ileawde" (learned and lewd, *i.e.* clerk and lay), and explains that he confirms all that his "raedesmen (councillors), alle other the moere dael of heom (all or the more part of them) . . . habbeth idon and schullen don" (have done and shall do) . . . these things shall "beo stedefast and ilestinde (lasting) in alle thinge abuten (without) ende !"   You see it is not so very difficult to make out ; it is merely a sort of inflected English.

Having sworn to abide by this agreement, Henry soon took steps to evade it ; and the first step was to get papal absolution from his oath.   This was readily granted. Meanwhile, we begin to hear of Prince Edward, now a high-spirited young man of nineteen, devotedly attached to his father and mother, and to his noble young wife, Eleanor of Castile ; he had already been endowed with the Earldom of Chester, and set to govern the troublesome Welsh marches.   In 1259 we see him attempting some sort of mediation between his father and the barons, who are slow at getting their measures of reform translated into fact.   By 1261 he is wholly for his father ; the royalist party is getting stronger ; the barons are quarrelling over their scheme, and civil war is near.   Simon is abroad for long periods, and in his absence no attempt is made to organise resistance. But, in 1263, he returns and begins to get to work. London now, as in 1215, is strongly on the baronial side, and feels the full weight of the King's displeasure in the shape of heavy "tallage" on its citizens.

After a vain attempt at getting the King of France to arbitrate, the sword is drawn and, in 1264, an unexpected stroke of luck at the battle of Lewes throws the whole kingdom into Simon's hands. Prince Edward, who led one wing of the royal army, pursued too far a charge against Simon's London contingent, and came back to find his father and uncle captives in the hands of the Earl. The Prince honourably gave himself up as a hostage for his father; but Simon, less honourably, did not liberate Henry. A fresh scheme of reform, of a much more oligarchical character and probably much more Simon's own work, was produced. By this the whole power was put in the hands of three persons —Simon, the Earl of Gloucester, and the Bishop of Chichester—who were to choose the King nine counsellors to control him absolutely.

From May 1264 to August 1265 Simon governed England in the captive King's name, and quarrelled with the Earl of Gloucester as a matter of course. His government was, however, rendered illustrious by the summoning for the first time of the House of Commons as an adjunct to the baronial Parliament, very much in the form in which it continued down to 1832. Probably this excited little attention at the time. " Knights of the shire," that is to say two, or three, or one knight (a word then equivalent to our "country gentleman ") had been elected to represent each county in parliamentary assemblies several times during Henry's reign. Citizens or " burgesses" from some towns had been called as far back as 1213. But now for the first time two knights from each shire and two burgesses from each borough in the kingdom were to come. What was really represented here was not the "people with a big P," but the counties, or, rather, the county courts. In every county were one or more boroughs, which sent representatives to the regular meeting of the county court (*e.g.* to meet the justices when they came on circuit); so townsmen and country gentlemen were already accustomed to act in common, and England was in a fair way to escape that fatal division between rural and urban populations which has wrought so much evil in France. To call representatives from those county courts to a central assembly was the best way to learn of what grievances the different localities in the realm complained; it was also the most convenient way of learning what taxes they were prepared to pay. The King (or Simon) might have gone round to each county court and learned the same things, but it would obviously have been a less convenient method.

No share in legislation falls as yet to this body of men; they are not yet an integral part of Parliament, only a temporary adjunct to it. No share in the supreme judicature is ever to be theirs; that is a matter for the Most High *Court* of Parliament alone. But whether the full meaning of a central assembly of representatives from county courts was or was not understood at the time, it was a great step towards national self-government, and there was a young man at hand who would profit by the lesson.

Simon did not liberate this young man, nor his father; he did quarrel with the Earl of Gloucester; he intrigued with the native prince of North Wales, Llewellyn; he showed himself grasping and greedy. Against papal pressure, however, he stood firm, and here the nation cordially supported him. When the Pope sent over bulls of excommunication, these solemn sheepskins were torn up and thrown into the sea, and "Master Martin," who brought them, was ducked in Dover harbour. At last Prince Edward escaped from his captivity at Ludlow, rallied the royalist forces, and overthrew and slew Simon at the battle of Evesham, August 1265.

Considerable vengeance, though not of a bloody

kind, was taken on those who had engaged in the rebellion ; the bishops who had supported Simon had to make an abject submission to Rome; the Londoners were heavily fined, their mayor imprisoned, and their walls thrown down. A few irreconcilables, who held out in the island fastness of Ely till 1267, were pardoned only after paying five years' rent of their lands. But, compared to the results of any unsuccessful rebellion in the next two centuries, these punishments were almost nothing. The last five years of the reign were tranquil; the old King for the most part allowed Edward to govern in his name, but the Prince was away on a crusade when Henry died on 16th November 1272.

CHAPTER XIII

EDWARD I

THE contrast between Edward I. and his father is great. His name attracts us at once; he was of course called after the Confessor; and he stands out on the canvas of history with William I. and Henry II. as one of the three greatest of our mediæval kings. In one respect he was the greatest of these three, for he was much more consciously than the other two, the servant of his people; his aims were much more national; his moral character was loftier. But, above all, he owes his fame to his having thoroughly grasped—first, the principle of government through parliament; and secondly, the idea of direct sovereignty over all the British Islands. But he was not the inventor of either of these. He could not have prevented the system of parliamentary government taking root if he had tried to do so; and the chance of making an united Britain fell to him as it fell to none of his predecessors or successors till the seventeenth century. He was merely a strong, resolute man who seized at the gifts that fortune held out to him.

Edward was tall and spare and warlike; a hard, just, upright man, a true product of the thirteenth century, far more truly pious than his father, but quite antipapal in his views of the relations of Church and State; with all the mediæval belief in crusades, and a strong hater of Jews, infidels, and heretics; a devoted husband to his noble Spanish wife, Eleanor (who died in 1290, before the critical period of his reign began); capable of fierce

passion, and by no means always able to control it; an
earnest student of war, yet avoiding war except as a final
means to gain a great end; above all, with a most
thorough belief in the righteousness of his cause, and a
steady disbelief in the righteousness of those who opposed
him. This last characteristic led him into his worst mistakes, and it was he who began the fatal practice of
executions for "high treason." Let us try and understand the reasons and the results of this. The game of
feudal rebellion was indeed over; we have seen that
hitherto it had been played by both sides according to a
set of fairly merciful rules; but, as the Crown had come
to be invested with greater and greater sanctity in the
eyes of the nation at large, the sin of "rebellion" assumed
greater proportions, and began to be branded with the
name of "treason." Treason literally means a betrayal
of your faith, a breach of your "allegiance" to your
lord. It is obviously no use to conspire against the King
unless you have a fairly numerous body of followers to
do it with, so if you turn "traitor" you lead astray a
number of other men. Hence in the eyes of the lawyers
treason becomes *the* crime that is worse than all other
crimes; and its punishment (they cut you up alive for it)
more horrible than all other punishments. Edward was
the first king who systematically employed capital punishment for high treason, and did it with all legal forms.
And that which renders his use of it peculiarly odious is
that he put it in force against Welshmen and Scots taken
in arms against him, because certain Scottish or Welsh
princes had sworn oaths of allegiance to him. In the
next reign, and in all the succeeding reigns almost to the
end of the seventeenth century, the crime of treason
grew to enormous proportions; and the lawyers defined
it to mean "levying war against the King," "adhering
to the King's enemies," &c., &c. Vague words these,

for what is "war"? who are "the King's enemies"? what is "adherence" to them? Any sort of riot may very easily be construed into one of these offences, and often is.

Edward then appears to us as rather a narrow, angular character, but right English at that ; he does not seem to have been much of a judge of men, or he would not have been so badly served by his lieutenants in Scotland ; probably he kept every one who worked under him at a great pitch and strain all his life, and was without the good-humour which had made Henry II.'s fierce activity tolerable. Certainly he left no one behind him who could continue his work. It was not to be expected that such a man would not occasionally come into conflict with his subjects, for his great aims were expensive to support, and he used strong measures to extort money for them. But his subjects knew that they were great aims and not selfish ones, for he took them into his confidence.

The new parliamentary system of government gave Edward and his subjects frequent opportunities of meeting face to face. One can fancy him stalking into Westminster Hall, and sitting down on the throne, and haranguing a full Parliament of clergy, barons, and commons in the French language, while his chancellor repeats the same ideas in bad Latin. Much of what he says is probably distasteful to his audience, but it is clear and intelligible and straightforward ; it generally tends to mean : "I have got to hold down Wales and to conquer Scotland, to hold on to Aquitaine (at the gates of which the King of France is ever knocking) ; to secure the open door for our wool trade with Flanders ; the Pope is giving trouble, as you gentlemen in lawn sleeves know only too well" (here the bishops begin to look rather uncomfortable). "I shall require at least an eighth part of the property of every one of my lay subjects, and a fifth—yes, I think quite a fifth—of that of the clergy. I shall take one army to Flanders, and every one who has land to the value of £20 a year must come and serve in the cavalry (my foot will consist of German auxiliaries); and my sheriffs will collect another army of 10,000 men from the northern counties, ready to cross the border on my return from Flanders. My chancellor will lay before you certain laws to which I desire your assent—one for restraining the acquisition of lands by the clergy, who already own too much land; one for enforcing the bearing of arms by all my subjects in proportion to their wealth; one for the protection of merchants all over the kingdom, and to make it easier for them to get their debts paid" (loud applause from the burgess members). And so on.

Edward varied the composition and the form of summons of Parliament from time to time, but after many experiments he settled, in 1295, on what we may call the normal form, or almost the normal form, of later parliaments. In that year we find the clergy sending all the bishops, 67 abbots, an archdeacon with two "proctors" (procurator, "person who cares for") from each diocese, a prior with one proctor from each cathedral chapter. The baronage send 8 earls and 41 barons (a smaller number than usual, many were fighting abroad); the commons send 74 knights (two from each of 37 shires) and 220 burgesses (two from each of 110 cities and boroughs). This would have remained the permanent form, but that the clergy kicked against having to pay regular taxes. The Papacy, at the very height of its pretensions, under Boniface VIII., suddenly sprang upon the Kings of England and France the startling statement that under no circumstances might clergymen pay any taxes at all. Both kings were naturally furious, and Philip IV. answered with private and violent attacks on the person and character of the Pope; but Edward was more politic. Good Archbishop Winchelsey felt himself in a very awkward position between his loyalty to the Crown and his loyalty to the Head of Christendom; but Edward, after much bullying (once he threatened to outlaw the whole clergy of England), forced him to a compromise, which was that the contribution of the clergy was not to be called a tax, but a "voluntary gift"; that the clergy as a whole should not be included in Parliament, but should sit apart in two provincial assemblies or "convocations" of Canterbury and York, which should always be summoned whenever Parliament was summoned; when Parliament made the King a grant of money, the clergy were to make their "voluntary gift" at the same time; and, to save them the trouble of wrangling over the amount, Edward III. obligingly fixed it at £20,000 at a time when the ordinary parliamentary grant was under £40,000. The clergy lost much influence in the State by this arrangement, for they lost the power of influencing legislation except through the bishops and greater abbots who continued to attend Parliament. The convocations could continue to legislate for the clergy down to 1531, when even that power was taken from them. Convocations still sit and hold learned and interesting debates, but these have no influence on legislation. The right of making the separate "voluntary gift" remained to them till 1664.

The main principle which lies at the root of parliamentary government is, that he who pays taxes should have a voice in the granting of them. This principle we have seen in embryo in the 12th and 14th articles of Magna Carta. King Edward gave a general assent to it by the mere fact of summoning and consulting his Parliament ; but he was a little inclined to evade it when very hard pressed ; and once, in 1297, his immense demands for money led to an open quarrel with his Parliament, in which the Earls of Hereford and Norfolk stood forth as the champions of resistance, and things looked for a moment like civil war. But the matter ended in Edward giving an explicit promise that in future he would not attempt to take direct taxes except with consent of a full Parliament. This promise is known as the "Confirmatio Cartarum," and is practically a much fuller reinsertion of those articles of the Charter which had been omitted in 1216. One would have expected that subsequent kings would have been wise enough to abide by this contract ; they very seldom were, but the fault was not wholly theirs. For you must consider that, as a country increases in prosperity, two things usually happen. First, the business of government becomes more expensive, but the nation, by its spokesmen in Parliament, usually fails to see this ; it will give what its ancestors gave, but not a penny more. Secondly, money falls in value—that is to say, a pound will no longer purchase half of what it would purchase two hundred years before. This, also, the nation will long refuse to see. The revenue of King Edward III. will no longer suffice King Henry VIII. or King Charles I., not necessarily because these kings are extravagant, but because they have much more governing to do, and because a pound in the sixteenth or seventeenth centuries will not purchase half what it purchased in the fourteenth. The result has been a long series of quarrels between kings and parliaments mainly upon the question of money.

In his dealings with "our dear adversary" of France Edward showed considerable statesmanship. His reign is not marked by great foreign wars or great victories, like those of his grandson; but then we must remember that, unlike his grandson, he had to deal with a French king, Philip IV., who was even greater and abler than Henry II.'s opponent, Philip II.; and, on the whole, Edward more than held his own. Philip's two great objects were the annihilation of the independence of Flanders and the reconquest of English Aquitaine. Edward's quarrel with Scotland came most opportunely to Philip's aid, for it gave France an ally who could always divert the attention of the King of England. The independence of Flanders under its own Counts was of paramount importance to England, for it secured us the open door for the export of our main produce— wool. All the good clothes worn in Northern Europe were made on Flemish looms with English wool, and so great was the trade that Edward was able as early as 1275 to levy a tax of 6s. 8d. on every sack of wool exported from England This tax remained the largest source of Crown revenue down to the sixteenth century. Edward more than once went to Flanders in person and enlisted German princes as his auxiliaries in the struggle; but, while the German princes quarrelled over their pay, the real defence of the country rested on the valiant Flemish burgesses, whose spearmen gave the French knights a terrible lesson at the battle of Courtrai, 1302, in which England took no part.

Still more keen was Edward on preserving the last remains of the inheritance of Eleanor of Aquitaine, *i.e.* the country between the Charente and the Pyrenees, which had been left to England by the treaty of 1259. Without much open war, and by incessant negotiation and fortress building, Edward succeeded in drawing round this territory a girdle of fortresses of such strength that it resisted all the efforts which the French kings

could bring against it for more than half a century.
One can hardly call Aquitaine, as a whole, loyal to
Edward, or a very satisfactory possession.   It would
have been wiser, no doubt, to give it up, and to concentrate all the English strength in the Channel.   But
this was too much to expect of a mediæval king ; and,
on the other hand, the city of Bordeaux was loyal and
its trade with England was very important and rich.
It remained English in sympathy far into the fifteenth
century.   The possession of Aquitaine also enabled
Edward to keep the friendship of his brother-in-law of
Castile and of all the Spanish peninsula.

But it is time to turn to the really interesting point
in Edward's reign—his attempt at reducing Britain to
complete union and subjection to himself.   He began
with Wales.   Ever since the days of Richard I. the
princes of North Wales had been growing stronger, but
not much more civilised.   That they were feudal vassals
of the Kings of England no one of them attempted to
deny ; they occasionally put in an appearance at the
English Court and did homage.   One Llewellyn was
the ally of the barons against John.   His grandson had
already given Edward trouble when Edward was Earl
of Chester.   He was in perpetual quarrel with the
"Lords Marchers," and he was now to begin the last
struggle for the independence of Wales.   He had been
betrothed to the daughter of Simon de Montfort, and
during the civil war had rendered valuable assistance
to the baronial cause ; he had seized Shrewsbury, and
not given it up till 1267.   On one pretext or another
he had avoided doing homage to Edward.   Perhaps
he thought, in his stupid isolation, that the "barons'
wars" were still going on.   Edward, in 1276, resolved
to point out his mistake to him.

The Wales over which Llewellyn ruled was confined

to the modern counties of Denbigh, Merioneth, and Carnarvon, with a strip of Montgomery. All to the south and east of this was already made into English shires, or else was "Marchland" held by the Lords Marchers, of whom the Mortimers were the leading family. But Llewellyn's real strength centred in Carnarvonshire, and especially in the wild district round Snowdon. Any English king who wished to beat him must hold the valleys of the Dee and Mawddach on a curve from Chester to Barmouth ; he must send a fleet to blockade the Menai Straits, and so cut the Welsh off from Anglesey (whence they got their corn), and must, as far as possible, build castles along the northern shore. This was, in fact, Edward's plan, but it had to be repeated twice. In 1277 a great road was cut from Chester to Conway, where a castle was built. Llewellyn thereon submitted, and was pardoned on surrendering the modern county of Denbigh, while Edward proceeded to build castles at Rhuddlan, Hawarden, Carnarvon, Harlech, and Aberystwyth. David, the brother of Llewellyn, who up till 1277 had taken Edward's part, was endowed with lands in Denbigh. But Edward the lawgiver and administrator was not content to rest on the work of Edward the soldier. He proceeded at once to upset the old Welsh laws and customs (which were no doubt barbarous) in the ceded districts, and to replace them by English law; and it well illustrates his narrow and unsympathetic nature that he pushed on this work too fast. The result was a fierce outbreak of David and Llewellyn, in 1282, which gave Edward the opportunity (for which he had perhaps been scheming) of overthrowing the last remnant of Welsh independence. Acting on the plan of campaign described above, and going slowly and methodically to work at it, Edward was by the autumn of 1283 completely victorious.

Llewellyn was killed in a skirmish ; David taken and hung as a "traitor." True, there was a Madoc, a son of Llewellyn, who made a little fuss in 1294, but he was speedily taken and imprisoned for life in the Tower. With Llewellyn Wales really ended.

The twelve counties into which it was eventually divided were not represented in the English Parliament till the reign of Henry VIII. The title of "Prince of Wales," borne by the eldest sons of subsequent Kings of England, reminds us of the one joke which is recorded of the grim king ; for he who was afterwards Edward II. was born in Carnarvon Castle, in 1284, and presented immediately to the Welsh people as their prince, "who could not speak a word of English."

Not very much to regret was taken away when this last remnant of the "Britons" submitted to the English yoke ; the long border warfare had had very bad results on the temper of the barons who had to carry it on. A certain amount of poetry and legend clung to the Welsh name, though less, I think, than to that of any other mountain people. Welshmen have remained thoroughly loyal to the English Crown, and Welsh soldiers have fought valiantly for it on many fields ; Welsh agriculture and mining industries have been carefully and successfully carried on, and Wales is a rich country ; but it is remarkable how few great men Wales has produced, and how little it has contributed to our history. This has been mainly because of the stubborn pride which has refused to allow its common people to learn the English language. Of recent years this absurd self-renunciation has been flattered by political agitators, with disastrous results on the character of the Welsh people.

When Edward I. undertook the conquest of Scotland he probably imagined that he had only to deal with a

much larger Wales.   He started with the advantage of
having in Southern Scotland a large number of barons
who were well affected to his cause, and who held lands
in England as well.   He was soon to find out his mistake.
The history of the sufferings and revenge of Scotland is
indeed a great contrast to the uninteresting subsequent
history of Wales.   By all the laws of nature Scotland
ought to bear to the English Crown the most virulent
hatred, instead of the most passionate loyalty.   For 300
years she saw her southern provinces desolated with
fire and sword as the result of the policy of Edward I. ;
for 300 years she repaid that injury with interest on the
North of England.   When, after the end of the ravages,
an accident of marriage brought her own royal race to
the throne of Great Britain, she found herself oppressed
by that race almost as much as by the first three Edwards ;
when that race had made itself impossible in England,
much of what was best in Scotland still clung to it with
touching fidelity, and still refused to recognise the
foreign race that was brought in by the English to
rule over both countries.   Largely Celtic in blood, Scotland has accepted the fertilising stream of Teutonic
civilisation, and has turned it to such account that she
has contributed to the arms, the arts, the commerce,
and the literature of Great Britain a number of distinguished names infinitely out of proportion to her
population or her natural resources; and more wonderful still, the loyalty of even the most purely Celtic
portion of her population is exactly in inverse proportion to the treatment that was meted out to her for
500 years.

For almost the whole of that period Scotland suffered from impoverishment directly brought about
by the border wars.   For more than half of it the
lands on each side of the border were a desert producing

O

nothing but peel-towers and armed men. The North of England suffered equally with Scotland, if not more. Hexham, one of the finest and largest of Northumbrian churches, was left roofless for 200 years; " it was not worth while to rebuild the roof, as the Scots would come and burn it again directly." But far and near in Scotland the towns were ruined, the sea-borne commerce annihilated, the people rendered savage and barbarous. A terrible result ? It would have been better for Scotland to have submitted to King Edward, and received the blessings of union and incorporation at once ? Well, possibly it would have been better for the material welfare of the Scotland of that time. But, on the whole, the Empire would have been infinitely poorer at the present day—poorer by the loss of the great history of a noble struggle for independence—poorer by the loss of that iron character of the Scottish people, which grew in them by and out of the struggle—poorer by the loss of a thousand noble examples of patriotism.

Mind, the resistance came from Lowland *and* Highland, and from Galloway no less than from Lothian : and it came not from the nobles but from the people, the small poor farmers and freeholders of the South and the small poor gentry of the North. Nearly all the nobles were at one time or another traitors, and those who were not were too often playing a self-seeking game. One of the strangest results of the struggle was the alliance between Scotland and France, to which the Scots gave everything and the French nothing but a little bad architecture and a few humorous corruptions of Scottish speech. The negative influence of France was seen in the aversion on the part of Scotland from accepting English legal or parliamentary systems.

The male line of Malcolm and Saint Margaret came to an end at the death of King Alexander III., who was killed by an accident in 1286. For eighty years Scotland had been steadily growing in prosperity. The natural antagonism between Highlanders and Lowlanders had been steadily diminishing. A last and very belated Viking invasion had come and gone, crushed by Alexander at the battle of Largs, 1263 ; the Hebrides had been ceded by Norway to the Scottish Crown ; in the Lowlands the land was held everywhere upon ordinary feudal tenure. The large estates of the Church were particularly well cultivated ; the boroughs had charters and self-government on the English model, and a considerable trade with England, Scandinavia, and the Continent ; taxation was light, for the kings had no foreign wars to speak of ; there was a great council of barons, which was rapidly on its way to develop into a parliament ; traces of the jury system in the county court are found quite as early as in England ; the sheriff was clearly copied from England, but he was spreading everywhere and was beginning to check the too great power of the barons. The beautiful pointed style of architecture was already highly developed, as may be seen in the melancholy ruins of the few Scottish cathedrals. All this Scotland threw away, and threw away with her eyes open, in her struggle for independence. Who shall dare to say that she was not more than right ?

Alexander's daughter had married a Norwegian prince, and had died, leaving a daughter, Margaret, the " Maid of Norway," aged three years. Edward suggested to the regents, who held Scotland for her, that the most natural thing in the world was to marry her to his infant son ; the union of the two crowns would then come about peaceably, and against such a fair proposal nothing could be said. In 1290 an agreement on this basis was made, and Edward sent a large ship of Yarmouth to escort the little maid to Scotland. But she died in the Orkneys, on her homeward voyage, and the Scottish throne was vacant.

Several possible claimants at once presented themselves, barons who had connections more or less remote with the old royal line ; and Edward was asked, or suggested that he should be asked, to act as arbitrator. The barons of Scotland, nearly all of Norman or English descent, and many of them holding lands on both sides of the border, raised no objection to signing a document which acknowledged Edward as overlord of Scotland. In this capacity, and as president of a large court of arbitration, Edward adjudged the crown, in 1292, to John Balliol, who undoubtedly had the best claims in strict feudal law. Another prominent claimant was Robert Bruce, an oldish man, whose Scottish estates lay in Annandale and Carrick. The new king did full homage for the kingdom of Scotland, and Edward seemed to be at the summit of his ambition. But a war with France broke out in the next year, and Edward demanded from his new vassal large sums of money, and bullied him in various ways. The Scottish barons found that they had made a grave mistake, and had given their country an overlord who meant to make his power a very real and interfering one. In 1294 Balliol suddenly concluded an alliance with France, and almost the whole of Scotland supported him.

Three critical years followed before Edward was able to avenge this insult, and during those years all Edward's enemies were springing at him at once. Wales, Aquitaine, Flanders, the Scots border, all had to be guarded or held down by force. The Pope seized the chance of adding to the chaos. The French sacked Dover, and Edward's heavy taxation produced the attempt at baronial revolt in England noticed above.

Not till 1296 was Edward able to leave the other theatres of disturbance, and cross the border with a large army ; but, when he did, he swept the Scots before him. The battle of Dunbar was the first of a series of defeats from which the Scots learned to prepare fresh resistance. John Balliol and many barons tamely submitted ; but the vassal king was deposed, and the vassal kingdom was to be incorporated under Edward's direct rule.   The Scottish crown and the sacred stone of Scone—believed to have been the pillow of the patriarch Jacob when he saw the vision of angels—were carried to Westminster ; and, after a march to the shores of the Moray Firth, Edward came back to turn his victorious arms once more against France, leaving an English regent to govern Scotland.

Then came the great surprise of his life.   His lieutenants governed Scotland cruelly, and seem to have been stupid men besides : and so, in May 1297, without any baronial support, a small Lanarkshire landowner, William Wallace, arose and called the nation to arms. The nation answered him, and, almost without cavalry, certainly without archers, Wallace cut in half and broke a large English army at the battle of Cambuskenneth, near Stirling (Sept. 1297).   The Earl of Moray and several barons at once joined Wallace, whose spearmen swept over Northumberland in an awful raid for which there is no parallel since King Malcolm's time.   But the majority of the Scots barons hated Wallace, and Edward was not slow to take advantage of this.   Patient and prudent as ever, the King of England waited till he could strike in overwhelming force, and his second great expedition to Scotland fearfully avenged the raid of Wallace, who was defeated with great loss at the battle of Falkirk (1298).   Falkirk is the first battle where we hear of the skilful combination of the long-bow with cavalry : whenever these two arms were successfully combined the English were generally victorious ; but where the long-bow was unsupported by cavalry, or *vice versâ*, the Scottish spearmen were the more effective troops.   Great victory as Falkirk was, it was a fruitless one, for the country was eaten up, and even Edward's great skill as an organiser of commissariat was not equal to feeding a large army in a barren land.   So, from the end of 1298 to 1303, the "conquest" of Scotland could only go on very slowly, and it consisted mainly of sieges, while the French war engaged Edward's own attention. But the fall of Stirling, in 1304, seemed almost to finish the business, and Edward proceeded to treat the "conquered" country as he had treated Wales : he divided it up into counties, and appointed English sheriffs ; judges were sent on circuit ; all the paraphernalia of English government were introduced ; all Scots caught in arms were hanged or vivisected as "traitors," including Wallace (in 1305).   The whole nation writhed under this treatment, and the bolder spirits took to the hills and murdered isolated English officials.   But no leader was found till 1306, when Robert Bruce, grandson of the old claimant, having cleared the way by the murder of a possible rival, John Comyn, in the Kirk of Dumfries, suddenly proclaimed himself King of Scotland, and was crowned by the hands of a noble Scottish lady at Scone.

Ambition rather than patriotism was undoubtedly Bruce's main impulse at first.   He had been a partisan of Edward's and had sworn oaths to him, and Edward considered him a perjured traitor, even as William had considered Harold.   He had certainly been a sacrilegious murderer, but murder was not an infrequent crime among the Scottish barons, and was going to be dismally frequent during the next three centuries.   But he was forced from mere necessity to appeal to every patriotic feeling in the heart of every Scot; and in the time of adversity he showed himself a true patriot and a most able king and soldier.   Driven almost at once by the English armies into the Western Islands, he reappeared in Carrick, in 1307, and the West rose as one man to greet him.   Edward resolved, old as he was (sixty-nine), to take the field in person once more, and died by the Solway, within sight of the Scottish shore, July 7, 1307.   With his latest breath he ordered his coffin to be carried in the van of his host against the rebel Bruce.   But Edward II. was not the man to carry out this or any of his father's wishes; and though almost every castle in Scotland was still in English hands, the War of Independence had begun, and begun under a leader well qualified to carry it to its glorious issue.

We must not be too hard on the Scottish barons as a whole; up till now they had hardly grasped the principle of a Scottish nationality as opposed to an English. The baron of mixed descent was, to my mind, usually an honest, rather stupid, brave man, into whose mind new ideas did not readily penetrate.   He had a keen grip of property, and was loth to lose his English lands as his great-grandfather had lost his Norman lands.   He loathed wild Highlanders and wild Galwegians, and did not perceive that his sturdy Lothian tenants were developing into a nation which could only continue to exist through union with Galwegians and Highlanders.   He was apt to be a fiercer man than an English baron, because he had more extensive feudal jurisdiction, more private war, less restraint from the central government, a poorer soil, a more hardy tenantry.   The experience of the next three centuries was wholly bad for such a man; it encouraged his fierceness, and, as he grew poorer and poorer, it also encouraged his greed, and prompted him to sell his soul to the king of England whenever that king happened to be victorious or offered him gold. His own kings, after the death of Robert Bruce, were with few exceptions, weak men who controlled his feuds very little ; and the result was that while the Scottish nation was making one of the noblest fights for independence ever made on earth, it was left practically without leaders, or with leaders who used the state of war only to gratify their greed or their private revenges.

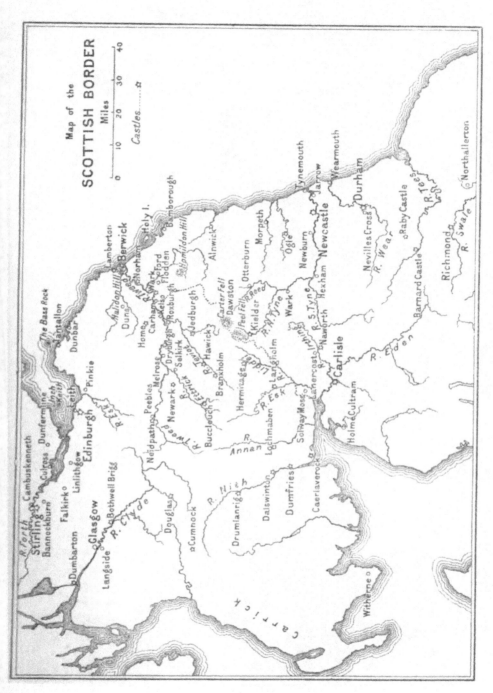

Map of the
SCOTTISH BORDER

Miles

0   10   20   30   40

Castles......⚜

To face page 216

CHAPTER XIV

THE LEGAL AND SOCIAL SYSTEM OF THE THIRTEENTH CENTURY

To any one looking back, say at the time of the Wars of the Roses, the thirteenth century must have appeared as a golden age, an age of peace and prosperity, of learning, of great men and great causes. And indeed there is much reason to regard it as a very great age indeed. Our own eyes are specially directed to it from the fact that both our parliamentary system and our legal system took definite root at that time. I have said enough about the former, and will not detain you long about the latter. But it is necessary to understand what we mean when we say that in the thirteenth century Common law finally triumphed over Roman law (which was getting the upper hand all over the rest of Europe), and to some extent over Canon law also.

You must understand, then, that all law, written or unwritten, has need of interpretation by professional judges, interpretation which will apply some known rule of law to the particular case to be decided. Written law will need far less interpretation, will be more intelligible, but it will be less elastic. Roman law is written law, and is exceedingly clear and simple ; it also makes in favour of absolute power of the sovereign, whom it regards as the sole lawgiver. Very little of our English law was then written ; at the death of Edward I. a small handful of statutes, passed in Parliament (beginning with the Great Charter), constituted our only written laws.

The law that the judges applied was based simply upon previous decisions given by previous judges in the King's courts. The coronation of Richard I. was selected as a convenient date behind which you "could not go" —*i.e.* you could not quote a "precedent" or "ruling" of a judge before that time. About the year 1258 Henry de Bracton, a judge of the King's court, wrote a law-book in which he quoted some 500 decided cases. Now every time a judge gives a decision, he is supposed to base it either upon a written statute or on a previous decision; but if the case before him does not exactly fit in with any previous decision, he must stretch that previous decision or modify it so as to meet the new case.

Let me illustrate this by two imaginary cases taken from modern life. It has come, after several important decisions, to be a rule of law that a man is liable for the acts of his servants. A bishop driving to church, in never so great a hurry, must pay damages if his coachman runs over a child who is too much occupied in staring at the splendours of the episcopal barouche to get out of the way. But one day, while his lordship is in church, the coachman, instead of waiting at the west door of the cathedral, as he has been told to do, picks up a friend and drives him round to a neighbouring hostelry, and on his way drives over a child. The parents of the child sue the bishop for damages. The case will not be decided upon any abstract grounds of right or justice; nay very likely some injustice to some individual will be done by the decision; but the question for Mr. Justice Bracton or Mr. Justice Blackstone to decide will be the question of the *limits of the bishop's liability;* and his decision will turn upon what previous cases have come before the courts in which the limits of such liability have been defined. Very likely it will be a very important decision; for Bracton or Blackstone is very likely to rule that a man cannot be held liable for the acts of his servants when they are not in actual execution of their duty.

Or, again, suppose a case in which you have, by long-established custom, a right to drive any "vehicle, coach, carriage, cart, wheelbarrow," &c., across a certain bridge in my grounds, and you suddenly take to driving a motor-car across it. By every principle of abstract justice I should be justified in stopping you and committing anything short of murder on you. But not by the Common law of England; when you bring an action against me for stopping you, it will simply be for the judge to decide whether a motor-car is a "vehicle" or not. If no Act of Parliament has yet defined the evil-smelling monster, if no previous decision involving any definition of it has been given, it must be given now. So you see the judges *make the law as they go along;* have in fact been making it from the thirteenth century until the present day; and this is "Common law."

The courts in which the Common law was applied were primarily the King's three "Common law Courts," in each of which he was supposed to be present himself, was in fact present in the person of his representative, the judge. They were called "the Exchequer," "the King's Bench," and "the Common Pleas"; they had gradually acquired a separate existence and a separate "roll" of decided cases (written in barbarous Latin), and, by the end of the century, a separate staff of judges, at the head of whom was the "Chief Justice" of the "King's Bench," the nearest representative of the now extinct "Great Justiciar." The judges of these courts sit by turns at Westminster, and by turns go on "circuit" to hold "assizes" at the County Courts. When they go on circuit the sheriff will convoke the whole County Court to meet them, and the business done will be chiefly trying criminals, always with some sort of jury. It is very difficult to say what "civil suits" will be tried at the assizes, but they will be comparatively few. It is also very difficult to say to what civil suits, tried at Westminster, the jury principle will be applied; and lastly, it is not at all easy to see in which of the three courts at Westminster any ordinary civil suit of Smith *v.* Brown will be tried. There will be an appeal from the civil courts in some cases to the House of Lords, in some perhaps (in the fourteenth century, but not after) to the "King in Council."

But the Common lawyers were queer, crabbed fellows, who seem to have tried to make their science as great a mystery as possible; a layman who should try to penetrate this mystery would resemble the famous "blind man groping in a dark cellar for a black hat which isn't there." They did not wish to make it too easy or too cheap for litigants, and they would often refuse to entertain suits of any kind to which they were not accustomed; thus in the Middle Ages a foreigner could not plead in the King's courts at all, murder on the high seas was not a "crime," a married woman could have no property, land could only be bequeathed to your eldest son, and so on.

In order, then, that justice should be done in such cases as these, we find the idea growing that the King in person, or by some special representative other than the Common law judges, is to take some steps; hence his Chancellor (then always an ecclesiastic) will begin to hear "petitions of special grace and favour," and do justice to the petitioners according to a different set of rules, which have more of Roman law in them, which come to be called "Equity"; and the "Court of Chancery" grows up to administer these rules to certain classes of cases. This Equity court will develop side by side with the Common law courts, and sometimes in conflict with them, down to 1875, when the two will be fused. Or, again, the King in his Privy Council will begin hearing lawsuits in very special cases, and out of this practice will grow, in the fifteenth and sixteenth centuries, the ''Court of Star Chamber,'' and several similar courts, which have much more drastic methods of doing justice than either the Common law or the Equity courts.

Then there were the Ecclesiastical courts — Archdeacon's, Bishop's, Archbishop's courts—one above the other, with a final appeal to Rome. These were not, in effect, royal courts at all ; their law was not the King's law but the Pope's, or the ''Canon'' law, which the Popes had laid down for the determining of all disputes between clergymen, or about clerical property, all over Christendom. In certain cases laymen might be summoned before these courts, fined, and made to do penance. This jurisdiction was hated with a right English hatred of priestcraft. · But the mediæval clergy were passionately litigious, and bishops and abbots were for ever riding off to Rome to prosecute appeals against each other or against the Crown. Both Parliament and Common law courts were very jealous of the Canon lawyers, and incessantly interfered with their competence, by statutes and judicial decisions, right down to the Reformation.

Litigiousness and a certain amount of legal knowledge were by no means confined to the lawyers and the clergy. King, baron, squire, merchant, freeholder, all seem to have had something of legal education, and all were prodigiously active in legal and other business. The notion that mediæval Englishmen were inactive, or ''sunk in the night of ignorance and superstition,'' as we are often told, is one of the most groundless of fables. The more I look at it, the more I realise that all classes were incessantly on the move, and that intelligence and a certain standard of education were very widely diffused at the close of the thirteenth century. Even the villein, so soon as he was asked to bear arms for the King (in the reign of Henry III.), must have frequently travelled beyond the bounds of his village. The Roman roads were still in fairly good repair, and must have presented a lively scene.

The towns had nearly all got charters, and trades in them were governed by "gilds," or associations of handicraftsmen or merchants, which regulated wages and prices, provided for sickness and old age, performed devotions to some special patron saint, and saw that good articles were produced—at least they were supposed to do this last, though we may fairly suppose that tricks of the trade were no more unknown to the mediæval shopkeeper than to the modern. If there had been sugar, they would no doubt have put sand in it ; if there had been tea, it would have been adulterated with sloe leaves. Yet the temptation to such tricks would naturally be less when prices were fixed not by competition among the tradesmen, but by custom. The towns enjoyed a certain measure of self-government ; if we look at their written charters, we shall get the idea that they enjoyed a great deal. A thirteenth-century charter, say, to the citizens of Oxford, will grant (1) the right of collecting all the King's dues and tolls within the walls, and paying down a lump sum to the King for them ; (2) the right of electing their own mayor and sheriff ; (3) the right of holding some sort of a court for small disputes (often called a husting or house-thing) ; (4) the right of freedom from tolls in other places, and of taking toll from all non-Oxonians coming to trade in the city. Perhaps there will be, further, the right of holding an annual fair, or (very rarely) of exemption from direct taxes. A great many ancient privileges will no doubt be confirmed by the same charter, but this will mean very little. As a matter of fact, the principle of one law for town and country alike, enforced by the constant visits of the justices of assize, reduced the privileges of the towns very considerably; the King, too, was very apt to cancel or suspend a charter if the burgesses showed themselves too stiff. London had its charter suspended for several years together at various times in the thirteenth century. So the English towns never attained that almost republican power which was characteristic of the great cities of Germany, Italy, and Southern France.

I do not think that the towns constituted, by any means, the most progressive or most enlightened factor in national life at that time. London, the Cinque Ports, and a few other seaports, had an extensive foreign trade in wine with Bordeaux and Spain, in furs with the Baltic, in cloth with Flanders, in silks, spices, and other Eastern goods with Italy, by way of Flanders. Spices, we must remember, were of enormous importance to a people which lived largely on salt meat. Most of these things were brought to England in ships belonging to the great German cities on the North Sea, by men of the "Hansa" or "Hanseatic League," who had a special wharf and house of business in London, called the "Steelyard," just above London Bridge, and extensive privileges of trade with our other ports. It is probable that the Bordeaux trade was carried on in English or in Gascon ships; but I think it is almost certain that our "mercantile marine" was in a very backward condition. The sea swarmed with pirates till a much later date, and we, who were to become the most maritime nation in the world, were one of the latest

European states to have a large mercantile fleet of our own. In return for imported articles of luxury, the main exports which the foreign traders carried away with them were tin, hides, and, above all, wool, wool, wool.

Rough homespun cloth, sufficient to clothe Higg the son of Snell, must at all times have been woven at home, probably by Mrs. Higg herself in the winter evenings; but every one above the lowest rank would wear clothes woven in Flanders. Neither in the towns nor in the villages was there much of what we should call comfort, still less of luxury. One may safely say that there were no drains at all, and as the towns were closely packed within their walls, and as all the houses were of wood, the conditions of life must have been most insanitary; all dirt was thrown into the gutter which ran down the middle of the street, and pigs and dogs were the principal scavengers. Rain and fire—and fire was unquestionably frequent—would occasionally make a clean sweep of refuse heaps, which, without them, were too apt to breed pestilence; yet pestilence, when it did come, was quite as destructive in the villages as in the towns. The townsmen had one marked peculiarity—they were excessively jealous of their brethren in all the neighbouring towns, whom they branded as "foreigners" (what we call foreigners they called "aliens"); they rather rejoiced if their neighbours were burnt out or heavily fined; the patriotism of the townsman was very keen, but it was entirely concentrated upon his own little narrow community. Edward I. systematically tried to break down this isolation, and his grandson went even farther. They were the first kings to treat trade as a national concern. Edward kept custom-house officers in all the ports; his Parliaments regulated the export of wool; in the teeth of his Parliaments he allowed foreign merchants to come and trade freely in England, and thus over-rode the narrow views of the citizen class. Within thirty years of his death, Flemish weavers had settled in Norwich (no doubt to the intense disgust of the Norwiccians), and began to teach Englishmen how to weave fine cloth. Edward, moreover, made it possible for a merchant to sue for a debt in the King's courts at Westminster, from whatever city his debtor came. He expelled from England the greedy and bloodsucking race of Jewish usurers, and has been much blamed by posterity for so doing. It is true that the lending money on interest was illegal for Christians all over Europe, and, as merchants and kings must sometimes borrow money, other and less open means of getting it had to be discovered, and foreign bankers with elastic consciences took the place of the Jews. But the Jews had formed all over Europe a close corporation devoted to this one object, and almost every one was heavily indebted to them. Previous kings, especially Richard and John, had encouraged the Jews to fleece their subjects, and had then occasionally fleeced the Jews of their ill-gotten gains. Edward nobly forewent this resource, and received the gratitude of his people in return.

After all, in a primitive state of society it is not what a country exports or imports that constitutes its wealth, but what it produces, exchanges, and consumes within its own boundaries and by its own mouths. Do men feed well, and are they warmly clad? Can they afford to bring up their sons better than they themselves were brought up? We shall find that they can do and do these things. In spite of the exclusive attitude of the townsmen, the thirteenth century did witness a great development of internal trade from village to village, town to town, and town to village. The stewards of the monas-

P

teries and of the great barons were for ever on the move
buying and selling ; they and the traders from the whole
kingdom flocked to the great annual fairs of Winchester
and Stourbridge, and rode back with strings of laden
pack-horses behind them.   And all this was possible
owing to the "good peace" which the strong monarchy
had made.

If we turn to the agricultural districts we shall find
that Society in its lower grades is still based upon the
feudal tie between lord and vassal ; many of the descendants of our old friends, Higg and Pigg, are still
paying the same sort of diversified rents and services to
the descendants of Roger of Tubney as they paid to
Roger the first at the date of Domesday ; but all these
services are now immutably fixed, and all are annexed
not to Higg or to Pigg, but to the pieces of land they
hold.   If Higg has bought the "villein tenement" of
John, Higg, though a free man, will have to perform,
or get performed, the villein services that are owed by
it.   If John has thriven so much, that while legally
remaining a villein, he has bought a piece of Higg's
freehold, he will have to pay for it whatever free services (usually a small rent in money) Higg used to
pay.   All this is written down upon a strip of parchment called the "Court Roll," which Roger keeps in
his strong-box at the Hall.   Very likely Roger has
"emancipated" three or four of the better of his villeins ; these then become free men, and they pay
money rent instead of villein services for their land.
It certainly pays Roger better, as it must have been
exceedingly difficult to get the villeins to perform their
proper labour rents.   Tubney has been prospering exceedingly since we left it.   There are now four families
offreeholders, who pay only a small rent in money to
this Roger (the eighth of his name since the Conquest)

There are twenty-four villein families, and they occupy twice as much arable land altogether as the Domesday tenants occupied, though their individual holdings are no larger; they have broken up the waste land as far as the boundaries of Fyfield and Anglesham (the two neighbouring villages). One of these families still pays three days' labour a week; the others vary between two days, one day, a money-rent, and a rent in corn or hens or eggs or eels. All will have to do something extra at harvest-tide. The tenements of the freeholders have got names, and are giving the names to their owners. John holds the bull-croft, and because he holds it he has to go to the County Court at Lewes whenever it meets; it is a horrid bore for John, but that is the *rent* that he pays for his holding. If William bought the bull-croft he would have to go instead of John: the duty of going that long journey has got somehow or other attached to the soil of that particular croft on which the village bull is kept, instead of to the flesh and blood of its owner. Probably the name of that piece of land will stick to John's descendants, and they will be called Bullcraft David Hazelgrove is so called because his ancestors bought from one of the Rogers the thirty acres of woodland which went by that name. They thinned and planted and tended it well, and set up as village basket-makers; their name has been honoured for centuries in mid-Sussex; long may it be so. Roger the fourth was no sportsman, and he freed his villein, Hobb, on condition that Hobb should continue to supply the Hall with rabbits from the Warren. Hobb's great-grandson is now called Robert Warren. The Church encourages all these enfranchisements and commutations of labour rents for money rents; it is pleasing in the sight of God, and good for Roger's soul as well as for his pocket. The lawyers also encourage them, for enfranchisement is a legal act, and some lawyer will be paid for entering it on the court rolls.   Once these services are commuted, it will be impossible to change them back again ; it will always be impossible to make people pay more or harder services than their last immediate ancestor paid.   As the village increases in population and prosperity, Jack the Miller is perhaps, after the squire, the most important and prosperous person in it.   True, mill-stones are very expensive, and do not last long ; they cannot be bought nearer than Chichester, and it is a fearful job to get them across the soft, heavy tracks over the downs ; but wheeled carts must have been continually passing from towns to villages with these necessary articles, and with iron for William Smith to make ploughshares and horse-shoes and rough weapons.   The wool and the corn and the hides which Tubney "exports" to Chichester to pay for these could no doubt have been carried on pack-horses.   Salt must be imported from somewhere or other, for we salt all our meat for winter consumption—fat as we are, we seldom eat fresh meat.   Very likely the salt comes by sea from Chester or Bristol to that rising port, Shoreham. By sea certainly comes the wine that Roger drinks, the fine clothes that Roger wears, the catgut for the bowstrings of the village (the staves are made of yew wood from Kingly Vale, by John Bowyer), the finely tempered steel weapons and armour which Roger bears when he goes to serve King Edward.   Roger breeds his own horses, and occasionally imports a sire from Flanders or Normandy.

There must have been some, but perhaps not as yet much, transference of hands from village to town.   A villein could claim his freedom if he remained (no doubt after running away from home) for a year and a day in a chartered town ; but the "demand for hands" in the towns was not great before the fourteenth century, and the villein might run a fair chance of starving in a town unless he were a very clever fellow. Thus both his intelligence and his stupidity prompted him to remain at home. But his son would often be educated at a monastic school; the monasteries themselves were often recruited from the villein class, and certainly the two new brotherhoods of St. Dominic and St. Francis were largely so. The greatest age of monastic foundations was over, and the mind of the thirteenth century was turning to more practical forms of devotion. The first outcome of this was seen in these two brotherhoods of "Friars." Offshoots of these orders reached England early in the reign of Henry III. The Friars were to live in the world and to walk about in it, doing good, the Dominicans by preaching, the Franciscans by visiting the sick and the poor in their squalid homes. No such truly Christian ideal has been given to the world since the time of the Apostles : the friars were at first a standing protest against the wealth, the luxury, the greed, and the corruption of the monks and the higher clergy ; and Saint Francis himself remains the one truly beautiful and practical figure in the Church of the Middle Ages. One wonders that the Popes ever consented to the establishment of two orders which threw down such a direct challenge to the system on which the Church grew fat, and indeed it was not without hesitation that they had given their consent. A century later the Church definitely shut her doors on John Wyclif, who proposed very much the same sort of thing : two centuries later the Pope thought that the only two things to be done with Luther were to make him a cardinal or to burn him alive. When the Church had definitely shut her doors on reforming movements which came from within, she soon found that reform threatened her from without, and that it would be by no means mild. Meanwhile, however, down to the end of the reign of Henry III. the Franciscan Friars at least remained pure and unworldly; but, even before the fourteenth century dawned, their increasing popularity brought with it lavish gifts from the devout laity, and sloth and luxury came, as they must come to all celibate communities, in the train of increasing wealth. Before the close of that century "friar" was a by-word for all that was fat and lazy and sensual, as may be gathered from innumerable popular songs and from Chaucer's "Canterbury Tales."

But already a new development was in progress in the fertile age which we are considering—that of the foundation of colleges and schools. At first these were all attached to monasteries, and every great monastery kept a school of some sort, at which all but the very highest class would be educated. Many of the scholars from these schools would proceed to the now flourishing Universities of Oxford and Cambridge. We may dismiss the wild statements about "30,000 scholars at Oxford" in the thirteenth century, but we may reasonably conjecture that the numbers were at least as great as at the present day. But there were as yet no "Colleges" within the University; the students all lived in lodgings or in "hostels," and were often as turbulent as they were poor. They were at perpetual feud with the citizens, and the barons' war was preceded by a murderous "town and gown row." There were no endowments for teaching, and apparently any one who could hire a lecture-room might set up as a professor. The professors were paid wholly by fees of those who chose to attend their lectures, and therefore they really did lecture on useful subjects and at times convenient to the students. These students used to follow a popular man or a great teacher from one to the other of the many universities of Western Europe; and Oxford had an especially close connection with the then greater Universities of Paris and Bologna. It was Walter Merton, Edward I.'s chancellor, who early in the reign founded and gave his name to the first College at Oxford, and Hugh of Balsham soon followed him with the foundation of Peterhouse at Cambridge. These colleges differed from monasteries in that the scholars, though they lived in common, took no monastic vows and were not all necessarily intended for the clerical profession. The great majority, however, were no doubt so intended, for it was the surest avenue to wealth and fame—perhaps to the chair of St. Peter himself—for any one who was not nobly born as well as for many who were. The Canon lawyers, all of whom would be clerics of some sort, as yet far outnumbered the Common lawyers, and all the emoluments in the King's Chancery were open to them. Many collegiate foundations at both Universities, and some few outside them, followed Merton and Peterhouse during the next two centuries, and from them issued a constant stream of men well qualified, in the wise words of Archbishop Chicheley, "to serve God in Church and State."

While mercantile and rural and clerical life was thus actively developing, the natural career for the upper classes was the soldier's. The crusades had immensely widened the mental horizon of the few who returned from them, but the day of the crusades was over. St. Louis of France and Edward I. were the last true crusaders; and the latter went to Palestine more as to a set field, where immortal honour was to be attained and the crown of immortal life to be won, than with any real hope of delivering the Holy Sepulchre. But war on the borders of England or on those of the English holdings in France was never long suspended, and you might also keep your war-horse in exercise by an occasional tournament, though the good sense of most of the English kings made them very loth to consent to these silly and costly displays of prowess. But not merely the upper classes but the whole community of freemen, and, from the reign of Henry III., of the villeins also, was obliged to bear arms and was liable to be called out to use them. The enactments of the Parliaments of Henry III. and Edward I. are quite clear on this point. The "Assize of Arms" was re-enacted again and again, and Edward's great "Statute of Winchester" (1285) only improved upon it. The principle of this Act is a graduation of the whole adult male population according to wealth and irrespective of feudal obligation. "If you have land worth £20 a year," says Edward, "you must serve in my cavalry. I don't care whose tenant you are, or by what tenure you hold your lands. You will provide your own horses and armour and weapons. If you have less than this you will serve in the infantry with the weapons which your wealth warrants. I do not specify where or for how long I shall require your services. I shall not call you all out at one time, but I shall send 'Commissioners of Array' to each county to raise me a goodly number of men from it, and those who are not called out will have to contribute to the wages of those who are." Thus the army that fought in Scottish and Welsh wars was essentially a national, or, as we should now say, a "citizen army." England was as yet spared the doubtful blessing of a class of professional soldiers ; but the French wars of the fourteenth century rapidly led to the formation of something very like one ; and the professional soldier in due time begat the tight uniform and the drill-book and the War Office.

Feudalism and the crusades, however, completed the military education of the upper classes, and made it possible for the kings who welded the nation together to undertake national warfare on a big scale. It was, for instance, in the crusades that the real art of castle-building was first learned. The castle of the twelfth century had been little more than a square tower or a "shell-keep"; the thirteenth-century castle is nearly always round, and consists of at least two "wards" (walled and fortified courtyards), with a "keep" in the centre of the inner ward. The keep becomes the last resort of a garrison driven from the outworks, and on these outworks themselves the primary defence rests. These works are now provided with towers at the angles and at intervals along the walls, and these towers stick out from the wall-line so as to enable you to shoot sideways at people who are moving to attack you in front. The next development was to run a projecting gallery of wood or stone round the top of these towers, with holes cut in its floor, so that you could pour something humorous in the way of melted lead or boiling oil on your assailants. This is called "machicolation," and the holes are "machicoulis." As successive wards are added to the castle, each defended by a deep ditch and crossed only by a drawbridge, it is a great point that each inner ward should "command" the one outside it, *i.e.* should be on a higher elevation; the keep, the innermost defence of all, should therefore stand very high.

To capture such a castle as Carnarvon or Caerphilly, before the days of gunpowder, will be extraordinarily difficult. But you may try in several ways, and probably will try them successively or all at once

before you succeed. (1) You may fill up the ditches,
and batter the walls with huge blocks of timber called
battering - rams, sometimes shod with an iron point
and then called "cats," because they clawed their way
into the wall. (2) You may dig down and mine under
the ditches and walls. (3) You may build a huge
wooden tower on wheels till it is as high as the wall,
and from it you may shoot great blocks of stone or
wood or barrels of lighted pitch from a clumsy machine
called an "arblast" (a sort of gigantic cross-bow). (4) Or
from the same tower you may let down a platform on
to the walls and rush over it. None of these plans
are agreeable while the garrison can shoot at you
comfortably from under cover. You may therefore
possibly devise a sort of covered gallery under which
your battering-rammers and your miners may work,
and move it about on wheels wherever it is wanted;
but the besieged will very probably set it on fire before
it is finished. And so, after all, your best plan is to
starve out the garrison, lengthy process as this may
prove to be; unless indeed you can get a traitor inside
to open a postern gate to you some dark night. It is
thus easy to understand how often in the Middle Ages
the weak were able to defy the strong; a very small
garrison to defy a very large army. Every individual
soldier in a faithful garrison was of enormous importance, every separate ward of a castle might be defended
tower by tower, door by door, foot by foot; whereas,
in a modern siege, once a breach is made by artillery
fire the whole place must capitulate at once.

To make the defence stronger than the attack was
the object of the thirteenth-century armourers, as well
as of the castle-builders. During the most part of the
twelfth century body and head had been armed much
in the same way as in the eleventh, except that the shirt

of ring-mail had grown longer and was supported by extra quilting underneath. Next came stockings and shoes of the same material. But the most notable change was in the headpiece, which grew at the end of the twelfth century into the huge iron "helm," like a saucepan without a handle turned bottom upward; it had slits for the eyes in a movable plate called a "vizor." So great was the weight of this article that it was made to rest upon the shoulders, and was only put on in actual battle. Before the end of the century it grew conical instead of flat at the top. Over the shirt of ring-mail was worn a long flowing garment called the surcoat, obviously copied from the "bournous" of the Arab sheikhs: which proves that the slavish following of foreign fashions is not confined to our own day. The white "bournous," useful in Syria as a protection against heat, was ridiculous in Europe. "Arms" were embroidered on the surcoats and crests affixed to the pot-helmet early in the thirteenth century. Soon we find thin plates of iron fixed outside the ring-mail, in order to protect particularly vulnerable parts like the knees, elbows, and neck joints, and perhaps the breastplate may be found before the death of Edward I. Early in the fourteenth century this combination of plate and chain armour was the universal wear, for arrows which might have made an ugly dint in the chain would glance off the plate.

The immense efficiency attained at this time by the new weapon of the English, the long-bow, is well known; the bow which the Norman archers had used at Hastings was the short-bow, drawn only to the breast, not to the ear. The cross-bow or "arbalest," though used by English soldiers in the later twelfth and the thirteenth centuries, was essentially a foreign weapon, and it was the mercenary troops of the first three

Plantagenets who introduced it; but the English long-bow, the real origin of which is doubtful, first appears in legend as the weapon of Robin Hood and his friends who,

> ". . . in merry Sherwood,
> Sent with preterhuman luck
> Missiles not of steel but fir-wood
> Through the two-mile-distant buck."

This was the six-foot bow made of yew, the effective range of which was nearly 150 yards. Edward first seriously employed it in his Welsh and Scottish wars. Hardly had it come into use when it met, in the latter of these quarrels, an offensive weapon that was to out-last it—the Scottish spear, which was the true parent of the steel hedgehog of " puissant pikes " against which no horse would charge. At Falkirk, as we have seen, the two offensive weapons met face to face and the bow won, but won only because it could be supported by a cavalry charge. At Bannockburn, where they next met, the spear beat the bow because the ground was unfavourable for such a charge.

CHAPTER XV

EDWARD II. AND THE BEGINNINGS OF DECADENCE

ONE is at first at a loss to explain the great contrast between the steady growth of the nation in power, in manfulness, in unity and prosperity, which from the Conquest to the close of the thirteenth century had been almost uninterrupted, and the miserable lack of all or most of these qualities which is so often visible in the England of the fourteenth and fifteenth centuries. That the fault lay with the natural leaders of the people—kings, barons, and churchmen—is fairly evident ; but how or why these leaders had so fallen off in character it is not easy to understand.

I can only suggest one or two answers to the question, and I do not by any means feel that they are adequate.

(1) In the first place, the constitutional system—that is, the system of parliamentary government, or "self-government"—was an exceedingly delicate piece of machinery, and it needed a really strong king like Edward I. to keep it in working order. And when you take away the hand of a strong guide, and leave any delicate piece of machinery to a lot of overgrown boys to manage, they will break it and quarrel over the job. The barons were the overgrown boys ; the machinery of the Constitution soon got out of gear, and, by the reign of Edward IV., simply existed to register the decrees of that party of the barons which had for the moment got the upper hand.

(2) There were too few barons, and these few were too powerful and too rich. They kept courts of their own, of splendour almost equal to that of the King. As the old families died out, their lands fell in to the Crown, and the Crown gave their lands and earldoms to the younger scions of the royal house ; or, if there were female heiresses left, the Crown married these scions to these heiresses. I have already pointed out, in speaking of the children of Henry II., the difficulty of dealing with the younger sons of a king. But Henry III., Edward I., and above all Edward III., systematically absorbed the great earldoms and their heiresses into the royal family. Thus a new class of barons grew up, "princes of the blood-royal"; it was sure to be a discontented and grasping class. The few remaining barons of non-royal blood naturally imitated the turbulence and extravagance of the princes; and the insolence of these last became so great as to flout and finally to upset the throne itself.

(3) The third answer is closely connected with the second. There was a good deal of uncertainty of title to lands all over England, and therefore disputes between neighbours, often verging upon private war, were frequent. Wilfred of Ivanhoe (to take a familiar instance) was very apt to return from Palestine after some years' absence to find that Athelstan *had* married Rowena after all, and that the son of Athelstan was reigning at Rotherwood. Wilfred would have amazing difficulty in getting his identity recognised by anybody but the faithful fool Wamba. Even after the crusades were over, the French wars provided another stage on which the incident of "missing heirs" was quite a common one. This was aggravated by the fact that, if I died leaving two or three, or any number of daughters, but no son, my lands had to be divided equally between

my daughters, and consequently between their husbands. And my earldom, or earldoms? Hear the story of the Bohun lands.

At the end of King Edward III.'s reign died the last male of the great house of Bohun, Earls of Hereford, Essex, and Northampton. He left two daughters, Mary and Eleanor. Mary married Henry of Derby, afterwards King Henry IV. Eleanor married Henry's uncle, Thomas, the youngest son of Edward III., ancestor of the Staffords and Buckinghams. Henry and Thomas conspired, more or less, all their lives against Richard II., and Richard from time to time laid hold on their lands, as lands of traitors were held to "escheat" to the Crown. Henry became king in 1399, and at once entered on all lands then held by the Crown. He ought, of course, to have restored, to the heirs of Thomas, Eleanor's share of the Bohun lands. In fact, he expressly promised to do so. He never did. Nor did Henry V., though, if he had lived longer, he might have done so. The regency of Henry VI. was too weak, and too poor, to restore anything to anybody, and so the lands of the old earldom of Hereford were held as Crown lands by the three Lancastrian kings in succession. What did the Stafford family do? They simply turned Yorkist. They helped King Edward IV. to the throne, again in return for an express promise of the restoration of the lands of Eleanor Bohun. Do you think Edward IV. was the man to loose his grip on any property—to be bound by any promise? He was not. So the Duke of Buckingham, in 1483, entered into close compact with crook-back Richard to upset little Edward V., and make Richard king; and the price was once more to be "Eleanor Bohun's lands." Disappointed as usual of his price, there was nothing left for the Duke of Buckingham but to turn Lancastrian. "Off with his head, so much for Buckingham," said Richard. The lands finally rested in the strong grip of the Tudor monarchs.   It is a weary tale, but illustrative of what was going on on a greater or lesser scale throughout England in these two dismal centuries ; and it is easy to see that the baronage deteriorated frightfully in the process.

(4) The French and Scottish wars also exerted a demoralising influence. The latter were on the whole unsuccessful for England, though they became by long repetition a national necessity, if only in order to defend the northern frontier ; but they were border wars in a barren district, varied by fierce plundering raids, and as such were bound to breed cruelty. The French war had periods of great success, and periods of disastrous failure. It was undoubtedly at first forced on Edward III., in order to defend our trade with Flanders and to save Aquitaine ; but the longer it went on, the less of a national necessity and the more of a gamble it became, while its very success under Edward III. and Henry V. could lead, in a country like France, in which settlement of the conqueror was impossible, only to extensive plunder. Wars for plunder breed savage professional soldiers, like the Spaniards in the New World, or the men of the French revolutionary armies. During the intervals of failure and truce these men sulked in England, or engaged in feuds and stabbing affrays.

(5) With these materials for civil war at hand, an ostensible cause will not long be wanting. " Parties " or "factions " in the State appear early. Edward II. governed very badly ; the barons, headed by a prince of the blood, hated and killed his favourites. Edward sought and got a bloody vengeance, for which a few years later a bloodier vengeance was exacted by his enemies. Revenge went on from generation to generation. " Lancaster and

York" are already there *in posse*, if not *in esse*, before the death of Edward II. There is a brilliant interval during the whole reign of Edward III., but it is only an interval. A parliamentary system is a farce when worked by such men as Thomas of Lancaster, and Thomas of Gloucester, and Richard, Earl of Warwick, the "king-maker," who kept a private army.

(6) The Church was not in much better plight. The middle of the thirteenth century had seen the crash of the mediæval "Empire," the end of it was to see the crash of the mediæval Papacy. The system of Europe had in theory rested on the idea of two powers, one spiritual and one temporal, above kings and nations alike. England and France had always steadily refused to believe in the "one temporal power," or to recognise in the German Emperor the successor of Augustus or Constantine; but they had been obliged to recognise and more or less to believe in the "one spiritual power" as being above all national churches. In practice they had both fought against the extremest pretensions of this papal power, but the entire corporation of the clergy had often been obliged to support the Popes.

But when the emissaries of the King of France put Pope Boniface the Eighth on a donkey, with his face to the tail, and in that position pelted him with filth and dragged him through the streets of one of his own cities; when the fierce old man died of rage and grief and shame; when King Philip terrified the cardinals into electing one of his own creatures as Pope, and made that creature come and live at the very door of France, then the world-renown of the Papacy was over. The new Popes would be mere tame cats of the French king; cats that could indeed be taught to make hideous noises at, and even to scratch their master's enemies; but cats they remained till 1378. When in that year the universal

Q

horror of Christendom began to be too openly expressed,
when even the Popes themselves began to feel the degra-
dation of their position, the period of schism succeeded
to the period of captivity. One Pope was elected at Rome
and another at Avignon, and the schism lasted till 1415.
When it was ended by the Council of Constance, the
Popes, on getting finally back to Rome, came back to
little more than a rich Italian prince-bishopric.

Naturally, in such conditions, the leaders of the
English Church were somewhat at sea. They could
not, as Englishmen, pay much regard to the threats of
a French Pope ; but, as churchmen, they felt keenly
the need of some sort of Pope to whom some sort
of obedience should be paid. They began to fear
lest the Crown should follow the impulse of the nation,
and break with the Papacy altogether ; and hence,
abdicating their old share in the leadership of the
English people, they threw themselves rather blindly
on the mercy of the Crown, and besought it to take
care of their consciences for them, but, above all, to
protect their pockets. The laity began to perceive this
very clearly, and to growl more and more ominously
against clerical wealth and clerical pretensions. The
growl spread from barons to squires, and from them
down to the very lowest class of all.

(7) But, you will say, did not the "Commons"—the
squires, the townsmen, the freeholders, and the villeins
actually profit by this state of things ? To some extent
it is true they did—witness the power of the Lower
House in the reigns of Edward III. and Henry IV.;
witness again the considerable level of material prosperity attained in the fifteenth century, which was
very little affected even by the Wars of the Roses.
But that prosperity was nothing like so considerable
as it would have been under a series of strong kings

and continuously free Parliaments. The cleavage of classes became infinitely greater than it had been in the thirteenth century; and even the practical abolition of villeinage, blessing as it was for the future, dissolved many a tie between "lord" and "man," while the wealth to be derived from sheep farming, which needs few hands, caused the uprooting from the soil of many industrious families for which there was as yet not much outlet in other fields of labour.

And so a lack of leaders and a "lack of governance" is characteristic of the two dismal centuries before us, over which we will now hurry as fast as we decently may.

The reign of Edward II. is somewhat of a puzzle. He was the fourth son born to his father and the noble Eleanor of Castille; but in all his actions we find that he is totally unworthy of his parents. He shirks all the hardships of campaigning, though he is a good lance in the tilt-yard. He is fond of pomp and splendour like Henry III., but it is vulgar pomp, and leads to heartless extravagance. He is a "dressy" man; he is illiterate. He is fond of witty courtiers, who make heartless jokes on the sober fighting barons who had borne the brunt of his father's wars. One of these courtiers, called Gaveston, renders himself intolerable to the entire baronage; but when Edward goes abroad to marry Isabel of France, he actually leaves the Regency to this Gascon knight, and presently makes him governor of Ireland.

The Scottish expedition had been given up at once (July 1307), and King Robert's power naturally grew apace—castle after castle fell to him. Grievances were presented in Parliament, on this and other scores, in great plenty; and at last, in 1310, a proposal was made by the barons, headed by Lancaster, Pembroke, and

Warwick, for the appointment of a "Commission of Government," like that of 1258, to supersede the King's authority for a time.   Thomas, Earl of Lancaster, Leicester, and Lincoln, was the son of that unlucky Edmund whom the Pope and Henry III. had tried to make King of Sicily.   He was a bad, ambitious man, who saw in the weakness of his King and cousin the chance of playing a popular game.   He who opposes a bad king is sure of the votes of the vulgar herd, whatever his own character may be ; and the house of Lancaster was particularly fortunate in this respect, for it succeeded to a popular "tradition" in favour of opposition, which dated back to 1258 or even to 1215.

The "Lords Ordainers," as Lancaster's Commission was called, did nothing to redress the various abuses of which Parliament complained.   The King resented their appointment but was powerless to prevent it.   To avoid meeting them he rushed on a Scottish expedition, which penetrated to the Forth ; but King Robert prudently avoided battle.   The Ordainers contented themselves with the banishment of Gaveston ; but Edward soon recalled him and loaded him with favours, whereupon Lancaster and Warwick caught the favourite at Scarborough and beheaded him without form of trial.   This was the first actual blood shed in *party* warfare (1312), but it began to feed a stream which grew in volume till the last scions of the Plantagenet house were swept away by it.

The position of the King was for the next ten years quite different from that of any of his predecessors. He had been flouted by his own barons without any open defeat in the field, and he had seemed to acquiesce in the flouting.   Lancaster governed England in his name.   King Robert was carrying all before him in the North ; and Stirling Castle, the last English strong-

hold in Scotland, was in grave danger. Edward could
not avoid taking the field for its deliverance, and in
1314, he gathered a large army and advanced to Stirling.
King Robert, however, was an admirable " chooser of
ground," and he took post to the south-west of Stirling,
with his front resting on a bog and the Bannock b.
Allowing for all usual exaggeration, the English
was far larger than the Scottish; but lack of gen
ship prevented the proper combination of archers
cavalry, and, through lack of scouting, Edward fa
to discover that the ground was in fact impractic
for cavalry. The few Scots horse, by a rapid f
movement, managed to cut up the English arcl
before these had done much damage; and the Eng
horse got in motion too late to outflank them. Wl
they did get in motion they were unable to strug
through the heavy ground in front, or fell on the ri
into a line of pits which Robert had dug, and whi
he had filled with " crawtaes," or calthrops, to lan
the horses. Those who floundered through charge
the Scots spearmen gallantly, but were unable to break
their line, and, when reinforcements of Scottish foot
were seen coming over the hill, the whole army of King
Edward broke and fled. King Edward fled himself,
among the first, and rode off to Dunbar. Robert's
success had left him master of all Scotland, and he
proceeded to carry the war into England, and even
into Ireland, where for a short time he got his brother,
Edward Bruce, recognised and crowned as King. But
this move was a mistake, and Edward Bruce was defeated
and killed in 1317.

Neither Lancaster nor Warwick had been at Bannockburn, and the former at least cannot be cleared
of treasonable complicity with the Scots. Both had
refused to follow the King's standard, under the plea

that: had not properly submitted to the "Ordinances"
of 1o. On his return, in defeat and discredit, Edward
fou himself more than ever at Lancaster's mercy;
an we now begin to hear of private war breaking out
b een Lancaster's adherents and some few royalist
l on the congenial soil of the Welsh marches.
re ruled Roger Mortimer, Lord of Wigmore, who was
1 to become notorious. Edward, however, found
nds in the two Despencers, father and son, whose
cent came from a leading baron of Simon de Mont-
t's time. The details of the struggle are repulsive
d uninteresting until, by a sudden dash in 1322,
lward managed to capture Thomas of Lancaster, in
orkshire. After the scantiest form of trial, Thomas
as beheaded; and eight barons of his party, with a
rge number of knights, suffered death at the same
me. This vindictiveness was quite new in English
history, and showed at once the deterioration of national
character to which I have referred. The Parliament
apparently agreed to all this as readily as it had agreed
to the Ordinances in the hour of Lancaster's triumph.
It expressly repealed the Ordinances, and passed the
celebrated "Statute of York," which declared that all
matters touching the estate of the King and kingdom
should be brought before Parliament, and that no law
should be enacted without consent thereof.

There was a nominal truce with Scotland in 1320,
and again in 1323; but the border warfare was little
checked thereby. Once, in 1322, we find that Edward
himself narrowly escaped being taken prisoner. We
hear also of an Earl of Carlisle, one of Lancaster's
party, betraying the city of Carlisle to the Scots, and
paying for his treason with his head. And we are
getting very tired of Edward II. and his unpleasant
ways.

The final mischief came from abroad. The Despencers do not seem to have given the barons any very serious cause of complaint; but they feathered their own nests, as the favourites of a weak king are apt to do, and they certainly incurred the hatred of the Queen. When King Philip IV. of France died, in 1314, he was succeeded by his three sons in succession; and the last of these three, Charles IV., in 1323, contrived to evade receiving the homage of the King of England for Aquitaine, and even overran one of its outlying provinces. The Despencers were afraid to let Edward go abroad to settle the matter, and, in 1325, the Queen was sent instead. She seems to have played into the hands of her French countrymen, very possibly at the instigation of Roger Mortimer and the Bishop of Hereford, Adam Orlton, who appears as the wire-puller of the revolution that was coming. Next, Prince Edward was sent to join his mother and to perform the lawful homage for Aquitaine. The boy was only thirteen, but he was a precocious boy, and must have known what was going on.

What was going on was that the remnants of Lancaster's party were flocking to the Queen, who in 1326 moved to Hainault, in the Low Countries; there she was living in open adultery with Mortimer; there, too, Prince Edward was betrothed to Philippa of Hainault, whose father, the Count, lent troops for the projected invasion of England. And the invasion was intended to overthrow not merely the Despencers, but their master also. Isabel landed in September, openly avowing herself to be the avenger of Lancaster. She was rapidly joined by almost every one of name or position in England. Henry of Lancaster, the brother of the late Earl; the Bishops of Lincoln, Hereford, Norwich; the Archbishop of Canterbury; Edward's own half-brother, the Earl of Kent; his best friend, Henry Beaumont—all came over to the Queen's cause in turn. Not all the factitious popularity of Lancaster will explain these sudden desertions from the Crown. It looks almost as if some secret about Edward II. had been revealed to the conspirators, one after the other; but if that secret had been, as has been hinted, that Edward II. was not really the son of Edward I., but a changeling, the knowledge of it would have operated equally against Edward III. Perhaps, after all, the fact was that the man Edward had made himself impossible as king, in days when a king was all important. Every intelligent person must have felt that. His cruelty, coupled with his hopeless failure in Scotland, had hardened all hearts, and he was thrown to the wolves as unscrupulously as he had thrown Lancaster, or as Lancaster had thrown Gaveston. The Despencers were caught and put to death.

Parliament met in January 1327, and only four bishops protested when an Act was hurried through deposing King Edward II., and declaring that the Crown had devolved on King Edward III. The dethroned king was soon after murdered in Berkeley Castle. He was the first (but he was not to be the last) king deposed since law and order were known in England.

For four years the wicked Queen and Mortimer who soon grabbed for himself the Earldom of March, governed in the name of the young Edward; they did their best to associate Henry of Lancaster with them, but Henry soon began to perceive that he was only being used as a tool. After a frightful and unavenged raid of the Douglases into England, peace with the Scots was at length made by the Treaty of Northampton, 1328, by which England renounced all the pretensions of Edward I., and acknowledged Robert as King of

Scots. This peace, sensible and necessary though it was, did not add to the popularity of the Government, and there were rumours being spread abroad that Edward II. was still alive. For acting on one of these rumours Edmund, Earl of Kent, the son of King Edward I. by his second wife, was executed without trial, in 1330; and Lancaster, whose head was beginning to feel shaky on his shoulders, thereupon stirred up the young king to assert himself and get rid of his mother's scandalous favourite. He contrived to have Mortimer surprised and condemned to death, in October 1330, and with this event the real reign of Edward III. begins.

CHAPTER XVI

THE REIGN OF EDWARD III

EDWARD has been rather mocked by sober historians as a mere knight-errant who plunged England into war for his own ambitions, and did not know what to do with his conquests when he had made them; and as a recklessly extravagant king, who never paid his debts, and did not care whom he ruined by his dishonesty. On the other hand he has been extolled as the "ideal King of Chivalry," the national champion of a national war, the true founder of English industry and commerce. Where does the truth lie? Two or three things are very clear to us: (1) That, after the most dismal reign in English history, with a fierce baronage already trained to imbrue its hands in its own blood and in that of its king, Edward contrived, apparently without difficulty, to suspend the baronial feuds for fifty years, and to leave his reign memorable as the last one for over two centuries in which there was no attempt to set up a rival king or to disturb the internal peace of the country. (2) That by the most deliberate policy he succeeded in breaking down the exclusiveness of English merchants, and getting foreigners to settle and remain undisturbed in England, from which time began our woollen manufactures in the Eastern counties; that he took the House of Commons into full confidence on this and on all other commercial matters, and left it with the deliberate habit of commercial legislation on a grand scale. (3) That he asserted and maintained for many years the sovereignty of the seas as no king had done before him. (4) Finally, however badly the French wars turned out in the century after his death, we cannot shut our eyes to the position assumed by Edward III. in the eyes of Europe.

In estimating this position we must not forget the immense overweight of the Kings of France during the preceding century. No country had compared with France in power, riches, and civilisation. All this prestige Edward III. simply shattered to pieces, and left the firm (and quite new) conviction in the minds of his subjects that one Englishman can beat three Frenchmen. France is a country that recovers from war and disaster more quickly than any other; but we may well doubt whether she had entirely recovered from the Edwardian wars before the seventeenth century. It is true that Edward exhausted England in the process of ruining France, and that the war engendered the very worst conceivable spirit, that of the mercenary soldier and the professional plunderer. "They took and robbed and brennt it clean" is the ordinary way in which the entry of an English army into a French town is described by the good Froissart, secretary of Queen Philippa, who wrote perhaps the most famous chronicle of the whole Middle Ages. Very rarely "they robbed without the brenning." "The granges full of corn, the houses full of all riches, rich burgesses, carts and chariots, horses, swine, muttons, and other beasts; they took what them list and brought it into the King's host; but the soldiers made no count to the King nor to none of his officers of the gold and the silver they did get; that they kept to themselves." How many families were founded in England out of the plunder of the French wars and the ransoms of French knights and barons! Some of such plunder occasionally went to found chantries and colleges, for even a successful mercenary captain was apt to have twinges about his future when he came to the end of life. Good Archbishop Chicheley did well to found, in his great College of the Souls of all faithful departed people, masses for the souls of those who fell in the French wars; for, if all tales be true, forgiveness was much needed by some of them.

Still we must remember that hostilities were at first forced upon Edward. There are three main causes of the commencement of the " Hundred Years' War " between England and France : first, the growing conviction in English minds that the conquest of Scotland was hopeless while France was so powerful; secondly, the deliberate intention of the French kings to absorb English Aquitaine; and thirdly, the determination of England to maintain the " open door " into Flanders for her wool.

King Robert of Scotland died in 1329, at the age of fifty-five, leaving a son, David, barely five years old. Robert had done his work so thoroughly that even the weakness of his successors could not wholly undo it. His only mistakes had been his attempt on Ireland, and the fact that he rewarded the patriotic party among the barons somewhat lavishly; this was especially the case with the great house of Douglas. Randolph, Earl of Moray, was Regent for little David; he died shortly after King Robert, and meanwhile the "disinherited barons " of the old English (Balliol's) party were clamouring for readmission to their estates. The Scottish regency, however, held this to be impossible, and the disinherited turned to Edward Balliol, son of the late King John, who was in exile at the English Court. The Treaty of Northampton had been very unpopular in England, and King Edward III. was fully alive to the necessity of subduing Scotland at some date or other. He accordingly supplied Balliol with money and troops; but it was mainly with refugees of his own party that Balliol landed in Fife and won the battle of Dupplin Moor, in September 1332; he then took Perth, and was crowned King, while the little David was sent to France for safety. Expelled again by patriots, Balliol again returned with King Edward and a large English army, which inflicted on the Scots the terrible defeat of Halidon Hill, near Berwick, July 1333. But Balliol had to buy English help by the cession of the border fortresses, and of part of the counties of Berwick and Roxburgh. To maintain a puppet king in Scotland for any serious length of time was entirely beyond the resources of Edward III. Twice more before 1337 he invaded Scotland on behalf of his ally; but whatever success he gained melted away as soon as his back was turned. In 1338, Robert Fitzalan, the "Steward," who had married Robert Bruce's daughter Marjory, became Regent; he recovered all the Southern strongholds, and recalled King David in 1341. By that time Edward III. was busy elsewhere.

The natural and laudable efforts of all French governments have been directed, as I have already said, towards securing for France the boundaries of old Gaul, the Rhine, the Alps, the Pyrenees, and the Ocean. For 150 years before the accession of Edward in England, France had been steadily marching in these directions. The strong fortification of English Aquitaine by Edward I. opposed a serious barrier in the south-west, and Charles IV. had begun to hammer at it. With the death of that king, in 1328, ended the elder branch of the house of Capet. If a female could inherit or transmit the succession, the heir was the young King of Navarre; and after him Edward of England, in right of Isabel, his mother, who was the daughter of

Philip IV. A female, however, had never yet either inherited or transmitted the succession to the French throne; and the entire national spirit of France was against the recognition of a foreign king, whether of Navarre or of England. The so-called "Salic Law" was therefore now deliberately invented by the French lawyers to exclude all female successions or transmissions, and the leading "Prince of the Blood," Philip of Valois, was elected as Philip VI. He was descended in the male line from Louis IX. The Valois were spirited, active, rather vain fellows, who rapidly deteriorated when they found themselves on a throne; with two exceptions they showed little of the craft and tenacity of purpose of the earlier French kings, and unfortunately they ruled France for over 250 years. Edward had made some sort of protest against Philip's election, and had talked about the claims of his mother, Isabel; but had since then twice done homage for Aquitaine, once with all full formalities. Not the slightest intention of claiming the crown of France can be traced in his first measures; but, if Aquitaine should be attacked, defend it he must and would.

We have long ago seen the Counts of Flanders as intimate friends of England, but that attitude was now changing. As the German "Empire" weakened and French strength grew, all the princes of the "Low Countries" were being drawn into the orbit of France, and French influence was steadily making its way into the old Imperial lands on the borders of the Rhine. Philip III. and IV. had seemed to be in a fair way to swallow the whole of what is now Belgium, when suddenly the resistance, which the princes of that country no longer cared to make, was made by the sturdy burghers of the Flemish towns, especially of Ghent, Bruges, and Ypres. These burghers were now always quarrelling with their counts, and the counts were consequently driven to rely on French help against their own subjects. Philip IV. and the Count of Flanders were defeated by the burghers at Courtrai, in 1302, after which the towns came to rely more and more upon English help. Philip VI. avenged Courtrai at the battle of Cassel, 1328, and followed up his success by getting the Count to arrest all the English merchants who were in Flanders. This wanton piece of irritation to England was answered by Edward with an embargo laid upon the export of English wool, which at once produced a famine in Ghent, just as now a famine would be produced in Manchester if America stopped the export of her cotton. It only needed this to move the burgesses to a definite and permanent resistance to French aggression, and to a close alliance with England. War between England and France was inevitable, and King Edward at first prepared for it very much in the same way as his grandfather had done.

That is to say, he made an alliance with the Emperor, subsidised German troops, took off the embargo on English wool, received and fêted magnificently the spokesman of the Flemish towns, Jacques van Arteveld, a Flemish noble who had been enrolled in the Weavers' gild of Ghent ; and finally, when nothing else would satisfy his Flemish allies, he took the title and quartered the arms of the King of France, 1340. Older causes of quarrel were not wanting ; for years before this, the piracy of French ships, and of Genoese ships in French pay, had been going on in the Channel, and had provoked sharp reprisals from England. Several other doors into France were soon opened to our troops ; one by a discontented Count of Artois, one by a claimant of the Duchy of Brittany. This last door remained open almost till Edward's death ; but the fighting in

Brittany, such as it was, had little effect on the main struggle. That at first was confined to the Flemish frontier, and the first years were uneventful except for the great naval victory of Sluys, off the Flemish coast, where Edward routed a French and Genoese fleet in 1340, because the French admiral committed the blunder of allowing his captains to begin the battle from an anchorage on a lee shore. Yet in 1342 a truce was patched up, and the war seemed likely to produce little more result than previous wars between the two countries had produced.

All this was changed three years later by a brilliant raid by the Earl of Derby (now the heir of the house of Lancaster), from Bordeaux in the direction of Poitiers. The utter failure of all Philip's attempts to check this revealed to Edward's eye the military weakness of the splendid French king. An immense army of heavy cavalry had been got into unwieldy motion to check Derby, and had got as far south as Aiguillon, when Edward, in the summer of 1346, sailed from Southampton to the relief of Aquitaine. On the voyage a certain Norman noble, Godfrey Harcourt, persuaded the King of England to land in Normandy by way of effecting a diversion, and so, in July, the future army of Crecy disembarked in the Côtentin.

Now Paris was then, as it still is, *the* place in France at which an invader should strike, and the natural mediæval idea would be a triple advance upon Paris from Aquitaine, from Flanders, and from some point in Normandy or Brittany ; these three " bases of operation " are, however, so far apart that it was most unlikely that convergent movements from all three, or even from two of the three, would ever be successfully effected. There should have been ample time for a French king, acting from his centre, to destroy one of the converging armies, and thus to leave the other or others "in the air," as the soldiers say. Edward seems to have had only the vaguest notions of co-operating with Derby or with any one else, and if there were any strategy in his head at all, it was probably only that of a dash upon Paris and a capture of Philip's person before the large French army could return from the south-west. If this were his idea, he spoilt it by wasting too much time in "brenning" the rich province of Normandy.

But while the English army is disembarking on the sands of St. Vaast-la-Hogue, let us take a glimpse at its composition and at that of its opponents. Before beginning the war in earnest Edward had issued a circular letter to the sheriffs, which was to be read in every parish church in England, setting forth the causes of the war and his own "rightful" claim to the crown of France. Thus, right or wrong, he fully took his people into his confidence. Philip did nothing of the sort. Further, Edward entered into contracts with certain great lords to supply him with volunteer troops for certain definite sums of money. There was no question of calling out the militia, or of issuing " commissions of array," such as he would use for a Welsh or Scottish war, nor even of calling out the feudal levy. The army was a volunteer army pure and simple, and, as each purveyor of volunteers looked after the pay and equipment and clothing of his own men, we have here the origin of the English regimental system, in which each regiment is a little separate corporation, with a keen spirit of honour and of rivalry with other regiments. Unfortunately, in the intervals of peace in the fourteenth century, the "proprietors," if one may so call them, of these regiments were apt to offer their services to other princes than their own,

R

and to become, in fact, leaders of those "Free Companies" of which we shall soon hear too much.

The pay of this army was exceedingly high. The "men at arms," *i.e.* knights (who were probably about 2000), were paid at least 2s. a day (say 26s. of modern money); out of this, however, remember that the knight had to provide his heavy armour and certainly two if not three war-horses, and pay the men who looked after them. The 5000 archers were paid 3d. or 6d. a day, according as they were or were not mounted (say 3s. 3d. and 6s. 6d. respectively); they provided, of course, their own bows and arrows. The 5000 Welsh and Irish "knife-men" came lowest on the scale; they received 2d. a day (say 2s. 2d.); their business no doubt was to stick the French knights when they were unhorsed, or to stab the poor horses from underneath. One cannot say for certain that these numbers are correct; the army, when it fought at Crecy, was certainly smaller than this owing to the natural "waste of war," though Edward did not weaken it by leaving garrisons behind him. "Keeping open a line of communications" was a duty entirely unknown to a mediæval general, though, if Froissart speaks truly, the art of scouting was very well understood by the English. Edward no doubt reckoned that, if baffled, he could escape to Flanders or the sea.

The French army, when fully called out, was reckoned at anything from twenty to fifty thousand knights of the feudal levy (a number impossible to manœuvre effectively with the tactics of those days), some 7000 Genoese cross-bowmen, and a very large but varying number of "milices communales" (*i.e.* militia of the towns and villages, armed with pikes and spears and short-bows). The pay of these last men is said to have been as low as ½d. a day, but the French coinage

varied so constantly in value that it is difficult to ascer-
tain the true value of such a sum. The knights served
at their own cost.

Knight for knight, and footman for footman, there
should have been little disparity in the stuff of the
armies, except for the immense superiority of the
long-bow over all other infantry weapons; and yet,
for nearly a hundred years after this campaign, no
French army inflicted, in open field, any serious defeat
on an English army of equal strength; while over and
over again inferior numbers of English beat superior
numbers of French. This can be attributed only to
one fact—the comparative absence of class feeling in
England; the much greater unity of the English nation,
which was yet so much more diverse in blood than the
French. For the French knights would not co-operate
with the footmen; they would, and did often dismount
and fight on foot themselves; but it was as individual
knights, not as parts of a whole army. The English
leaders, though they may have been bad strategists, were
generally good tacticians, *i.e.* they knew the way to
combine " missile tactics " and " shock tactics," arrows
and lances, and they had realised that the days of " heavy
cavalry " battles were over.

The failure of the French to realise this last truth
was, perhaps, because France had been so pre-eminently
the nation of the crusades, and it was in the crusades
that the spirit of " knighthood " and " chivalry " was
first developed; a spirit which, in spite of many beautiful English examples, never quite mastered the robust
common sense of the English army. The " very perfect
gentle knight," whether French or English, was often
too apt to be thinking of doing bigger deeds of personal
valour than any one else, to care much how the battle
went; and, if he was not very " perfect and gentle," he

was apt to despise any one who did not come up to his own standard in pedigree, or in manner of fighting. But enough of this spirit did spread to England to put occasional restraint on the worst of men's brute passions, to teach tenderness to women, to make the investiture with knighthood a religious as well as a social act. King Edward himself, his nobler son the Black Prince, Sir John Chandos, Seneschal of Aquitaine, Sir Walter Manny, and, in much later times, Sir Philip Sidney, are the true English examples of the "flower of all knighthood."

Up to his overwhelming victory at Crecy, Edward's "ride through France" must have seemed to those who watched him the maddest affair. Philip waited quietly at Paris, and called up every available man for the defence. Edward failed to take anything that was seriously held against him (*e.g.* Rouen), though he plundered some very large cities which were ill-defended (*e.g.* Caen). His army, gorged with the spoil of the rich Norman province, lumbered along the Seine to Paris, outside which he sat for weeks calling upon Philip to come out and fight him like a gentleman. At last, despairing of this, he managed to repair the broken bridge over the Seine at Poissy, and lumbered along again north-eastwards, in the direction of Flanders. Cut adrift from any base that he had ever had, he could hope for safety only by regaining touch with his fleet, or by getting behind the screen of the Flemish cities. Philip, by this time in full strength, moved out of his capital, and marched parallel to Edward till he reached the slow deep river of Somme, where he broke down all the bridges except that of Amiens, which he held in force. Edward seemed to be completely in a trap, until a daring dash over a tidal ford carried his army across at Blanchetaque, his archers driving off a body of French cavalry which had molested the passage. Once safely across he determined to risk a battle.

Crecy lies on the Calais road, some thirteen miles north of Abbeville. Edward, burning for fight, took post on the slope of a rolling down, with an impenetrable forest covering his right, and the village of Wadicourt on his left, while his front faced the Abbeville road, by which alone the French could advance. The drawing up of the armies on August 26th in three "battles," that is, wedges almost as deep as long, was common to both sides; but the English front was composed of archers interspersed with dismounted knights, while on the French side the Genoese cross-bowmen were all in front, and unsupported. It seems certain that the impetuosity of the first French "battle" led its knights to charge even before their order was complete, and before the cross-bowmen could get into action at all. These were, moreover, wet through, and so were their bow-strings. An English archer could shoot six arrows for one of a cross-bowman's bolts and he aimed always at the horses, which experience had not yet taught the knights to protect with defensive armour. Galled to madness by the arrows, the French cavalry rode forward through and over their own infantry; but, practically, not half of them ever succeeded in reaching the English lines at all. Even so the first line, where the fifteen-year-old Prince Edward was winning his spurs, was for some time in grave danger; yet the expert King Edward refused to advance his reserve, which was not in action all day. The dismounted English knights of the first and second battles, aided by the archers from the flanks, did their work before the evening, and the French losses were overwhelming. The "milices communales," who were not on the field, but in the rear, were cut to pieces in the pursuit that followed the battle.

Flushed with this success, Edward resolved to lay siege to the great city of Calais, which, as a nest of pirates and privateers, had long plagued the English merchant shipping. This enterprise was not so mad as it seemed; for some ten miles round Calais, the country was flat and very marshy: only three causeway roads crossed it, one leading south-west to Boulogne, one north-east to Dunkirk, and one south to St. Omer and Abbeville. If Edward could hold these roads, and if his fleet could blockade the town by sea, relief was impossible. The possession of the city would secure to England the mastery of the Channel, and an ever-open road to Flanders. Edward built outside the beleaguered walls a regular wooden town, which he named Villeneuve-le-Hardi ("Newtown the Bold"), and there, well supplied by his fleet, he sat for eight months, easily beating off Philip's clumsy efforts at relief, till he had starved out the men of Calais.

Meanwhile Derby, when relieved of the presence of the great French army, had taken Poitiers, though he made no attempt to hold it; while at the same time Queen Philippa had obtained, in October 1346, a great victory over the King of Scots. Poor little David, who had been restored to Scotland in 1341, pluckily attempted a diversion in favour of his French allies, and, after raiding as far as Durham, was caught, beaten, and captured at Neville's Cross. Froissart tells an amusing story of the English squire, John Copeland, who took the King of Scots. He rode out of the battle with him as prisoner for fifteen leagues, till he came to a castle called "Orgueilleux" (which turns out to be only Ogle Castle); he swore he would deliver his prisoner to no man or woman living, except the King of England.

The Queen sent expressly to Master John to bid him surrender David; but John, who perhaps had little faith in the generosity of ladies, proceeded to ride post to Dover, and thence take ship for Calais.   There he told his tale, and then said King Edward: "John, the good service you have done is so much worth that it must countervail your trespass," &c.; but, nevertheless, bade him hurry back and hand over David to Philippa. But John was right in his calculations, for the King gave him £100 a year in land at once.   David was sent to the Tower, and spent the next eleven years in honourable captivity in England; he was not much missed in Scotland, where Robert the Steward ruled in his stead.   And Queen Philippa came to Dover, and took ship for Calais, she and many ladies and damosels with her, and no doubt they spent a delightful winter and spring with their husbands and lovers in Newtown the Bold.

When Calais was on the point of surrender, Edward either showed himself unusually cruel, or else, as is more likely, determined on a great theatrical performance for the glory of his good Philippa.   He demanded that the six leading burgesses of Calais should surrender themselves to be hanged, and promised that only then would he admit the rest of the city to his mercy.   It was not in the least like Edward to punish gallant opponents whom no one could possibly accuse of breaking faith with him; and, if he pretended to turn a deaf ear to the prayers of Sir Walter Manny and all his knights, it was no doubt in order that the Queen, being great with child, should come and kneel at his feet and beg the lives of these men.   So the good Queen did, and the King yielded to her prayer, and she took the six burgesses and feasted them royally; and Calais became an English possession.

Edward made a futile attempt to repeople it with Londoners, even as Henry II. had tried to colonise Dublin with Bristol men; but the Londoners would not stay, and the French population gradually drifted back, though it does not seem to have given much trouble afterwards. And so for two hundred years Calais was ours. "Calais and Dover are the two eyes of England," said the Emperor Sigismund to Henry V. "Leave Calais alone," said the dying Louis XI. to his son, when all the rest of France had been won back from the English. Yet it may well be doubted whether Calais was not, after all, a mere white elephant to the English Crown. In the first place, that command of the narrow seas which it gave came too easily to us. The defence of an island like ours lies in its fleet; but it was not till we lost those stone walls of Calais that we learned really to trust to our wooden ones. In the second place, it was a terrible drain on the resources of a Crown that was often (*e.g.* in fifteenth century) very, very poor. The county of Calais, as finally ceded to us, comprised, besides the city itself, a considerable stretch of territory, with four great, and a few smaller outlying fortifications, and it cost fabulous sums of money to keep all these in repair. In the third place, its enormous garrison, which was in effect a little standing army, and the only thing of its kind in the King's dominions, was often a serious menace to law and order in our island. Twice during the Wars of the Roses it was shipped across the strait under the command of a disaffected or ambitious "Captain of Calais," and on each occasion it changed the fortune of the war.

From the fall of Calais in 1347 till the year 1355 the war with France was almost at a standstill; only the Breton quarrel kept it alive at all. For a new and terrible scourge was making itself felt by both nations and left them little time to reflect on peace or war at all. There had been pestilential epidemics before, but never, before or after, anything like the "Black Death," which appeared in England (at Weymouth), in August 1348. The population at the date of Domesday has been guessed at about two millions; and, though this is probably well outside the mark, we may fairly assume that, whatever it had been in 1086, it had doubled by the middle of the fourteenth century. The Black Death reduced it in a year by something between a half and a third. This plague came from the East, where it still smoulders; it recurred from time to time in England down to the last outbreak in 1665, but never upon anything like the scale of its first appearance. The impossibility of fighting it arose both from complete ignorance of medical science and from complete indifference to sanitary precautions. Increase of luxury often produces decrease of ability to resist the attacks of disease; but, whereas in later pestilences the upper classes—who could escape from infected quarters to the open air, or, still better, go and live on the water—got off comparatively free, there was no flying from the Black Death. The Archbishop of Canterbury and many of the highest clergy died of it; the peasants who lived in open air were quite as badly off as the townsmen who inhaled the effluvia of the gutter. The population of England probably did not recover its thirteenth-century figures before the end of Elizabeth's reign. And the results upon the relations of classes were most far-reaching.

In a country which was still almost purely agricultural, what were you to do if the labouring population was suddenly diminished by one-half? Your crops would be unreaped, your fields unsown; you and your tenants would starve. Say you are a fourteenth-century landlord who has already emancipated his villeins. These quondam villeins are now freemen who pay you a small fixed money rent for their land (a later generation will call them " copyholders "), and who work for you or for any one else who will give them good wages. But suddenly you find that half these labourers have died ; that half the corn-lands of England are unreaped, and that the crops (of 1349) lie rotting on the ground. The first thing that will happen is that the price of corn will leap up to double the price of 1348. The twopence which you used to pay John Hodge for a day's harvest work will no longer support him and his family : he demands fourpence. Neither he nor you quite understand what is happening. It is not to be expected that either of you should be acquainted with the "Laws of Political Economy"—all you say to Hodge, therefore, is : " ridiculous—get you gone and starve if you like." But you find on inquiry that no one of the labourers who have survived the plague will work for less, and that one of your neighbours, a shrewder and richer man than yourself, is actually paying his men fourpence, though he tries to conceal the fact. When, in 1351, you at last meet your fellow-squires in Parliament, all that your collective wisdom can do is to make a heroic effort to put back the clock. You enact the famous "Statute of Labourers," which forbids labourers to migrate from place to place in search of higher wages, forbids any one to give or take higher wages than were current in 1347, and decrees that any man who refuses to work for such wages shall be adjudged as a bondman to the person who offers such wages to him. But to make things quite all right, you also attempt to fix prices at what they were in the year 1347. If a quarter of wheat were then worth three shillings, it *shall* be worth three shillings still, and no man shall ask more for it.

But the goddess of Political Economy—an ugly female at best—is not only ugly but, like Justice, she is blind and, like Justice, she holds a pair of scales : in the one lie "prices" and in the other "wages," and she is always seeking to adjust them one to other. It took the world a long time to learn this tolerably obvious truth (and there are some fools who have not learnt it yet). Time after time this absurd "Statute of Labourers" was re-enacted, but no statute was ever more hopelessly disobeyed. Landlords who had not emancipated their villeins were little better off than those who had, for they could not increase the labour rents of the survivors, and not enough men survived to do the field work of the manors. Some, who had emancipated, tried to ignore the fact and to demand again the old labour rents. The villeins laughed in their faces ; they were masters of the situation. Slowly, very slowly, the wage-scale adjusted itself to the price-scale during the next twenty or thirty years, and slowly, very slowly, prices began to fall again. The idea of wages and prices fixed by law could not be got out of the heads of the landowners, and the mistake was repeated again in the sixteenth century.[1]

The more prudent of the landlords recognised that some great change, which they could not understand, had come over the country, and gave up the attempt to cultivate their fields on the old scale and in the old fashion. They might instead do one of several things : (1) they might sell the whole or a portion of their land outright—it would be bought either by small freeholders, or by the villeins enriched by the rise in wages, or by soldiers returned from the wars laden

---

[1] The idea of prices fixed by law was not wholly a new one even in 1351 ; the craft-gilds had always tried to regulate the prices of manufactured articles ; what was new at this time was the attempt to enforce a fixed (and totally absurd) price for the necessaries of life all over the country.

with French spoil, or by townsmen who had made
their fortunes as wool-brokers; (2) they might lease
their lands for a greater or lesser period to one or
several of such people, and get a yearly rent paid for
them; (3) or they might give up corn-growing and take
to sheep-farming—in fact, turn wool-brokers themselves.   All these three changes took place sooner or
later all over England, and the result was that society
came to be held together far more by the tie of mere
money contracts than by the older and kindlier tie of
mutual interests in the village lands between landlord
and labourer.   In due time—perhaps by the seventeenth century—something of the spirit of the older tie
came back, and landlord, farmer, and labourer began
again to live in mutual interests as of old; but the
"progress" of the nineteenth century shattered it all
again.   Meanwhile, in the fifteenth and sixteenth the
cleavage of classes was deep and hateful, and led to
several frightful outbreaks, notably one in 1381, which
almost assumed the proportions of an agrarian war.
It led to a great migration of labour into the nasty,
stuffy towns; and it certainly created the class of
'sturdy beggars" who are the ancestors of the very
unsturdy tramps of our own day.

While it was only in Brittany that the hostilities
between England and France smouldered on in these
dismal years, it was in Brittany also that the "Free
Companies" originated, in the disbanded—or rather not
disbanded—regiments of the earlier part of the war;
companies commanded by professional adventurers like
Knollys, Calverly, and Hawkwood, who went on making
war on their own account simply as a matter of profit;
but who would at once rally to England if the war
were to begin again on a big scale.   In 1355 we find
Edward raiding Picardy from Calais, and the Black

Prince raiding northwards from Bordeaux; in 1356 Edward was over the Scottish border, John of Gaunt (his third son) was raiding from Cherbourg, and the Black Prince was on the grand raid of all, by which he reached the very centre of France and the River Loire. But the new French king, John (Philip died in 1350), hurried to meet Prince Edward with an overwhelming force. The Prince turned, none too fast, and began to crawl back through Poitou towards Bordeaux. His army of perhaps 6000, of whom not 2000 were knights and the rest archers, laden with inestimable plunder, could not outstrip the chivalry of France burning to avenge the defeat of Crecy : " for there was all the flower of France, none durst abide at home without he should be shamed for ever." Froissart's figures are, as usual, incredible, but we may fairly allow the French to have been at least five to one. Prince Edward, who positively revelled in odds of three to one, thought that on this occasion discretion would be the better part of valour, and offered, by the mediation of a certain French cardinal, to abandon all his conquests, plunder and prisoners, in return for an unmolested retreat to Bordeaux—nay, he was ready to promise not to serve against France for seven years to come. John demanded the surrender of the whole army. Sunday, 18th September, was passed in a series of fruitless negotiations, but also in the fortifying, by Sir John Chandos and the Prince, of the very excellent situation known as the gap of Maupertuis, a few miles from Poitiers. When the fortification was completed King John's demands were found excessive. His best plan would obviously have been to blockade the English and starve them into surrender, for in spite of their plunder they had no food with them ; but such a plan did not commend itself to the " flower of France," nor to their king.   John therefore elected to storm the position in three "battles," *i.e.* wedge after wedge of heavy men should be thrown upon it. · He prudently dismounted most of his knights for the purpose, and he sent them to charge up a narrow muddy lane, between hedges and vineyards lined with dismounted English knights and archers.   A small detachment of French knights on horseback, having been despatched to brush these insects out of the path, proved to be the immediate cause of the rout of the whole French army ; for their wounded horses recoiled upon their own advancing heavy infantry, and the English archers and knights (both with the advantage of the ground) made a frightful havoc of the first two "battles," which at length took to their heels, after losing a quarter of their numbers.   Chandos and the Prince at once resolved on a charge on the third battle, which was itself larger than the whole English army.   "Advance banner, in the name of God and St. George," cried Edward ; and down they poured in line rather than in column.   In that third battle fought King John in person, with his thirteen-year-old son Philip (ever afterwards called "the Bold ") guarding his father's back.   John performed "prodigies of valour " (kings always do in battle), though as futilely as our King Stephen at the battle of Lincoln, and seemed quite to forget the defeat of his army in admiring his own prowess.   But our archers simply shot holes in the French line, and our knights poured into the gaps thus created and laid about them.   Froissart cannot contain his delight at the noble feats of arms that there were done.   As Kinglake wishes to give the heroic actions of every individual officer at Inkermann, so our dear mediæval chronicler tells us exultingly of the shrewd handstrokes of the gentle Sir Thomas or the tragic death of the great Earl Walter.

But there were Thomases and Walters there without handles to their names, who died for St. George and St. Denys with equal goodwill. At last. what was left of the third French "battle" turned tail and fled like the first and the second. Overpowered by numbers, John yielded himself prisoner among the very last, and a hot dispute, as to who actually took him, had to be referred to the Prince, who ultimately referred it to his father in England.

Every one knows of the chivalrous courtesy whereby the Prince overwhelmed the King of France with compliments, told him that the palm of valour of the day rested with him alone, feasted him royally (on his own mutton and claret, one must presume, since the English had nothing to eat on the day of the battle), and waited on him at table in person ; since which event the noble motto of "Ich Dien" (I serve) has for ever graced the scutcheon of the Princes of Wales. Slowly the English army moved back to Bordeaux with its huge train of prisoners, though all who could ransom themselves or who would promise ransom, were let go at once on the "true faith of knighthood." King John soon afterwards accompanied the Prince to England, and remained in joyful captivity for four years, and "went a-hunting and a-hawking in Windsor forest at his pleasure," while his ransom was being extorted from Frenchmen. His son the Dauphin, afterwards Charles V., governed in his name. Raid after raid desolated France up till the treaty of Bretigny in 1360 ; but the Regent was a very different man from his father and grandfather, and he began to formulate the plan which was ultimately to turn the tide and to save France : "no battles ; let the English ride through the land, and let us devote ourselves to fortifying our cities and to cutting off hostile detachments." It was a frightful alternative, but it was better than surrender; by shutting his eyes to the misery of his country Charles ultimately saved its independence.

The treaty of Bretigny, 1360, fixed an enormous ransom for King John, not half of which could ever be paid, and further gave to Edward, in exchange for his surrender of the title of "King of France," almost the whole of the old inheritance of Henry II.'s Queen Eleanor (*i.e.* Poitou in addition to Edward I.'s Aquitaine), as well as the County of Calais, and the County of Ponthieu on the Somme; and all this not on feudal tenure from the Crown of France as in old days, but in full independent sovereignty. It was either too little or too much for the victors of Crecy and Poitiers to claim; and it would be impossible to hold it all for any long period of time, with any force which England could command. King David of Scotland had also been released for an enormous ransom in 1357, and spent the rest of his rather futile life in trying to raise the sum. He died in 1371, and was succeeded by Robert II., the first of the "Stewarts," son of Robert the "Steward," who had been regent and had married Marjory Bruce. King John also died in England, in 1364, for he came back as his knightly word had pledged him to come, in default of his ransom being paid in full. No doubt he found the honourable captivity of Windsor more to his taste than his own wasted land, where the Free Companies and a frightful peasant insurrection were rendering life intolerable for a "real gentleman."

The sorrowful close of the reign of Edward III. is soon told. Prince Edward was created Duke of Aquitaine, and sent to govern his Duchy from Bordeaux—sent to the task in which Richard I. and Simon de Montfort had so signally failed, and in which our very perfect gentle knight failed also. The Gascon barons, the d'Albrets, the "d'Artagnans," and their kind were no more amenable to law and order than their ancestors in the twelfth century. The Kings of Arragon and Navarre were to prove hostile, and the King of Castile, called Pedro the Cruel, a peculiarly repulsive specimen of his race, was just being driven from his throne by his bastard brother Henry, who had obtained French aid. It was absolutely necessary for the ruler of Aquitaine to have a friendly Castile. The Free Companies were pillaging all the frontiers of the Duchy; again and again Edward drove them over his borders into France, into Avignon (where they almost held the Pope to ransom and evilly entreated some fat cardinals), into Italy; but again and again they came back. While even the worst of them regarded the Black Prince with dread as the first captain of Christendom, the best of them could hardly help seeing in him a power not altogether dissimilar to their own; and they knew that, if war broke out again he would immediately call them to his standards. Bordeaux, indeed, where he kept the most magnificent court in Europe, benefited greatly by the increase of trade with England, and perhaps his experiment in government might have proved a temporary success but for the disastrous Spanish war of 1367.

That evil man, Pedro, had been evicted from Castile in the previous year, having alienated the hearts of all his subjects by his horrible cruelties and murders; and he came to ask Prince Edward's aid. The Prince, we are told, considered Pedro's to be the "Cause of Kings"—"a bastard should not disinherit a rightful sovereign." But the fact that the new King Henry had been enthroned by French aid, and that the long friendship between England and Castile must therefore be necessarily broken, probably counted for more in Edward's mind.

S

Yet the wise Chandos warned his master against putting any faith in Pedro or supporting him in any way; it were better, in his view, to strengthen the Pyrenean frontier. The lust of battle, however, was awake in Edward's heart, and needed stimulating as little as it heeded warnings. So the banner was advanced across the Pyrenean passes, knee deep in snow, in February 1367. Pedro promised to find funds in abundance—"not just at the moment, however; his treasures were all safely locked up at Sevile." Edward rashly pledged himself to advance the necessary sums, and the Free Companies flocked to join his standard. A large English and Gascon army reached the Ebro in April, and inflicted a frightful defeat on King Henry at the battle of Navarete. Pedro was crowned at Burgos and went back to Sevile to find his treasures. But, whether he ever found any or not, he never paid his debts to the Prince; the summer that followed was hot, and the English army was decimated by fever and dysentery. Edward himself contracted a mortal disease from which he was to die nine years later. Wasted with sickness, he led his wasted army back across the mountains and home to Bordeaux. The Companies, in default of pay, began again to pillage the Duchy: Edward was obliged to impose heavy taxation on all his subjects; the towns on the whole responded cheerfully, but if there was one thing that Gascon barons would not suffer, it was to be taxed like "common men." The "financial honesty of their government" was nothing to them. They appealed to the King of France.

The King of France was ready to listen. Beside Charles V. stood already one of the grand figures of French history, Sir Bertrand du Guesclin, a rough Breton knight whose name came to be a watchword to the coming generations, not only for all noble

knightly faith and bravery and mercy, but also for
scientific warfare, for study of advantageous positions,
cunning stratagems, night surprises, escalades of towns,
and the like. While du Guesclin's personal valour is
well illustrated by the story of his forsaking a tournament and going to challenge the peasants to fight
him in a barn, because they were "stronger men
than he could find at the tournament," his great idea
of war was, like Napoleon's, to fight only when and
where he was in greater force than his enemy. In him
King Charles placed the fullest confidence; his own
hand was so infirm that it could not hold a weapon,
but he sat in his closet at Paris and planned the
campaigns that du Guesclin, as Constable of France,
was to execute. Charles wisely grasped the English
principle of paying his soldiers. He paid the feudal
lords for defending their own castles, "for he that lets
himself be paid ends by letting himself be commanded,"
and indeed the first need now for a French king was
to be master of his own chivalrous barons, and to
prevent them from throwing away whole armies of
themselves, as at Crecy and Poitiers. He further
obliged each town to keep a company of cross-bowmen or spearmen; while the smaller nobles were
organised in paid companies (regiments) commanded
by captains nominated by the King.

Even before the Spanish war the main issue had
been reopened between France and England by a fresh
flare-up of the quarrel in Brittany. The Prince of
Wales had sent assistance to the English faction there,
and Chandos had defeated and captured du Guesclin at
the battle of Auray; but du Guesclin was, after some
delay, admitted to ransom, and the craft of the French
king managed to patch up a peace in Brittany. Charles
had then addressed himself, and with more success than

Prince Edward, to the task of getting rid of the Free Companies, which were pillaging all over France. Some few of them took service in France and settled down on wasted lands to become French subjects, but the largest and worst were eventually packed off to Italy. And so extensively had these companies been recruited in England, that Charles had little difficulty in blending the cry of his subjects against them with a cry for the breach of the treaty of Bretigny and for revenge on the English. No sooner was the Prince of Wales back in Bordeaux than du Guesclin was over the Pyrenees re-establishing King Henry in Castile. Pedro was murdered, and henceforth Castile was French in sympathy for many years to come.

So the toils were fast closing round the sick lion at Bordeaux : Chandos, his right-hand man, went off to defend Poitou, and was killed in an obscure skirmish (1370) ; civil war had been raging in the Duchy since 1369 ; finally the King of France took the decisive step and summoned the Prince (as if Aquitaine were still a fief of France, which, by the treaty of Bretigny, it was not) to answer the complaints of his barons at the royal court at Paris. "Sirs," answered Edward to the messengers of this summons, "we will gladly go to Paris to see our uncle ; but I assure you it shall be with basnet on our head, and with sixty thousand men in our company." It was an empty threat, but not altogether an unworthy or an ungracious one. With a tenth of that number Edward had made the crown of France rock on the head of Charles' father. In 1370 two great French armies converged upon Aquitaine ; du Guesclin overran the province of Agenais, the Duke of Berri took Limoges. Everywhere on the border lands the French were welcomed as deliverers ; but this was not so much the case when they penetrated

Map of
FRANCE
to illustrate the
100 YEARS WAR

English Aquitaine
as by Treaty of 1259. ——————

Edward III's
possessions by Treaty
of Bretigny 1360. ——————

Miles

0   20   40   60   80   100

farther into the heart of old English Aquitaine; the coast towns especially were wholly English in sympathy. The Prince turned fiercely on the track of the Duke of Berri, and sacked, with horrid slaughter, the "rebel" city of Limoges, thereby incurring the one stain of cruelty which rests upon his memory. In January 1371 he returned to England completely broken in health; though he lingered for five years more, he lived in retirement till his last year. He left his brother, John of Gaunt, as his lieutenant in Aquitaine. John did nothing to defend the country; he contracted a marriage with a daughter of the deceased Pedro of Castile, and set off to claim the crown of that kingdom in right of his wife. By the end of 1372 all Poitou was in French hands; by 1374 all the highlands of Guienne and Gascony. Then a truce was made till 1377, but only a few days before the death of King Edward (June 1377) a French and Castilian fleet swept the Channel, burnt Rye, Winchelsea, Lewes, Dartmouth, and Plymouth, and insulted Southampton, Dover, and Calais; it kept the sea till 1380, once even penetrating the estuary of the Thames. The last fearful raid of John of Gaunt—a "ride" from Calais to Bordeaux in 1373 —had produced simply no effect, and, when King Edward died, Bordeaux, Bayonne, and Dax were all that remained of English Aquitaine.

What a change! King Edward's last years, which were thus closing in disaster abroad, were a record of shame at home as well. His good Queen had died in 1369, and he gave himself up to unworthy favourites; his second surviving son, John of Gaunt, aspired to fill the place in his father's councils that his nobler brother Edward had held till sickness incapacitated him. John somewhat recalls Henry III. in his restlessness and his futility, though not in the blameless character of that prince's private life.   He was immoral, and set an immoral tone to the Court.   There was a spirit of unrest in the air, which, in the next reign, was to break out openly in the Lollard movement.   When John returned to England, in 1374, he set himself to overthrow his father's wise minister, William of Wykeham (Bishop of Winchester, and founder of the oldest English public school).·   He hounded on all the discontented elements of Society to an attack on clerical property, merely from a desire to acquire popularity.   His ambitious designs were so manifest that his brother Edward, dying as he was, was driven to come forward and oppose them in the Parliament of 1376.   It is possible that John already aimed at the crown ; he was Duke of Lancaster, for he had married as his first wife Earl Henry's daughter, and the name of " Lancaster" was still something to conjure with.   But Parliament rallied as one man round the ten-year-old heir of the Black Prince, and, lest the old King should be talked over by Prince John, it made a clean sweep of the court favourites and impeached several bad ministers ; it even went so far as to appoint a large commission of reform, somewhat on the lines of those of 1310 and 1258.   The Black Prince died, 8th June 1376, while Parliament was still sitting ; John of Gaunt at once set aside all its acts, imprisoned its leading members, and for a year governed the kingdom very badly in his father's name. A year after his eldest son's death, King Edward followed him to the grave, June 23, 1377.

> " Mighty victor, Mighty Lord,
> Low on his funeral couch he lies.
> No pitying eye, no heart afford
> A tear to grace his obsequies.
> Is the sable warrior fled ?
> Thy son is gone.   He rests among the dead.
> The swarm that in thy noontide beam were born,
> Gone to salute the rising morn."

So Gray's Welsh bard wove in burning prophecy the winding-sheet of the race of that first Edward who had extinguished the independence of Wales. And the King passes, a doubtful figure, across the stage of history. But it is not so much to Edward III. as to his son that the thoughts of all Englishmen turn when they seek to recall the man who first made " British Infantry " a word to conjure with on the Continent. When his last hour had come, the Black Prince asked to see once more the faithful companions who had fought round him, and asked pardon of them all if he had offended any, and then he committed his son to their care ; and so died. You may see his helmet and his tattered surcoat yet hanging above his tomb in Canterbury Cathedral, " the veritable arms worn by the first great English soldier."

Edward III.'s reign is remarkable for the great increase of the legislative work of Parliament and the greatly increased power — one might almost say the preponderance—of the House of Commons, in which from this time men with purely English surnames form the large majority. These gentlemen were fond of describing themselves as the " poor silly Commons, who did not understand such matters," when Edward consulted them (as he invariably did) upon any big matter of foreign policy; but in reality their control of the purse gave them the yea and nay to every serious question. Though it is not till Henry IV.'s reign an established principle that only in the House of Commons can a tax be first voted, it is a regular practice throughout the latter part of Edward III.'s. One may well ask how Edward found money for his wars ; and the answer is— by the export of raw wool. The more the Continent was desolated, the more precious English wool became ; the price of a sack of wool varied from £2 to £8, and yet Parliament was able on one occasion to lay on an export duty of £5 per sack.   Fancy the feelings of the Flemish merchants at this !   But they had to pay, or go without the wool.   Of course they raised the price of cloth all over Europe, and so those who wore clothes had to pay more for them.   Extra taxes on imports (nearly all luxuries) also afforded Edward a considerable revenue ; we once find £1, 13s. 4d. levied on the tun or barrel of wine, and 6s. 8d. is a not infrequent rate. We must remember, however, that for the future the return from import customs will increase, while that from export customs will decrease, as Englishmen begin to use their own wool for weaving their own cloth ; but this is a change hardly felt by the revenue before the middle of the fifteenth century.

The direct land-and-property tax, which we have met in the twelfth and thirteenth centuries under various names, gets itself finally fixed in Edward's reign as a "tenth-and-fifteenth," and professes to be a tax of a tenth of your income if you live in a town or on the King's "demesne" land, and a fifteenth if you live elsewhere.   If it had really been kept up to this, it would have been a gigantic income-tax, and would have made the Crown very rich, as land went on increasing in value.   But it would have been necessary for the Crown to make the most searching inquiries every year into the actual value of men's lands and personal property ;   and so, to avoid this trouble, in 1334 the plan was adopted of fixing what a " tenth-and-fifteenth " ought to produce ; it was found to be £38,000.   If in that year you paid 3s. and I paid 2s., we should go on paying the same sum and no more, every time that Parliament voted the King a tenth-and-fifteenth. Seldom over £32,000 was actually produced by this tax, for some of us had been burnt out and some of us had been flooded out, and the plague had hit some of us too hard, and the King was almost as bad at collecting his debts as at paying them. Very rarely Parliament voted to raise a "Poll-tax," that is a fixed sum *per* head of the whole population; such a tax was never really profitable to the Crown. The result was that, as far as direct taxation was concerned, England remained a very lightly taxed country till the great civil war of the seventeenth century.

The surrender of the royal right to "tallage" from the towns and the royal demesne (1340), and the regulation of the import duties by the "Statute of the Staple" (1353), completed the control of Parliament over taxation.

There is a Parliament in most years; indeed, there is an Act of 1330 which says there shall be one every year. Parliament is divided into the two Houses, which sit separately from 1339, if not earlier. The members of the Lower House are paid wages—4s. a day for a knight of the shire, and 2s. a day for a burgess, and these sums are raised from their constituents. Some towns object so much to pay these wages that they petition to get off sending members; it shows how little the glorious privilege of "heckling his Majesty's Government" was valued in those days. Some actually did drop out of the list, including Birmingham—a fact which is apt to make one smile when one reflects that it was Birmingham which, in 1832, led the cry for the Reform Bill.

Before the death of Edward III. it was usual, though not absolutely necessary, that both Houses of Parliament should consent to the general tenour of all laws to be passed, but the form to be given to the laws still rested with the King. Not before Henry IV. or Henry V. was it laid down that the King must legislate in the actual form of words of the "Bill" which had passed both

Houses. Further, both Houses, but especially the Commons, thoroughly made good their right to inquire into, and demand redress of all abuses of the King's administration. In particular, this weapon was directed against the extravagance of the Court, which in Edward's later days was very great. The Commons audited the King's accounts; and, once at least, they appointed two citizens of London to receive the taxes voted for the war, and to see that they were applied to the war and to that only. In 1376 the "Good Parliament" exercised for the first time that curious right of "impeachment," *i.e.* of bringing to trial before the House of Lords, at the petition of the House of Commons, sundry of the King's ministers and favourites. This established the doctrine of the "responsibility of ministers to Parliament," and was to grow into the modern doctrine that "there is no act for which the King is, or some minister is not, responsible." You see it is really a way of shielding the King. When you impeach Lord Latimer, chamberlain to King Edward III., of "high crimes and misdemeanours," or the Earl of Strafford (in Charles I.'s time) of high treason, you are really striking at the King's own misgovernment. In your heart you know that it is the King who has ordered Latimer or Strafford to commit the crimes or the treason alleged; but it won't do to say so. It would lead to constant revolutions if you did. So the King shall be inviolable, but the agents of his misgovernment shall be extremely violable. This is a most useful weapon if Parliament is loyal; but in the hands of factious men it is a very dangerous one; it may be used to paralyse all government.

The other most remarkable pieces of legislation of the reign of Edward are the Statutes of "Provisors" (1351) and "Praemunire" (1353). Both are directed against papal pretensions, and neither of them pleases the clergy. "Provisors" enacts that the Pope shall not in future appoint to any bishoprics or benefices in England; and "Praemunire" is to some extent a corollary of "Provisors." It declares the penalties of imprisonment and forfeiture of goods against any person bringing in papal bulls or letters without the leave of the Crown, or suing in the papal court on any matters in which the royal courts have lawful jurisdiction. It is easy to see that the motive for both these acts was the fact that the Pope was now the tool of the French king. Neither statute was very carefully observed, and the Kings themselves were constantly driven to get the help of the Popes in forcing the cathedral chapters to elect to bishoprics persons acceptable to the Crown.

Genealogies are very tiresome things, but I fear it is quite necessary for our future guidance to understand rightly the lines of the descendants of Edward III. He had many children, of whom five are of first-rate importance.

(1) The Black Prince married Joan of Kent, daughter of that Earl of Kent who was put to death in 1330. He left one son, Richard II., who died without heirs of his body, and so his line came to an end.

(2) Lionel, Duke of Clarence, died before his father; he married a great Irish heiress of the de Burgh family, and left one daughter, Philippa, who married Edmund Mortimer, Earl of March (grandson of the traitor), and Philippa and Edmund left one son, Roger, who was consequently the next heir to the crown after Richard II. This Roger left a son, Edmund, who died childless in 1424, and a daughter, Anne, who married her cousin, Richard, Earl of Cambridge, and became *ancestress of the House of York in the first or female line.*

(3) John of Gaunt was thrice married. By Blanche

of Lancaster he had Henry, Earl of Derby, afterwards Henry IV., and so was the *ancestor of the House of Lancaster;* by Constance of Castile he had no sons; by Catherine Swynford he had John Beaufort, Earl of Somerset, who, though born before wedlock, was legitimated by an Act of Parliament; and from him descended Margaret Beaufort, mother of Henry VII.; and so John of Gaunt was also *ancestor of the House of Tudor.*

(4) Edmund, Duke of York, had two sons, the Duke of Aumale who died childless, and Richard, Earl of Cambridge, who married Anne Mortimer (see above, No. 2), and their son was Richard, Duke of York, father of Edward IV. So Edmund was *ancestor of the House of York in the second or male line.* Remember that by English law the girls of an elder son inherit before the boys of a younger son, and so the Yorkist claim is really derived not from Edmund of York, but from Lionel of Clarence.[1]

(5) Thomas, Duke of Gloucester, ancestor of the Earls of Stafford and Dukes of Buckingham.

These sons of King Edward and their descendants owned between them more than half the earldoms and baronies of England, and were very soon going to fall out about them. Edward had "busied giddy minds with foreign quarrels," but when Edward was gone and the foreign quarrels slept, the giddy minds began to busy themselves about domestic quarrels instead, so the prospects of the reign of little Richard were anything but rosy when his grandfather died.

---

[1] I have, here and elsewhere, followed the received view as to the descent of the crown: but we must remember that in 1399, there was, with respect to the claims of the houses of March and Lancaster, no actual precedent. Stephen and Henry II. had both claimed through females, but there were then no possible male heirs. In 1461 the precedent of 1399 was upset, and the rule of 1461 has been maintained ever since; e.g. in 1837 when Queen Victoria succeeded to the exclusion of her uncle the King of Hanover.

CHAPTER XVII

RICHARD II. AND THE GERM OF PROTESTANTISM

THE twenty-two years of Richard II.'s reign are about the most unintelligible in the whole of our history. As regards mere "politics," the difficulty consists in the character of the King ; but as regards war and national life, it is by no means easy to explain the contrast between the vigour and activity displayed (even in wrong directions, such as rebellion and massacre) by nearly all classes of the nation, and the apparent failure of the nation all round. Let us clear away the dreary politics before passing to the social and religious history of the period.

Richard appears by turns merciful and savage, patient and impetuous, brave and cowardly. In Shakespeare's play, of which he is the hero, something of this complexity of character is shown ; but we must remember that the poet had at once to uphold the semi-divine character of anointed kingship, and to signalise the triumph of the House of Lancaster. He was writing in the reign of Elizabeth Tudor, and the Tudors were in their own eyes before all things Lancastrians ; yet to glorify Lancaster meant in this case to glorify usurpation. So, if Richard is at one time "the skipping king that ambled up and down with shallow jesters and rash bavin wits," "landlord of England, not king," "who hath pilled the commons with grievous taxes, and allto lost their hearts," who "hath spent more in peace than his ancestors in wars," at other times he is "Richard, that sweet lovely rose," "the deputy elected by the Lord," from whom "not all the water in the rough rude sea can wash the balm." When the end comes, the poet makes him take it philosophically ; he professes himself ready to change his "gorgeous palace for a hermitage " ; he declares that

> " With my own tears I wash away my balm,
> With my own hands I give away my crown,
> With my own tongue deny my sacred state."

Yet he displays occasional spurts of sacred rage against the impious usurper. Then we have the Bishop of Carlisle, who alone stood up for the deposed monarch, uttering the terrible and true prophecy of how, for this usurpation—

> " The blood of English shall manure the ground,
> And future ages groan for this foul act,
> . . . and this land be called
> The field of Golgotha and dead men's skulls."

The poet was right to concentrate all the action of his play on the last three years of the reign, for it is these alone that are intelligible from a political point of view.

As far as the war was concerned, there was little peace and little fighting. John of Gaunt made two more futile attempts on the crown of Castile (1377 and 1386), and on the latter occasion was absent for four years. The warlike Bishop of Norwich headed a raid in Flanders in 1383, which he had the impudence to call a crusade because it was nominally directed against the adherents of the French Pope (there was a Roman Pope, too, now); but no effectual help was given to the latest rising of the Flemish cities against their Count and the King of France ; and Philip van Arteveld (son of Jacques), who headed it, was overpowered and killed at Roosebec (1382). The Breton alliance was finally lost in 1380; if Bordeaux and some other Gascon towns held out, it was mainly owing to the utter weakness of the French Government under Charles VI., who succeeded his father in 1380, and who soon went mad. Some hope of assistance from Germany was entertained when in 1382 Richard married Anne of Bohemia (a daughter of the Emperor), but no help came ; and we actually had to ask leave of the French fleet to · conduct the lady in safety from Calais to Dover. The Scots border raids continued with wearisome regularity, and we begin to hear of the great power of the Percies, Earls of Northumberland, whose retainers almost reached the dignity of a standing army. John of Gaunt remained nominal governor of a nominal Aquitaine, and occasionally visited Bordeaux, but all he did there was to drain it of money for his Spanish job. A long truce with France was finally concluded in 1396 when Richard married as his second wife the French child-princess Isabel. This series of complete failures is the more remarkable when we reflect that France was economically in a far worse state than England, and politically in as bad a state. In both countries the princes of the blood were flying at each other's throats, and shaking the crowns on the heads of their respective kings. In France these horrors continued till Henry V. in 1415 took advantage of them to renew the war.

In England the quarrels began almost from the coronation of Richard, a month after his grandfather's death. John of Gaunt was throughout his life an object of distrust to his nephew, and to the widowed Princess-mother, by whose councils Richard was at first largely guided; he was an object of hatred to the Londoners, who remembered his extortionate government during Edward's last years. He certainly was the enemy of the Church, or at least of the leading great churchmen, William of Wykeham, Courtenay Bishop of London, and of that very party which afterwards put his son on the throne. It was even believed that Richard had applauded the destruction of John's palace of "Savoy" by the London mob in 1381. Yet I find no evidence of actual disloyalty to Richard on his part, and from 1384 he took no active interest in English politics.

The other figures of mark are John's two brothers, Edmund, Duke of York, who was loyal to Richard from the beginning till almost the end of his reign, and who then suddenly and inexplicably deserted him ; and Thomas, Duke of Gloucester, who was disloyal throughout, and who played the same part to Richard as Thomas of Lancaster had played to Edward II. Then there is Henry of Bolingbroke, Earl of Derby and Duke of Hereford, afterwards King Henry IV., whose tortuous career of disloyalty and loyalty, and again disloyalty, was crowned by his usurpation of the throne in 1399 ; Roger, Earl of March, the real heir to the crown, who throughout seems to have hated the house of Lancaster more than he loved the King; he was killed in Ireland in 1398, but left children who were the rightful heirs. There is a shadowy Earl of Arundel, brother of an Archbishop Arundel—he is steadily disloyal ; a shadowy Earl of Warwick, steadily disloyal ; a shadowy Earl of Nottingham, created Duke of Norfolk, disloyal, loyal, disloyal, and dying in exile. But of one and all of these we may safely predicate that they were " over-mighty subjects," grasping at more earldoms and more riches, and not caring what they shattered in the process. Among the favourites of Richard only one bore an old historic name, Robert de Vere, Earl of Oxford, whom the King created Marquis of Dublin ; nothing good is known of him. Michael de la Pole,

Earl of Suffolk, was an old administrator of Edward III., and seems to have been an honest man. Tressilian was an upright, if very severe, judge. Most of the other favourites, like Sir Simon Burley, were old companions of the Black Prince. But they all seem to have rendered themselves obnoxious to the princes of the blood without ingratiating either themselves or their master with the Commons. The House of Commons during the reign has been well compared to the chorus in a Greek play, which keeps up a running fire of complaint against everything that happens.

The full force of faction hardly began to manifest itself before John of Gaunt's departure for Castile in 1386. In that year Richard was almost twenty, but was still childless, and Gloucester probably began to aim at the crown. At any rate he began the game by bringing forward in full Parliament a long string of charges against the King's favourites and ministers, and demanding the appointment of a Commission of Government on the model of that of 1310. Richard appeared to give way and retired to the west, but soon after took the not unnatural step of asking the judges their opinion as to the legality of the action of Gloucester, and of his own consent to the Commission. The judges unanimously replied in favour of the Crown, and the King returned to London to put his power to the test. But the Duke of Gloucester and his friends had surrounded London with troops, and the city was apparently hostile to the King. In November 1387 five peers, Gloucester, Warwick, Arundel, Nottingham, and Derby, accused of treason the entire body of the King's party, who fled as best they could. De Vere attempted civil war, but, being in command of only a few Cheshire loyalists, was easily overpowered at Radcot, near Oxford. The Parliament of January 1388 was entirely under Glou-

T

cester's influence, and condemned to death most of the King's friends, including Suffolk, Oxford, Tressilian, and Burley; as well as all the judges (though these were afterwards let off), the Archbishop of York, and a number of minor people. Not all were hanged, for some escaped to die in exile, but a whole sea of blood was shed. One mentions it only to show that a wholesale proscription of the defeated party had become a regular thing in " party government."

Richard acquiesced : a better man would have abdicated, a greater man would have cut his way through to Cheshire (where alone he appears to have had real adherents), and raised forces somewhere, somehow, or died sword in hand. But in acquiescing he only bided his time. He pretended to believe in Gloucester's loyalty, he employed him in diplomacy, in war, in Parliament; he won over Nottingham and Derby by slow degrees to betray their former friends. For eight years the King's tameness appeared to be complete ; then, in 1397, perhaps considering that he had given Gloucester rope enough, he suddenly arrested him and Warwick and Arundel, and Arundel's brother, the Archbishop. Gloucester was sent to Calais, where he was almost certainly murdered ; Arundel was publicly executed ; Warwick and the Archbishop were banished. The bloodshed was not so wholesale as in 1388, and no minor people suffered. But as in 1388 the victorious party had called on Parliament to ratify the proscriptions, so in 1398 the Parliament of Shrewsbury was made the instrument of vengeance. It passed four memorable Acts besides. By the first it made to the King the grant of the customs for life, whereas till now it had been the practice to grant them afresh in each Parliament ; by the second it delegated its powers to a small committee of twelve peers and six commoners, thus really voting itself out of existence and voting parliamentary government to be a sham; by the third it repealed in a lump all the Acts of 1388; by the fourth it declared it to be high treason ever to seek to upset the Acts of this present Parliament.

Thus Richard was practically left absolute. But unfortunately he had terrified, without striking down, the other princes of the blood and great earls. Derby and Nottingham, now respectively Dukes of Hereford and Norfolk, had been partners in the guilt of Gloucester and Arundel, and, though pardoned, they could hardly expect to feel safe under such a king. They are said to have met out riding, and to have communicated their fears to each other. Hereford betrayed Norfolk's confidence to the King; each called the other shocking names, which apparently each well deserved; and a set duel in the presence of the King was decided on. If two gentlemen in those days said to each other "You lie in your teeth," the best way of settling the matter was held to be an "appeal to the judgment of God," *i.e.* to duel. The lists were fixed at Coventry; but, just as the Dukes were preparing to fight, the King stopped the combat and banished both of them. Probably nothing discredited King Richard so much in the eye of the common people as this "unsportsmanlike" conduct; the actual belief in trial by battle being God's judgment was no longer strong, but the disappointment of the thousands who must have travelled long distances to see the fight (Sept. 1398) can well be imagined.

Richard possibly regarded himself as being at last master of his kingdom, at any rate he acted as such; he raised money by "forced loans" from rich people; he compelled all the adherents of the old opposition to buy their pardons, and to buy them very dear; and when John of Gaunt died, in February 1399, he confiscated

his vast estates, as he had already confiscated Gloucester's.   But he had expressly promised to Henry of
Hereford that, when his father died, he should succeed
to his titles and property even though banished.

The result was that Henry, who had gone to France,
only watched for the first opportunity of revenge.   This
chance Richard gave him by going to Ireland, in May
1399, to put down a revolt there.   Henry at once landed
in Yorkshire, professing to claim only his earldoms and
his father's Duchy of Lancaster.   Richard had left the
regency in England to his uncle of York, who exhibited
either utter incapacity or shameless treachery ; without
openly playing into Henry's hands, York allowed the
Duke to gather forces unopposed wherever he went,
and to act as if he were already king.   The Percies,
with all their northern army, joined Henry, who moved
about the kingdom displacing and imprisoning Richard's
officers.   Not till they reached Bristol did the heading
and hanging begin ; but, once begun, it went on vigorously—a regular proscription in revenge for 1397–98.
The house of Lancaster certainly waded to the throne
through blood, and the bloodshed was by no means
ended with the murder of Richard at Pontefract.

Richard had been detained some weeks in Ireland
by head winds, but at last he landed in Wales, where,
finding Henry's followers in too great force, he tamely
surrendered.   No word of his deposition was mentioned till he was brought to London, where an Act,
professing to be a voluntary abdication on his part,
was read in Parliament, and Henry IV. was elected
king.   Nor was a word spoken of the claims of the
rightful heir, little Edmund of March.   The exiled
Archbishop Arundel returned and placed the crown
on Henry's head.   Soon after this Richard "disappeared."   A bad king who had disgusted his people ?

Yes; and who was deposed by a bad baron, who did not please them much more or govern them much better.

Few revolutions have ever been taken so quietly by the country, and, had the house of Lancaster been as strong as it was at first popular, it might well have inaugurated a new era. For it was more the Government and a few of the great nobles that were rotten than the nation at large. When Richard ascended the throne the nation was steadily recovering from the economic crisis of thirty years before; prices were falling, and wages rising to meet them; landlords were rapidly adapting themselves to the changed conditions. But the country gentleman was isolated on his estate; the feudal tie between him and his tenants was dead; in his isolation he too often attached himself to the train of some great lord or prince of the blood, pledged himself to maintain his patron's quarrel, and thought no shame to wear his "livery"; hence, even when he came to Parliament, he came as a pledged partisan. The yeomen, the "franklins" of Chaucer's "Canterbury Tales," were rich and comfortable—it "snowed meat and drink in their houses"; but they were seldom called out in the militia, as they had been in the thirteenth century, so they became more and more money-getting and unwarlike, while the hired retainers of the nobles became more and more like professional soldiers. The once powerful sheriff was now a person of second-rate importance in his county; the judges had taken from him all his real judicial business, the "Commissions of Array" had weakened his military leadership, the justices of the peace (whose power had been greatly extended by Edward III.) were stripping him of his administration of "county business." He still presided at parliamentary elections, and still impanelled juries to meet the judges on circuit, but he was very apt to receive a letter from the Earl of Oxford or the Duke of Norfolk threatening him horribly if he did not procure the election to Parliament of some friend of theirs, or if he impanelled a jury which should presume to find a verdict against them in any lawsuit they might have.   In fact sheriff, jury, and often judge, were at the mercy of the great man of the county, whoever he might be.   The practice known as "maintenance and champerty" was open and avowed : the Duke of Gloucester would come forward and give evidence in open court on behalf of some tame murderer of his own, and would threaten bench, bar, and jury with open violence if the man were not let off.   And he usually was let off.   Even the King derived more strength from his possession of the Earldoms of Cornwall and Chester than from his royal crown.   Richard had his band of retainers, just like any other great earl, and they went about embroidered all over with " white harts."

The bishops and abbots were either trembling in their shoes at the outcry against clerical wealth, or were prosecuting their episcopal and abbatial lawsuits about property at distant Rome or Avignon.   Few of the clergy were like Chaucer's "poor parson of a town," who

> " Christ's lore, and His Apostles' twelve
> He taught, but first he followed it himself. "

See how the clerical society of that day is made to pass before us by the first great English poet in the Prologue to the "Canterbury Tales."   There is the friar "wanton and merry," who wanders over the country "hearing confessions sweetly" and "giving pleasant absolution " and "knowing the taverns well in every town " ; "summoners" and "pardoners" selling the

Pope's "licences to sin for a good twelvemonth"; the monk whose "favourite roast was a fat swan," and who thinks of nothing but eating and drinking and fine clothes; while the prioress, though she can sing divine service and "entune in her nose full seemly," and has good manners at table, is yet dressed up to her very grey eyes, and bears the extremely unreligious device of "*Amor vincit omnia*" on her gold brooch. True, there is the "clerk of Oxford," but he has not yet gotten him a benefice, not being worldly enough for one; but what can you expect of a man who prefers twenty volumes of Aristotle to rich robes, fiddle, and psaltery?

The lay society which accompanies these clerical pilgrims stands in distinct contrast to them. Chaucer is tolerant and satirical, as becomes a man of the world who has been in the household of good Queen Philippa and of John of Gaunt. He is not unduly severe against vice, whether clerical or lay: the miller is a thief—it is an old tradition about millers; the "doctor of physick" is a manifest humbug; the "sergeant-at-law" is too fond of unintelligible law phrases; the "wife of Bath" is a professional she-pilgrim, who has been thrice to Jerusalem and to every other fashionable pilgrimage in the world; the two stewards are grasping and subtle; but it would be hard to find in the whole range of satirical poetry more honest and honourable characters than the knight, the squire, the yeoman, the franklin, the merchant, the ploughman; if the sea-captain has a touch of piracy in him, it is mainly because the Government neglects to keep the sea clear of hostile pirates, and so one must act for oneself.

At the opposite pole of Society to Chaucer, the court favourite, comes William Langland, the half-crazy clerk, to whom everything is evil and all classes rotten

to the core, the clerical class worst of all.   The hope
of the poor is in the Crown alone.   Langland's "Vision
of Piers Plowman," followed by the "Creed" and
"Complaint" of the same, appeared at intervals from
1362 ; the wide diffusion of these works among the lower
classes proves that there were readers among them,
and is proved by the fact that "Piers the Plowman"
was a favourite watchword of the rebels of 1381.   If
Langland is furious against lawyers and hard landlords,
he is infinitely more so against all classes of churchmen ;
he denounces especially the system of penances, pilgrimages, and pardons sold for money ; much of his
work reminds one of the more sombre passages in the
Psalms, which he so often quotes.   But it was an age
of fierce lampoons and political songs, nine-tenths of
which were directed against the clergy.

Two things have rendered the reign of Richard really
memorable, and both were symptoms of a state of
unrest and discontent in a society that was still full
of vitality—the peasant revolt of 1381, and the beginning
of the English Reformation.

With one exception—that of John Ball, priest—
the leaders of the peasant revolt are obscure and unknown.   Ever since the attempts to enforce the "Statute
of Labourers" there had been growing up combinations
of peasants organised to defeat these attempts, and
striving to raise wages.   They had been very successful.
Leaders of these "strikes," Ball among them, travelled
far over Southern and Mid-England between 1377 and
1380 ; but it is a mistake to connect their work with
that of Wyclif's "poor priests" (of whom more anon),
for the latter were not organised till 1382.   There were
many disbanded soldiers and fugitive ex-villeins among
the strikers.   There is no truth in the view that it
was hunger and misery that caused the insurrection ;

Langland's evidence is directly to the contrary; wages, he says, were everywhere high in 1380, and the labourers were fat and idle.   Rather it was an all-round attempt to throw off the last vestiges of villeinage, on which stress was being laid by harsh or impoverished landlords, just because they were the last vestiges.   The poll-tax of 1380—the third poll-tax in three years, and almost the only instance of severe direct taxation that mediæval England ever knew—no doubt counted for something; but, above all, the peasants decided to throw off a multitude of small and vexatious grievances and petty "rents in kind"—the two hens at Easter, the dozen eggs at Michaelmas, the fine of fourpence for leave to marry a daughter, the necessity of bringing their corn to the lord's mill to be ground.   The destruction of manor rolls and title-deeds on which these vexatious little rents were written down, and of the lawyers who enforced them, were avowed objects of the peasants. Everything should be reduced to a money rent of fourpence per acre, was the cry.   Anything like communism, or forcible overthrow of property or destruction of the upper classes, is conspicuously absent from their programme.   Where landlords were reputed hard grinders of the poor they were murdered, and among the most hated landlords were the great monasteries, such as Chester, Bury, Peterborough and St. Albans, which all felt the fury of the revolt.   Lawyers were murdered wholesale, as were also foreigners (especially Flemings), and tax-collectors, and the agents of the King's bad Government.   The insurgents would not have been fourteenth-century Englishmen if they had not started with the rooted idea that, if only the King knew, he would do them justice; and in proportion to their devout belief in the King was their bitter hatred of his officers.   The Archbishop of Canterbury,

Simon of Sudbury, a mild old man of lowly origin, and very much under the thumb of the fierce Bishop Courtenay of London, was a special object of hatred; but it was as chancellor, not as archbishop. John Hales, the treasurer, was another specially odious person. The insurrection was not, as has been asserted, everywhere simultaneous; on the contrary it spread in regular fashion from county to county, and was over in London before it began in Yorkshire. But it was quick, and rather remarkably so, which looks as if it had been prepared. It began in Essex in the end of May 1381; a few days later it spread to Kent, and it has been called "Wat Tyler's" rebellion, from a Maidstone man who bore that name and who afterwards played a leading part in London. From the first it was signalised by sporadic murder, and by 10th June all the home counties were ablaze. It spread as far north as Yorkshire and as far west as Somerset, but was of very unequal violence in the different provinces. London was in the gravest danger, for it was occupied by the insurgents, who were admitted to the city by treachery. The London 'prentices sympathised with them and used the whole thing as a means of wreaking vengeance on the hated Flemish colony of weavers, and on John of Gaunt, whose palace of the Savoy was burned to the ground.

The King's "Government" shut themselves and him up in the Tower, for the authorities were everywhere paralysed except Walworth, the brave Mayor of London, and the fourteen-year-old King himself. The mob roamed over London for three days and nights, and behaved as mobs usually do. The King, being persuaded to go out and hold a conference with the rebel leaders at Mile End, showed great coolness and courage, but was obliged to promise all they asked.

During his absence the mob broke into the Tower and murdered the Archbishop and the Treasurer. At a second meeting, three days later, in Smithfield, it became evident that many of the peasants, trusting to the King's promises, had gone home ; the respectable classes in London had meanwhile been arming secretly, and Walworth had enlisted the services of Sir R. Knollys, one of the Black Prince's old companions. So when Tyler, as spokesman for the mob in Smithfield, began to put forward some fresh demands to Richard, the Mayor rode up and struck him to the ground, and he was immediately slain. For a moment every bow in the market-place was bent at the royal party, but, with surprising coolness, little Richard rode forward and said, "Tyler was a traitor—I am your leader," and they suffered him to lead them out to Clerkenwell fields. There they found themselves surrounded by armed knights, and surrendered at discretion. The rebellion smouldered for some weeks in the provinces, but the authorities everywhere took heart and put it down. At the next assizes bloody reprisals followed all over the country; the Government had received a rude shock, and avenged it rudely. The violation of all the promises made by the King at Mile End also followed. But villeinage was dead of itself ; a statute of 1390 recognised the impossibility of reviving it, and allowed wages to be fixed in each district by the justices of the peace. The rebellion had neither hastened nor retarded the economic change.

One result the rebellion had, and an evil one : it threw the churchmen more and more into the hands of the statesmen, and the statesmen into the hands of the churchmen. Though there was no real connection between the rebellion and the growth of free religious thought, the fact that the two had begun simultaneously

gave the bishops courage to confuse them, and to per-
secute new opinions.   Courtenay succeeded Sudbury
as archbishop and chancellor, and Arundel afterwards
succeeded Courtenay.   Both Courtenay and Arundel
were of the temper of persecutors.   It is in 1377 that we
first hear of a man arraigned for heresy in England;
the judge is Courtenay, and the man is called JOHN
WYCLIF.

The first real notice that we have of Wyclif is as
Master of Balliol College, in 1361; but he seems to have
been a Yorkshireman, and born about 1320.   Till 1374,
when he received the living of Lutterworth in Leicestershire, he resided principally in Oxford, and was known
mainly as the greatest logician of his day.   The dates
of his innumerable pamphlets are hard to determine,
but his most famous work, "De Dominio Civili," was
written in 1368.   He, if any one, carried on the opposition to the papacy begun by Grosseteste, in the thirteenth century.   He quotes Grosseteste freely, and looks
upon him as his master; but he relies mostly upon
Scripture and the early "Fathers," against the whole
tradition of the mediæval Church.   Before the end of
Edward's reign he had recommended disendowment of
the richer sections of the Church, and so rendered himself obnoxious to Courtenay and his party.   He allowed
himself to be used by John of Gaunt as a tool for this
purpose.   Twice in 1377 he was arraigned of heresy.
On the first occasion he was saved by John; on the
second, by John's deadliest enemy—the mob of London.
Neither of these facts are promising beginnings for a
reformer.   In 1382 he was again attacked, but not
arraigned in person, and, in 1384, he died in peace.
The legal power of the English bishops to condemn a
heretic to death was more than doubtful.   Had such
power been known to the law, it is almost certain it

would have been used in Wyclif's case, for he published his opinions quite openly; they spread widely before his death, and, though he was ready with logical explanations, he never recanted them. Finally, he attacked many of the cardinal doctrines of the mediæval Church. Attempts have been made to show that Wycliffism, or "Lollardry," as its nickname was (*i.e.* babbling), had no connection with, and little influence on our subsequent Reformation, but such attempts are quite hopeless. Wyclif was a Protestant, pure and simple, in nine out of ten theological positions that he took up. The only point in which he differs from the later reformers is in not denying purgatory. Let us try to realise his views as far as we can, and we shall see that they fall readily into line with those of such men as Latimer and Ridley. They are as follows :—

(1) The Pope, if not actually anti-Christ, is a totally unnecessary person, and not head of the Church at all. Christ is the Head of the Church.

(2) Masses for the souls of the dead, pilgrimages, penances, pardons at the hands of the clergy, are a delusion and a fraud—invented by the priests for the purpose of draining the laity of money.

(3) Holy Scripture is the sole rule of life, and should be in English; and Wyclif, or his followers, proceeded to translate it.

(4) Ceremonial is nothing, and is rather a hindrance than a help in man's personal relation to God, which is not bettered by the intervention of any priest. Man is to be saved by the mercy of God and faith in that mercy, and by living a good life.

(5) In the Mass, the bread and wine remain bread and wine after consecration, although spiritually they are, to the receiver, the most holy Body and Blood of Christ.

It is dreadful to have to discuss such mysteries as this last in a mere history book, yet we cannot understand the Reformation without doing so.   In reflecting on them, we may well pause before we speak harshly of those who persecuted the early reformers.   The daily miracle of the Mass, whereby every priest believed that he made every day, upon the altar, bread and wine into the most holy Body and Blood, had become the whole life of the Church.   If that were true, he who denied it was worthy of any death which human ingenuity could devise.   Take that away, and the whole foundations of the faith of Christendom seemed to crumble.   And all the persecutors firmly believed that to be true.   Wyclif refused to believe it to be true ; and he argued that, in its crudest shape, the belief could only be traced back a few centuries.   He firmly held, as nearly all subsequent Protestants have held, that in receiving the sacrament of bread and wine we do spiritually receive Our Saviour ; but that the bread remains bread and the wine remains wine.

In all the points above laid down Wyclif was truly what he has been called—"the Morning Star of the Reformation."   His merciless logic even carried him farther than these points, and he held that the validity of all sacraments depends on the goodness of the priest who administers them.   All churches have been obliged to reject this impossible position.   But for the most part Wyclif's doctrines are simple and intelligible to all.   The two main points that may be urged against him are : (1) that he was more destructive than constructive—he suggested no new form of Church government, though he was willing to pull down the existing one ; and (2) that towards the end of his life he even undervalued learning in the clergy.   His only foundation was his Order of " Poor Priests," and they were only to go about preaching; and he would have had them resemble the Apostles not only in their poverty, but in their ignorance of worldly learning, forgetful of the fact that it was the one learned Apostle, St. Paul, who really spread the Christian faith outside the narrow bounds of Syria. He saw with indifference the first attempt to root out his doctrines from his own University. Thus he appealed to the future, not to the present; one seems to see him in his study at Lutterworth looking dreamily "into the beyond," and having given up the expectation of immediate results. The beyond was undoubtedly his; and nothing made this more certain than his translation of the Bible into an English of a much more archaic type than that of Chaucer. There are comparatively few words of Latin derivation in this version, but all the same it is English and not late Anglo-Saxon (*e.g.* he calls the "resurrection of damnation" the "again-rising of doom"). There had been an Anglo-Saxon version, and there was a French version, but the main Bible of those days was the fifth-century Latin version of St. Jerome, known as the "Vulgate"; and the clergy had for centuries denied the laity full access even to that; in fact, with the exception of the Psalms (which every one knew) a layman needed episcopal licence to read scripture. Wyclif's Bible was seized and burnt wherever a bishop's hand could be laid on it, yet the existence of at least one hundred MSS. of it at the present day proves how very extensively copies of it must have been multiplied. And think of the enormous cost of multiplying before the invention of printing !

There was at first strong sympathy with Wyclif's doctrines in the upper classes, though not (as has been alleged) at Richard's Court. Richard was all for repression of free thought. But when these doctrines had been stamped out at Oxford in 1382, and again in 1409, the dissemination of them fell more and more into the hands of the unlearned, the field preachers, men of saintly evangelical life—often, after 1401, martyrs to the new faith—but not able to appeal to the educated laity as the learned reformers of the sixteenth century could. The "Lollards" were strongest in London, Leicestershire, and the diocese of Worcester; not till about 1415 did the movement take hold of the eastern counties (which were then far more intelligent that any part of England except London and Kent). The accession of the Lancastrians was marked by the definite commencement of real persecution, and Arundel was able to get through the Parliament of 1401 the Act "de Heretico Comburendo." By a later statute of 1414 heresy was made an offence at Common law, and sheriffs and justices were ordered to inquire after and arrest heretics, and to hand them over to the bishops for trial in the Church courts, which then handed them back to the sheriff to be burned alive. No one was to preach or teach without a licence from the bishop of his diocese. Not a great number of persons suffered death under these statutes before the commencement of the Tudor reigns; but Henry V., whose mind was of a narrow, fanatic type, was a fiercer persecutor than his father. A certain good Bishop Peacock who, in the year 1457, endeavoured to convert the Lollards instead of burning them, was very nearly burnt himself for advocating such a detestable heresy. After 1485 burnings multiplied, and, though the statutes were repealed in the brief reign of Edward VI., they were re-enacted under Mary; and her use of them gave her the nickname by which she has ever since been known. Elizabeth burned two heretics, and so did James I., but he was the last king who signed the bloody writ, and the statutes were finally repealed in the reign of Charles II.

CHAPTER XVIII

HENRY IV. AND HENRY V

THE "bad baron" who deposed Richard II. was not after all as bad a man as many of his contemporaries. His reign was a miserable one, because he was not strong enough to tame the forces which had put him on the throne, and which soon sought to put him off it. There is, I think, a strong family likeness running through the early Lancasters, and common to all of them except to the sainted Henry VI. From the Earl Thomas of Edward II.'s time onwards they are selfish, grasping, and unscrupulous; they are plausible, and hunters after popularity, which they generally manage to get. They are vindictive and cruel: Henry IV. was not specially so; before his accession he had been distinctly regarded as a "good fellow," in spite of some disgraceful acts of treachery (*e.g.* his betrayal of Norfolk in 1398). He had seen the world, had even been as far East as Prussia; he was fond of talking about Jerusalem and the crusades, and generally, until this his thirtieth year, had posed as a true chivalrous knight. After his accession it became at once manifest that the crown was too heavy a burden for him. He

> "himself knew well
> How troublesome it sat upon his head."

It had been purchased by bloodshed, and by bloodshed it had to be maintained. If Henry had a conscience—and we may suppose that he had—this may account for the melancholy and suspicious character

U

which he showed as king. His temperate private life and his anxiety to be honest in matters of finance, in spite of dire poverty, must be set to his credit. You may wonder at his poverty if you reflect upon the vast private estates of his house and the innumerable confiscations which every rebellion brought; but remember that for the lands of every disinherited person there were a dozen claimants who had helped the King to disinherit him. Only a very strong king like Henry II. can avoid rewarding his servants out of confiscations; and the king of a faction can never do so. If he does, they will simply go over to the opposite faction. Henry was always struggling with a load of debt, and always under the shadow of actual or possible treason. When open rebellions failed—and they were pretty well over by 1408—his enemies tried to poison his food, or hide in his bed weird instruments with sharp points to them. He fell ill of leprosy, and of that hideous disease known to modern cottagers as "bad leg"; he also suffered from epileptic fits. His younger sons were riotous, and his eldest son was ambitious and tried to induce him to abdicate. Among the baronial friends of his early days none stood by him when he became king. The rightful heir to the throne, the Earl of March, might be kept in safe confinement; but the mere name of "Mortimer" could, as Shakespeare said, make the usurper tremble.

Yet Henry's reign is memorable as a thoroughly "constitutional" one; the House of Commons was by no means liberal to him, but he was distinctly necessary to it; it knew itself his master, and, in a good-humoured way, it showed its teeth at him from time to time. He had to listen to long harangues from its speakers, to curtail his court, and to send away his second wife's Breton ladies at its orders. The House had genuinely hated Richard, though he had often been able to overawe it; it was a conservative and constitutional movement that had put Henry on the throne. It was also a clerical movement. But here he and the House differed, for the question of confiscating Church property was more than once mooted in Parliament, and Henry had some difficulty in staving it off. The privileges of freedom of debate and freedom from arrest of the members of both Houses were fairly won during the reign. Henry engaged, in 1406, to choose sixteen counsellors agreeable to Parliament to be about his person continually; in fact, he almost surrendered the nomination of members of his Privy Council to the two Houses. He gave the Lower House the sole right of bringing in bills concerning money (1407). He allowed it to audit his accounts, and to institute a regular system of "appropriation of supplies," under which each item of the revenue was to be devoted to a particular item of the expenses. The total revenue of Henry works out at just about £100,000 a year, of which Calais absorbed £30,000. Henry also allowed Parliament definitely to settle the succession to the Crown (1399, 1406). He also put the county franchise on a sound footing; knights of the shire were to be elected by all the freeholders of the county (1406). Twenty-four years later, an Act of Henry VI. defined the electors as freeholders possessing land worth forty shillings a year.

It all sounds very modern and "constitutional," but what was wanted was something the very reverse of this. A Henry II. was wanted, who would go about pulverising baronial castles and insolence, who would administer the law without fear or favour. Henry IV., busy man as he was, was quite incapable of this. In spite of his weak health, he travelled about his kingdom incessantly, and always at the call of duty;

but as soon as he was gone a few miles away, or even sometimes in his presence, the baronial influence asserted itself in private or civil war. There was no real peace in England any more than there was real peace with Scotland and France. What was the good of beautiful constitutional enactments when the French and Spaniards plundered all the sea-coasts, and the "keeping of the sea" had to be entrusted to an insurance company of merchants; when the Scots finally re-took Jedburgh (which England had retained since Neville's Cross), and even for a time held Berwick; when even a Welshman was in defiant and successful rebellion throughout the reign? It is true that these defeats and humiliations were wiped out in the next reign; whereas the constitutional enactments, being written on good durable parchment, survived to be used against the Stuarts in the seventeenth century.

The reign opens with a series of recriminations among those who had pulled down Richard. "Richard was alive"—in Cheshire; no, in Wales; no, in Scotland—it did not matter where; at any rate, March was alive. At Henry's first Parliament there were twenty gages of battle on the floor at once, flung at each other by fierce rival barons; "traitor" and "treason" were shouted across the "floor of the House" in a manner that would have appealed to modern "Irish members." The Acts of 1398 were repealed in the lump, as they deserved to be, but Henry contrived to avoid a wholesale proscription of Ricardians until an actual flag of rebellion was raised. He did not have to wait many weeks for this. False Richards — a "priest called Maudlin" was one of them — started up; one false Richard was long kept in Scotland as a bugbear to frighten the English king. Henry swooped down on the conspirators and hanged them up in rows, no less than eleven friars among them, which shocked his clerical friends. He went on to invade Scotland, the last King of England who did so in person. He reached the Forth, but had no other success. Robert III. of Scotland was a feeble prince, in ill-health, much governed by his brother, Albany, who was at feud with Robert's wild son, David of Rothesay. Albany caught Rothesay and starved him to death in Falkland Castle. Robert, in alarm, determined to send off his second son, James, to France, both to get him out of Albany's clutches and also to have him educated. The boy was captured on his voyage by an English ship and brought to Henry, who, remarking that "he could teach him French quite as well as King Charles," shut him up in the Tower (1405). Poor King Robert died on the receipt of this news, and Albany ruled Scotland. Henry V. transferred King James to Windsor, and he grew up in honourable captivity, made a love match with the English princess Joan Beaufort, wrote pretty verses, and returned to Scotland early in Henry VI.'s reign, to be the best King of Scotland since Robert Bruce.

The truce of 1396 with France had been confirmed in 1400, in terms somewhat contemptuous towards the English usurper, it is true; but there was nominal peace between the countries till 1410, and we cannot deny to Henry a strenuous desire to keep it. On the seas there was never peace at all, but the only good work on the English side was done by a famous pirate of Faversham, called Henry Pay, whom his enemies knew and dreaded as "Arripay." A Portuguese fleet appears occasionally lending aid to us in the Bay of Biscay; we can trace the connection between England and Portugal, her oldest and most constant ally, as far back as 1385.

Before Henry's return from Scotland Wales was ablaze under the famous Welsh squire, Owen Glendower, who claimed descent from the old line of Llewellyn, and who baffled Henry throughout his reign. It is amusing to read a proclamation of Henry against Welsh "bards, rhymers, and other vagabonds." Owen made war on the Mortimers, and took prisoner Sir Edward Mortimer, uncle of the Earl of March, and at once began to work upon the dynastic ambitions of that house. Henry, not feeling sorry that such a dangerous man as Mortimer should be under the lock and key even of a Welsh thief, refused to allow Sir Edward to be ransomed, and by-and-by Sir Edward ceased to wish it himself. Henry made two futile expeditions to Wales in 1401; but Owen was a statesman as well as a thief, and stirred up trouble from among all Henry's enemies, at home, in Scotland, and even in Ireland, where for a time three-quarters of the old Anglo-Irish families were up in arms. The Scots poured in on Northumberland, and were defeated by the Percies at Homildon Hill (August 1402), Archibald, Earl of Douglas, and Murdoch, son of Albany, being among their prisoners. Henry promptly demanded the surrender of these prisoners, and got Murdoch; but Henry Percy ("Hotspur"), son and heir of the Earl of Northumberland, who had done so much to put Henry on the throne, refused to surrender Douglas. Nay, he and his fierce old father broke out into a string of complaints against Henry's "ingratitude." Ingratitude indeed was more on the side of the Percies than the King. Hotspur had been made Warden of the Eastern Scots Marches, and Justiciar of North Wales and Cheshire, with vast salaries, castles, and "pickings." Northumberland was Constable of England and Warden of the Western Scots Marches, and had been given large confiscated estates. Between them father and son were supposed to have carried off Richard's hoard of £14,000—at any rate

Henry had never seen a penny of it. But Hotspur was Mortimer's brother-in-law, and, in December 1402, the two Percies came to terms with Sir E. Mortimer, with the Scots and Welsh, with Douglas and Glendower. No sympathy need be felt for them ; they proposed to partition England, "to restore the Heptarchy," anything to be revenged on Henry. They rose nominally for Richard if alive, for March if Richard were dead. Henry met and defeated them in a dogged hand-to-hand fight at Shrewsbury, 21st July 1403. Neither side showed a scrap of generalship, but the fifteen-year-old Prince Henry performed the usual "prodigies of valour." This was really the first battle of the Wars of the Roses, and, as in all subsequent cases, the order "heads off" was given after the battle, and the Earl of Worcester and two leading knights of the defeated party were executed. Hotspur fell on the field, and Douglas was taken prisoner. Neither Northumberland, Glendower, nor Sir E. Mortimer was present at the battle. Henry pardoned the old Earl, but gave his wardenship of the Marches to a man of the rival house of Neville of Raby, the Earl of Westmorland. For the subjugation of Wales the victory of Shrewsbury did nothing, and Owen was able to style himself Prince of Wales, and even to send envoys to negotiate with the French Court.

All 1404 the rebellion smouldered on, and broke out again in the north in 1405. This time Thomas Mowbray, son of the late Duke of Norfolk, stirred up old Northumberland, whose castles the King had been trying to reduce. They invoked Glendower's aid again, and got upon their side Richard Scrope, Archbishop of York, formerly an honest Ricardian, whose brother Henry had been decapitated in 1399. This rising was put down in detail, and Northumberland fled to the Scots. Scrope was taken, and, to the immense surprise of every one, was beheaded without trial. On the news of Scrope's danger, Archbishop Arundel, Henry's firmest friend, rode day and night to plead with the King against such an outrage on the feelings of the Church. It was a blunder, too, for Scrope alive was not nearly so dangerous a man as Northumberland, while, as a dead archbishop, he inevitably recalled Becket to men's minds : miracles, in fact, continued to be performed at Scrope's tomb down to the Reformation. Northumberland remained in Scotland till 1408, when he tried his luck once more, but was defeated and killed in battle at Bramham Moor. Mowbray had been beheaded in 1405.

The years 1406–1407 were almost wholly taken up with parliamentary business, and, as we have seen, it was the King's excessive poverty and weakness which gave the Commons such a hand over him. In the latter years of the reign we begin to perceive that even within the family of Lancaster divisions are likely to arise. As long as the King, whose health steadily fails, listens to Arundel, he will displease his half-brothers, the Beauforts, who turn more and more to the rising sun of the Prince of Wales. These Beauforts were the descendants of John of Gaunt by Catherine Swynford, and had been made legitimate by Act of Parliament. They were now represented by John Beaufort, Earl of Somerset, who died 1410 and was succeeded by his sons Henry (died 1418) and John (died 1444) ; by Henry, Bishop of Winchester (afterwards the famous Cardinal, who lived till 1447); and by Thomas, created Earl of Dorset 1412. It is difficult and needless to keep them all in one's head ; the important ones are the Cardinal, and the Earl or Duke of Somerset for the time being. These always pull together and always head a party ; they are very rich, and remain till the middle of the century the main props of the failing fortunes of the house of Lancaster. From them will come Lady Margaret Beaufort, the mother of Henry VII.

In 1409 the Prince of Wales and the Beauforts got the upper hand in the Council, and for nearly two years ruled at their pleasure. The stories about the Prince's wildness, which are so delightfully used by Shakespeare, may or may not be true, but he at least accumulated vast debts, which were not discharged at the end of his own reign. His brothers were certainly wild, and were several times found in affrays with the London citizens. In 1410 the Prince became Captain of Calais, and resolved to take advantage of the war of factions then raging in France between the Dukes of Burgundy and Orleans, both " princes of the blood." At first he interfered on the side of Burgundy, and it is interesting to see that 1200 English archers and knights could completely turn the tide of victory between French parties. An expedition of this size, being sent to the aid of the Burgundians, drove the Orleanists before it from Paris to the Loire (1411). Hardly was this accomplished when the Orleanists tried to outbid their rivals by offering Henry the old Duchy of Aquitaine (remember we still held Bordeaux and Bayonne and their districts). No English king could refuse such an offer, and Henry accordingly sent his second son, Clarence, with 1000 knights and 3000 archers, into the pay of the Orleanists. This no doubt led to a coolness between Henry and the Prince of Wales. We must remember that, if the Orleanist alliance meant the recovery of Aquitaine, that with Burgundy meant the open door in Flanders, for the Duke of Burgundy was now Count of Flanders and master of almost all the Low Countries. Clarence marched through Normandy ; but, before he had reached his appointed rendezvous at Blois, the two French factions had patched up a truce, and Clarence led his men home with their pockets full of French gold and their hearts lusting for more.   Both jobs were, in fact, disgraceful; the letting out of English soldiers as mercenaries to serve the factions of a neighbouring state did no doubt draw away some of the hot-heads from England, but it also revived the old war spirit which a prudent king should have sought to quiet.

The Prince, having ridden too roughshod over the feelings of his invalid father, found himself and his Beaufort partisans excluded from Henry's councils in 1411, probably because of an attempt to induce the King to abdicate, about which various conflicting stories are told. Henry reinstated Archbishop Arundel as his chief counsellor, and so matters stood when he died, on 20th March 1413. A death-bed reconciliation between the father and son is certain, but the terms of it are not known.

Henry V. was, beyond a doubt, the ablest of the race of Lancaster.   He was tall and strong, and excelled in all manly exercises.   If it is true that he had been wild in his youth, he did

> " Live to show the incredulous world
> The noble change that he had purposed,"

for a more sober, business-like king never sat upon a throne.   He became almost Spartan in his habits, and was fanatic in his attachment to the most rigid orthodoxy.   He had more than a full share of the craft and plausibility of his race, and knew admirably how to make the worse appear the better cause.   Thus he was popular all his days, and money was forthcoming from his Parliaments, and loans from his rich subjects, in a way that they had never been for his father, and never were to be for his son.   Henry Beaufort and the famous Richard Whittington, the Mayor of London, lent the King

enormous sums, which were never repaid. To the mass
of his people Henry was no usurper, but a legitimate
king, and so he was able to begin his reign by measures
of healing and reconciliation, such as the liberation of
the Earl of March, the restoration of the heirs of Norfolk
and Northumberland, a negotiation for the ransom of
the King of Scots and of Murdoch of Albany, and the
solemn transfer of the remains of the murdered Richard
to Westminster Abbey.

Nothing, in Henry's opinion, would contribute so
much to healing and reconciliation at home as to hurl
the whole strength of England upon the prostrate body
of unfortunate France; and for the moment the opinion
was justified. England showed once more of what
mighty feats of arms her soldiers were capable; her
fleets once more swept the narrow seas; her wool and
her gold purchased allies. But her national character,
which might have recovered during a period of peace or
of defensive warfare, received again a fearful stimulus
towards plunder and aggression. If the war should turn
out disastrous, as it did in the end, civil war would inevitably result, and be much fiercer than before. In Henry's
own case, his revival of a claim upon the French throne
was peculiarly odious. Even if Edward III.'s claims had
ever been good, not Henry, but Edmund of March was
the heir of them. An Act of the English Parliament might
put the Lancasters upon the English throne; it could
hardly justify their seizing the French throne also. But
worse—Henry deliberately posed as the champion of the
Most High God, raised up by Him to punish the sins of
France; with the most blasphemous hypocrisy he called
God to witness to his desire for peace at the very moment
(April 1415) when he was preparing his first invasion of
France. I do not, in the least, believe that he deceived him-
self in this matter, but it suited his policy to put forward

religious pretexts. The excuse has been made for him that his fanatical mediæval mind, which still believed in crusades and the duty of burning heretics, cannot be judged by our standards of morality; but everything else in his character was hard, practical, politic, and unscrupulous. In war he was no knight-errant, like the Edwards, but the thoroughgoing modern soldier. He began by doubling the pay of his archers, and even by paying his whole army a quarter's wages in advance. He sternly forbade plunder, because he knew it did not pay. He made terrible examples of "rebel" Scots, and, after he had become by treaty Regent of France, of "rebel" Frenchmen. He inaugurated the modern law of war which, until the other day, held it lawful to put to death a garrison that defends an indefensible place.

Nor do I think that Henry's religious attitude deceived his subjects. The unintelligent portion of them needed no hypocrisy to goad them into a war with France, for it seemed the natural duty and destiny of Englishmen; the intelligent minority accepted the war willingly from lower motives. If any excuse can be made for the King, it is that his warlike attitude was acclaimed by the whole nation, which was desirous of avenging the reverses of the last forty years. But, in fact, the lead distinctly came from the King himself; as early as August 1413 he was putting forward extravagant demands to the French Court—he knew that nothing would so effectually still all movements on behalf of the March family as a foreign war. The Church supported the war from another point of view, for the murmur against her riches had not been quieted by the burning of a few Lollards; and even now she was obliged to lighten her ship by throwing over the foundations called "alien priories" (i.e. small monasteries which were dependent upon great foreign monasteries, and paid tribute to them). These were declared confiscated to the Crown. The story, however, which makes good Archbishop Chicheley give Henry the diabolical advice to make war upon France in order to divert men's minds from Church plunder, and which Shakespeare has incorporated in his grand play of "Henry V.," is not found earlier than the sixteenth century.

The reign opened with a Lollard plot. Henry IV. had been afraid to touch those few among the upper classes who had been infected with "heresy," but his son resolved to proceed at once against Sir John Oldcastle, a leading Lollard, who had been a member of his own household. On his trial, Sir John confessed the full faith of later Protestantism, and described Anti-Christ as a beast whose head was the Pope, and whose tail was made of friars. He was sentenced to be burnt, but managed to escape from the Tower (Sept. 1413). Meanwhile his Kentish tenants, who loved him, and who were as good heretics as himself, had organised a rising for his release, and enlisted the sympathy of the London Lollards ; and such a rising actually came to a head in January 1414. It was a fatal error on the part of a religious party, for it enabled the Government to confuse Lollardry and treason. Henry took the most vigorous and obvious measures, and hanged thirty-seven of the rioters. Oldcastle was caught and executed.

In a Parliament at Leicester in the following April, the King took the very necessary and sensible step of condemning piracy, whether practised by his own subjects or those of his neighbours. Up till that time, whether you regarded "Arripay" and his kind as pirates or heroes depended upon whether you were a Frenchman or an Englishman ; in fact, both Governments had protected their own pirates. Henry now established "Conservators of the Peace" in every port, and ordered them to punish all acts of piracy, and to receive all prizes towed into English harbours, and determine whether they were lawful prizes or not. This was a real measure towards the safety of the sea, but it remained almost a dead letter for a couple of centuries to come. In his further measures for the same end, this king may lay some claim to be the first founder of the Royal, as opposed to the Cinque Port Navy. We find that he owned in 1417 sixteen great ships and "carracks" and eight barges. Probably these ships were the first that ever carried guns, but the sea-fights were still almost wholly boarding actions. The Cinque Port Navy still remained in full requisition as of old.

From the very beginning of his reign Henry had been in negotiation with both French factions. The Burgundians, headed by Duke John, were the more popular party, especially in Paris, where they had the fierce mob upon their side, but they were also the less national party, and afterwards proved it. The Orleanists were headed by the Gascon Count, Bernard of Armagnac, for Burgundy had murdered a Duke of Orleans in 1407, and the son of this murdered duke was still a minor. This was the party of the ignorant, fierce nobles who were destined to lose Agincourt, as they had already lost Crecy and Poitiers, from want of discipline. But for all that, they proved in the end to be the national party. The king, Charles VI., went mad every summer and recovered every winter. His sons, who died one after the other, were on the Orleanist side. His wife was a wicked woman. His daughter Katharine was destined to be the wife of Henry V.

We need not trouble ourselves much with the terms of Henry's overtures to the French leaders; we may be sure that he would have been bitterly disappointed if any of them had been accepted. Among other things, he

made the modest proposal that, in return for his surrender of the title of King of France, the French should
cede to England in full sovereignty all that Henry II.
and his Eleanor had ever possessed on feudal tenure,
together with the hand of Katharine, and a dowry of
800,000 crowns (a crown = about 3s. English).   The
Dauphin of the time being is reported to have sent
Henry in return a basket full of tennis balls, indicating
that play was all that he was fitted for.   If the story
be true, it was a wanton insult as well as a very poor
joke, and one does not wonder that Henry was angry.

In July 1415 we find Henry at Southampton preparing for war, with that earnest attention to details
which is the secret of success in all great soldiers.   While
he was there a plot was discovered.   Richard, Earl of
Cambridge, was the second son of Edmund, Duke of
York.   By his marriage with Anne Mortimer he had
united the lines of Clarence and York, and he had
an infant son, Richard, destined to be the father of
Edward IV.   He conspired with two other malcontents
on behalf of his brother-in-law, Edmund, Earl of
March, whom Henry had released from prison.   March
was a meek, and perhaps a sensible man, who had no
wish for a crown, and he himself betrayed the plot to
Henry.   Cambridge and his associates at once paid the
penalty with their heads.

On August 11th, Henry, leaving his brother John,
Duke of Bedford, as Regent in England, weighed
anchor from Portsmouth in the *Trinity Royal.*   He
took with him almost all the adult members of the
English baronage (thirty out of forty-one), and of lesser
fighting men two thousand knights with four horses
apiece, and six thousand archers; we hear of no
"knife-men," but there would be a lot of servants and
pages of sorts.   It took three days to disembark this

large army at the mouth of the Seine, and Henry at once proceeded to besiege Harfleur; he had miners and gunners with him, and some very heavy guns.

When I said that Henry was a hard, practical, modern soldier, I did not mean that the tasks which he set himself were practical or modern; only that, given the task, he would carry it out in a methodical spirit. Now, in his three expeditions to France (August to November 1415; July 1417 to February 1421; June 1421 till his death) he systematically set about the reduction of France north of the Loire, fortress by fortress, and we may guess that he discovered, before his death, that the task was beyond the strength of England to complete. The siege of Harfleur alone ought to have convinced him of this. Without relief from the French army the town held out, and held out against heavy fire, for five weeks, and Henry lost one-third of his men by sickness during the siege. The city fell on September 22nd. Henry left a garrison in it, and proceeded to seek battle outside it. He knew enough of the weakness of France to feel sure that he could give battle with advantage even with his army reduced by one-third; and he knew also that without a great victory the reduction of the north would be hopeless. Where he miscalculated was in supposing that, after his victory, French resistance would collapse at once; whereas, as a matter of fact, every stronghold in Normandy, Picardy, and the Île de France cost him a tough struggle.

When he set out from Harfleur he seems to have had only about 1000 knights and 3000 archers; he made, therefore, no attempt to take fortresses for the present, but passed on towards Calais, where he expected reinforcements. He advanced to the Somme, but discovered that the Constable of France (d'Albret) was thoroughly impregnated with du Guesclin's view, "let the English ride through France and starve as they go." Starvation was not far off : unable to cross at King Edward's old ford of Blanchetaque, Henry had to advance far up the river before he could get over, the French army marching parallel with him.   Some twenty miles south of Calais the Constable was overruled by the hot-heads among the French nobles, and threw himself across Henry's path, between the villages of Agincourt and Tramecourt (24th October, very wet weather).   The French were four to one, but, as usual, they had taken post on a ground far too narrow for their numbers.   Starving and small as the English army was, it was commanded by a consummate captain, and the victory was never doubtful.

On the 25th, afterwards to be the day of Balaclava, Henry formed his army in one line, with his archers in wedges on the front and the flank.   The Constable formed in the usual three wedges, with his cross-bowmen in the second of these (where, of course, they were useless).   Both armies were all on foot, except a small body of French knights, told off to execute Bruce's manœuvre of Bannockburn, and roll up the archers on the flanks ; but, as a matter of fact, these knights never got within striking distance of the archers.   The ground between the armies was heavy plough, trampled into a morass. The first French column charged gallantly, but sank to the knee in the soil, and was shot down at short range.   When the English and French knights met, our archers slung their bows on their backs and plunged into the mêlée with axes and leaden mallets.   Then the English charged the second wedge of Frenchmen, and here the fiercest fighting took place.   The King's brother, Humphrey, Duke of Gloucester, was knocked down, and Henry bestrode his body and slew the Duke of Alençon; half the crown on his helmet was shorn away ; but

X

gradually the French were forced back, and, on seeing this, their third wedge turned and, with some exceptions, fled. The battle lasted about three hours; pursuit was impossible, for the danger was still great; and when some French stragglers fell upon our baggage in the rear, Henry gave the word to "kill prisoners," lest a rally should reverse the fortune of the day. A good many were actually killed before the alarm passed off.

Agincourt was the first victory of thin English line over thick French column, and, for the third time within seventy years, the flower of France lay dead on the field. The English losses were under 200, but the starving and exhausted army had to hasten on to Calais. Henry's object was attained; he had replanted the banner of terror on French soil, and he concluded that the reduction of the north at least would follow as a matter of course. He entered London in triumph in November, and stayed in England more than eighteen months. During that time he received a visit from the Emperor Sigismund, who had just succeeded in putting an end to the great papal schism at the Council of Constance. Sigismund came professedly to mediate between England and France, and to see whether some common action of Christendom against the Turks could be undertaken. He ended by signing a treaty of alliance with Henry. Meanwhile Harfleur was besieged by the French, and rescued by Bedford, after a splendid naval victory won by the Earl of Huntingdon (May 1416). The Duke of Burgundy had taken no part in the Agincourt campaign, and was still fighting the Orleanists; but from this time he became more inclined to listen to Henry's proposals.

All efforts having failed to get the prisoners of Agincourt, who included the young Duke of Orleans, to recognise his title as King of France, Henry had to prepare for a war of sieges. So, in July 1417, he again mustered a large army (about 10,000 men) at Southampton, and crossed to France. There he found his task by no means so easy as he had expected. The siege of Caen took him a month; Falaise, ten weeks; Cherbourg, twenty weeks; and hardly a *bicoque* yielded in less than a week. Henry I.'s darling rock of Domfront held out to the last verge of starvation. The latter half of 1418 was wholly occupied in a fierce siege of Rouen, which did not fall till January 1419. Only with the fall of Rouen did anything like a panic set in among the governors of Norman castles; and then most of the lower Seine valley passed quickly into Henry's hands.

Every conquest had to be strongly garrisoned; the French people showed a dumb, dogged determination never to recognise the hated conqueror. Henry began to be very hard up for men; his Council wrote to him from England that he had already got every available lance and bow in the country. All this time the nominal government of France had been in the hands of, and resistance had been made in the name of Burgundians and Orleanists alternately, according as one or other of these factions got the upper hand. But on September 10, 1419, Duke John of Burgundy was murdered in the presence, and perhaps by the orders of the Dauphin Charles. John's son Philip at once signed a treaty with Henry, recognising him as King of France. Paris, as we have seen, was devoted to Burgundy, and the murder almost gave Henry the hearts of the Parisians. At last, in April 1420, the French Court, with the exception of the Dauphin, gave up the struggle and concluded the Treaty of Troyes.

Philip, the new Duke of Burgundy, signed this treaty with the Kings of England and France almost as an independent power. Henry was to be Regent and heir of France, the crown being left to Charles for his life. Both were to make war upon the Dauphin and the dregs of the Orleanist party. Henry was to marry Katharine with a very small dowry. The crowns of England and France were to be for ever united, but each country was to keep its own administration and laws.

All seemed over. Henry married Katharine in June, and at once proceeded to the reduction of the few strong places north of the Loire which were still held by the patriots. He towed the poor, old, insane king about with him, and could now with a good legal conscience hang "rebel" garrisons. He even sent for King James of Scotland to add a second puppet to the procession, in order that if he caught any Scots in the service of their "auld ally" he might hang them too. It is a dismal picture. Sens, Melun, Barbentan, were long valiantly held, but yielded in time. On December 31st, the two kings made a state entry into Paris, where the Burgundian sympathies of the mob secured them for once a fair reception. The English king garrisoned the famous Bastille, then not fifty years old, with English knights! In February 1421 Henry and Katharine went to England, and the Prince who was to be Henry VI. was born at Windsor on December 6th.

But resistance to this iniquitous settlement never died in North France. A valiant contingent of Scots landed at La Rochelle, the forerunners of many a band who were to give their lives for France on many a field right down to the eighteenth century; and they contributed largely to the defeat and death of Henry's brother, Clarence, at Beaugé, in March 1421. The Dauphin won over the Duke of Brittany, who had hitherto looked on in complacent neutrality. The treaty of Troyes was not over-pleasing to the English Parliament, but by this time Henry was in no mood to brook

opposition.   He returned to his sorry task in June, and
began with the difficult siege of Dreux.   When that fell,
he touched his farthest south at the Loire, but was
immediately obliged to retreat.   In October he began
the siege of Meaux.   That small place held out desperately, and ended by avenging the fatherland.   When
it finally fell, in May 1422, Henry was already very ill
of ague.   Dysentery followed ague, and, on 31st August,
he died at Vincennes, just outside Paris.

"Good Lord, Thou knowest that my intent was to
have built the walls of Jerusalem;" these were almost
his last words, and there is this much evidence that he
was sincere; he had borrowed from Lady Stafford the
"Chronicle of the First Crusade," and the book had not
been returned when he died.   In spite of his large
revenue, at that time almost touching £150,000 a year,
he died very heavily in debt.   Peace be to his ashes; he
won Agincourt.

CHAPTER XIX

HENRY VI. AND CIVIL WAR

AND so, at nine months old, Henry of Windsor was King of England and heir of France; at ten months he was King of France too, so far as treaties can make a king, for Charles died on 21st October. Besides his uncles, the Dukes of Bedford and Gloucester, the Bishop of Winchester and the other Beauforts stood behind his throne-cradle. Bishop Henry had been made a cardinal in 1417, but Henry V. had sternly forbidden him to wear his red hat in public. He was soon to put it on without scruple. "Henry VI.," says Bishop Stubbs, "was perhaps the most unfortunate king that ever lived. He outlived power and wealth and friends; he saw all who loved him perish for his sake . . . and he was, without doubt, innocent of most of the evils that befell England because of him. Pious, pure, generous, patient, simple, true and just; humble, merciful, fastidiously conscientious, he might have seemed made to rule a quiet people in quiet times. His devotion was exemplary, and unquestionably sincere. He left a mark on the hearts of Englishmen that was not soon erased . . . and it was no mere political feeling that led the rough yeomen of Yorkshire and Durham to worship before his statue, that dictated hymns and prayers in his honour, and that retained in the Primer, down to the Reformation, the prayers of the King who had perished for the sins of his fathers and of the nation."

How had such a beautiful character come to be

grafted upon such a bad stock? For Henry was come not only of the fierce and subtle Lancasters, but of the Valois, as bad a stock as any in Europe. Of Katharine herself we know almost nothing, except that she privately married, or did not marry, soon after Henry V.'s death, " Owen Tudor, a Welsh gentleman "; had by him, at any rate, two children, one of whom married Lady Margaret Beaufort and became the father of Henry VII.

At what period His Baby Majesty left his mother's lap we do not know. He was brought to London when he was two, and again when he was three, and publicly " processed " through the streets. In 1424 there appears on the records of the Privy Council the appointment of Dame Alice Butler as his nurse, and, in 1426, a second nurse, Joan Astley, was added. Both received £40 a year, which, it may be noted, was the same pay as was received by His Baby Majesty's judges! Dame Alice had leave given her "to reasonably chastise from time to time as the case may require." The Queen-mother died 1437. Henry had tutors given him by Parliament, Thomas Beaufort, Duke of Exeter, and on his death, in 1427, the Earl of Warwick (not the " King-maker," but the last but one of the " Beauchamp " Warwicks), a red-hot paladin of fighting and crusading. Warwick also is authorised to " chastise him when he trespasseth," and being a rough though an honest fellow, he may have used these powers so cruelly as to break the poor lad's spirit.[1] A learned education Henry certainly received, probably from his uncle, Humphrey, Duke of Gloucester, who, with all his vain, rash character, was a great patron of learning and learned men. Cardinal Beaufort would be

[1] It is but fair to state that Henry always showed attachment to Warwick, and that Warwick's son, who died young, appears to have been one of his greatest friends.

more likely to instruct him in the wiles of diplomacy and state-craft, but these were lessons by which Henry never profited. But as to who taught him the one priceless lesson which he really imbibed, that of patience and gentleness under suffering, of universal courtesy, of humanity to man and beast in a barbarous age, there is no record. Nor is there any record as to who inspired him with his immense zeal for the education of the young. Henry was really the first man to bend all his energies to this noble purpose without a thought either for his own glory or that of his family, or for the future welfare of his soul. Perhaps some instinct, or even inspiration, taught him to look through and beyond the seas of bloodshed that awaited the existing generation, and to provide solidly and permanently for the welfare of generations of English boys yet unborn. At the age of eleven and a half, Henry founded the University of Caen in Normandy ; at eighteen, all his thoughts were occupied with the foundation of Eton ; by the time he was twenty-six, King's College in Cambridge was completed !

His chaplain, John Blackman, has preserved some pretty stories of his private character : he naturally accentuates the King's devotion to the services of the Church, the early and long hours on his knees before particular shrines, but he also lays stress on his passion for reading, especially on his great knowledge of history. The King continually addressed personal letters to the worldly clergy of his realm, urging them to attend to their spiritual duties, "which surprised them very much." He tried to root out the ingrained custom of using the great churches for the transaction of secular business : (remember that the central aisle of St. Paul's, called "Paul's Walk," was the Royal Exchange and the Stock Exchange of that day). In an age of universal licentiousness, Henry was modesty itself ; once, when riding near Bath, he saw a gentleman sitting undressed in one of the hot springs there, and rebuked him severely (it seems a little hard, perhaps, that he should have expected his subjects to bathe in their clothes). In his dress he was uniformly plain, wearing "square-toed shoes of goat's hide, like a farmer's, a long gown with a round hat like a citizen's, and plain woollen stockings." He seems to have been fond of music, and to have been a good judge of painting.

Henry showed himself an excellent dispenser of ecclesiastical patronage. It was his great persistence that got William Waynflete, against strong opposition, made Bishop of Winchester. But, above all, it was on his schools that his heart was set. He was always coming down and talking to the first batches of collegers at Eton. "Be good boys, gentle and docile, and servants of the Lord," he used to say to them. Frequently he "tipped" them. He did not like them to come to Windsor, lest they should become corrupted by the wickedness of his courtiers, who, he complained, were always interrupting him with frivolities when he would fain be reading, and whom he constantly rebuked for strong language. His own strongest expressions, says Blackman, were "forsooth and forsooth," but I find him once swearing "by St. John" to a French ambassador. His royal predecessors used to swear by God's eyes, or God's teeth, or other parts of God's body.

The King's greatest characteristic, however, was his incorrigible mercifulness. He was continually not only pardoning capital sentences, but also remitting fines, and his Council complained constantly of it. As for the horrors perpetrated by the savage criminal laws of his time, he could not bear to look on them. Riding in at Cripplegate one day, he saw a nasty black thing stuck on a spike over the gateway, and asked "what it was?" "*Unum quarterium cujusdam proditoris,* so please your Majesty." "Take it away," said Henry; "no man shall suffer such cruel punishments for me." He was destined to be familiar with such sights before all was over. One suspects that all manner of impostors grew fat at Henry's expense. In 1437 I find him allowing twopence a day to a converted "Saracen." In 1441 some Abyssinian monks came to profess obedience to the Pope, and vaunted the attentions of their previous ruler to King Solomon, "whereas the Pope is much greater than Solomon." Henry hears the news, and his joy knows no bounds, "for Christendom is at last united." Of course, the real motive of these black gentlemen was to get Italian galleys to help them against the Turks. Henry corresponded incessantly with Popes, and cardinals, and councils. There was a big council sitting at Basle "to reform the papacy," in which he took the deepest interest. More natural and more English was his great zeal to effect the canonisation of King Alfred; but in this he failed.

Perhaps it would have been better for his generation if his eyes had been more fixed upon his own time and his own kingdom, for, before he had come to man's estate, things began to look very black in the said kingdom. In 1422 the prospect of a twenty-years' minority had at once to be faced. The late king had put all his trust in his brother, John of Bedford, and had left him instructions to act as Regent in France; the English regency he had left to his younger brother, Humphrey, Duke of Gloucester, but he had trusted to the Beauforts to hold their own against this impetuous person. The Privy Council, however, consisting of all the real leaders of English politics, refused to admit any Regency or even "Protectorate"; it acted as Regent itself, and Gloucester, though commonly spoken of as "Protector," was really only "second councillor, but first in Bedford's absence." The Council gave both Bedford and Gloucester large salaries, and did not forget to provide handsomely for its own members.

We must clearly understand that during the whole of the minority, and even for many years after, no movement against the house of Lancaster, as such, was made; no question of any other title to the crown was raised; whatever disturbances took place before 1450 were either private wars, or outbreaks against unpopular ministers. Perhaps no dynastic claims would ever have been raised, but for the fierce party feelings engendered by the split within the reigning family itself. That split was not long delayed. Gloucester was a vain fellow, whose character and career recall the futile ambitions of John of Gaunt. Bedford's whole honest, narrow soul was occupied in carrying out abroad the sorry task of Henry V. Cardinal Beaufort was wise in council, and was prodigal of his great riches (mainly acquired in the wool trade) in favour of the Government, but he seems to have been thoroughly unpopular. That healthy Erastian prejudice, for which England has so often had good cause to be thankful, branded him as a "haughty priest," and suspected that he played into the hands of the Pope.

Up till about 1429 the war went on the whole in favour of England; the Burgundians remained staunch to the alliance, and adopted Bedford's English tactics on many a stricken field. Gloucester gave the first shock to this alliance when, in 1423, he married a runaway princess from the Low Countries, Jacqueline, Duchess of Hainault. Hainault was almost surrounded by Burgundian territory, and Philip of Burgundy had no wish to see an English Duke in possession of it or of its Duchess. But this was what Gloucester wished, and on several occasions he diverted English soldiers and English gold to futile attempts to conquer Hainault. He even challenged Philip of Burgundy to a duel, and it is amusing to find that Prince (who was fond of good living) going into regular training for the combat. Bedford managed to patch up the matter, and by his marriage with Philip's sister, Anne, created a fresh tie between England and Burgundy.

Charles VII., a dreamy sluggish creature, was king only to the south of the Loire, and had never been crowned. In 1423 a French and Scottish force was defeated at Crevant, on the Yonne. In the next year the King of Scots was released from his long confinement, married Lady Joan Beaufort, and went back to begin that heroic struggle for order and good government in the North which only ended with his murder in 1437. To suppose that the release of James would obtain the recall of the Scots auxiliaries from France was quite a mistake. The terrible battle of Verneuil, the last great English victory in the Hundred Years' War, proved the valour and impetuosity of the Scots, but proved it in vain against the excellent tactics of Bedford. The war rolled backwards and forwards very much over the same ground, the southern frontier of Normandy and the Île de France, and the provinces of Maine and Champagne; Picardy was throughout held by our Burgundian allies. In 1425 Bedford was able to leave his command for a while and come to England to pacify the quarrel between Gloucester and Beaufort, which in that year had come to its first head. Duke Humphrey had complained that he was excluded from the Tower by a constable of Beaufort's choice; being popular in London, he had actually called the citizens to arms to support him, and thus the house of Lancaster was almost at civil war within itself only a few months after the death of the legitimate king, Edmund, Earl of March, who died without children, and whose silent claims were thus transferred to his nephew, Richard, Duke of York, who was just seven years older than Henry VI.

For the moment Bedford's prudence patched up a peace between the rivals. The Council snubbed Gloucester when, shortly after this, he demanded an extension of power, and he let himself be snubbed with impunity. Beaufort left England for a time, and 1427-28 were fairly quiet years. In October of the latter year the English were strong enough to begin the siege of Orleans, the key of the Loire and so of Southern France. It was valiantly defended by Dunois, the "Bastard of Orleans." The King of France was at Chinon, entirely in the hands of unworthy favourites, who actually sought to prevent his taking steps for the recovery of the North. Into his presence on March 9, 1429, an escort of six men conducted a peasant girl in male attire, who was to be known as Joan of Arc, the Maid of God. She announced to Charles that she was sent by God to relieve Orleans, and to conduct him to his coronation at Rheims. Perhaps the most astounding fact in the history of the Roman Church and of the French monarchy is, that Joan has had to wait till the twentieth century for the recognition of her saintship. But she has been canonised since the hour of her death in the hearts of the French people, and wherever since that day French soldiers have charged for the defence of their country, they have seen a vision of the Maid of God in shining armour in the thickest of the fight.

Joan's pretensions to a divine mission were carefully

scrutinised by Charles' bishops, who were not over-pleased with her answers. But the poor-spirited King thought he might as well give her a trial; while the practical men of war like Dunois, La Hire, and Xaintrailles either believed in her at once or saw the value of the popular enthusiasm which greeted her appearance. Of military genius she had absolutely none, but she could ride well and was utterly fearless. She claimed no free hand in the details of strategy or tactics, though her shrewd common-sense often proved of great service. All that "her saints said to her" was : "fight the English wherever you find them, till you have driven them from the land."

Early in May 1429 she managed to effect her entry into Orleans through the English lines; by the 8th she had stormed the blockading forts, and the English marched fearfully and sullenly away. The valley of the Loire was cleared when on 17th June the veteran English commander, Talbot, was overwhelmed and captured at Patay, from which battle Sir John Fastolf, another celebrated veteran, galloped away with his whole division without striking a blow. The discipline in our armies relaxed from that hour; they were already largely recruited from foreign adventurers, and no one relished the task of facing the Maid of God. Within a month after Patay the road to Rheims had been opened, and the Maid with her white banner stood behind King Charles at his coronation. Thereon she declared her mission accomplished, and asked to be allowed to return to her peasant home in Lorraine.

But her presence was too valuable to the French commanders to permit of this, and a cry went up for an instant advance on Paris. Charles' ignoble favourites, jealous of Joan's ascendency, actually prevented the success of the assault which was delivered on that city in September. The Maid was wounded. The King never faced the battle, and, after one failure, retired to the South again.

In that same year, 1429, on 6th November, little Henry was crowned at Westminster. Shockingly weary the poor boy must have been as he sat through the long coronation banquet in Westminster Hall, which included such delicacies as "boars' heads in castles of gold and armed, a red leche with lions carven therein, custard-royal with leopards of gold sitting therein and holding a fleur-de-lys, pig endored (gilt), crane roasted, great breme, jelly-pastie written and noted with ' *Te Deum Laudamus*,' and (somewhat of a bathos) boiled mutton "; our ancestors were gross feeders. But perhaps the little king woke up when Philip Dymock, the hereditary champion, rode into the Hall in full armour and publicly defied to mortal combat any one who should dispute His Majesty's title to both crowns.

A French coronation of some sort was also a necessity, but this was no easy task. Rheims was the only true "hallowing place" for French kings, who were always crowned with peculiarly sacred ceremonies and peculiarly sacred church-furniture. But Rheims was out of the question, and so Paris was selected. Even Paris was not easy to reach, since the Maid's victories had carried French raids far into the Île de France and Picardy. A little while before, Bedford, leaving Burgundy in Paris, had fallen back upon Rouen. But, while little Henry was waiting at Calais for an open road to Paris, the Maid was captured by Burgundian soldiers at Compiègne (24th May 1430). There were but two ways known to the Middle Ages of treating such a person. If she were not a saint, she must be a witch. Obviously it was to the interest of her enemies to take the latter view. Burgundians and English must share the blame of this infamy; could not both prove that their soldiers had fallen down from fright at the mere sight of her banner? and what, except witchcraft, could frighten such soldiers? But the largest share of blame must rest with the French clergy; even the patriots among them had never approved of Joan, and the University of Paris at once demanded that she should be given up to the Inquisition as a witch. Her king made no attempt even to offer ransom for her; only her soldier friends and the brave Duke of Alençon stood up for her. Philip of Burgundy, after some hesitation, sold her to the English, and by the end of the year she was in prison at Rouen.

Her trial for witchcraft before the Bishop of Beauvais was as great a farce as such things always must be. She had no sort of doubt that she had seen visions of saints and angels, not once nor twice, but repeatedly; she specified St. Michael, all in a flame of light, St. Margaret, and St. Katharine; she described their hair and their dresses; they spoke to her in French, "never in English." Such would necessarily be the form which a truly divine inspiration would take in a mind of such lofty simplicity as Joan's. Actual torture was not applied, but privation of all sorts, solitary confinement, horrible attempts upon her modesty, were steadily kept up for two months—anything and everything to make her confess herself a witch. At the end of May she signed some sort of recantation, but speedily withdrew it. On the 30th she was burnt alive in the old market-place at Rouen. "We are lost," said the English soldiers who saw her die; "we have burnt a saint." They had; and they were lost.

On December 10th of that horrible year little Henry was crowned in Notre Dame, but there was not nearly such a good dinner as at Westminster. Robbers and French partisans were prowling on all the highways round; the hearts of the Parisian mob had long been lost; no great Frenchmen were present, and it was the English cardinal who performed the ceremony. In fact, the whole thing was a mere piece of bravado— a dash on Paris, a crowning, and a cutting of the way back to Rouen. It was in that same year that the first voices on behalf of peace were heard in the English Parliament; we hear also of a fierce Lollard outbreak under one Jack Sharp, who boasted that he "would make priests' heads as cheap as sheep's heads—three a penny." In Maine and Normandy we steadily lost ground. Bedford's Duchess, Anne, died in 1432, and in 1433, in disgust at the perpetual quarrels between Beaufort and Gloucester, Bedford resolved to return and to take up the Regency in England. Yet for any suggestion of peace, or of abandonment of the English claims, we look as vainly to Bedford as to Gloucester. Before the middle of 1434 he was back in France, carrying fire and sword against the Norman "rebels."

In the next year came the crushing blow of the desertion of Burgundy. Philip made his peace with Charles, and received nearly all Picardy as his reward (treaty of Arras). Liberal offers had also been made by Charles to the English, who utterly rejected them. In September Bedford died of a broken heart. Gloucester at once blew up the flame of English "patriotism" to demand the continuance of the war at all costs; the young Duke of York succeeded to Bedford's chief command. But Beaufort was already wavering, and from this time we may date the formation of the peace and war parties which in time were definitely to become Lancastrian and Yorkist. Paris fell in April 1436. In the same year Calais was besieged, though in vain, by the Burgundians.

From 1437, when Henry, now sixteen years of age, began to transact business with his Council, things, instead of getting better, got steadily worse. His excessive desire to please and reconcile every one often led to self-contradictory decisions. His heart was set upon peace, and we may trace his hand in a fresh truce with Scotland, concluded immediately after the murder of James I. (James II., "James with the fiery face," was only seven years old at his accession); in a real attempt at peace-conferences with France in 1439; and, in 1440, in the liberation of the Duke of Orleans, who had been a prisoner since Agincourt. But Gloucester thwarted Henry's pacific desires at every turn, and the war of sieges dragged steadily on till 1444. The only English commanders of whom any good could be said were young Richard of York and the veteran Talbot. In 1443 we begin to hear of Edmund Beaufort, who succeeded his brother John as Duke of Somerset in the next year; and we begin also to hear of William de la Pole, Earl and soon Duke of Suffolk, the grandson of Richard II.'s favourite. And, whenever we hear of these two, it is as being strongly opposed to Gloucester and strongly opposed to York.

Suffolk was a soldier who had fought all through the war, and had once been taken prisoner by the Maid: one has no reason to suppose that he had at any time been an advocate for peace before 1444; but in that year the Beauforts, who, in spite of the retirement of the Cardinal from active life, had been steadily growing stronger, sent him to the French Court to negotiate for Henry's marriage on the basis of at least a truce. The lady selected was Margaret, a beautiful princess of the Angevin branch of the French royal family.

She was just sixteen years old ; her father, Réné, Duke of Lorraine, was titular King of Naples, Sicily, and Jerusalem, and titular Duke of Anjou and Maine, which last province had recently been the theatre of war. In such haste was King Henry for peace, that he instructed Suffolk not only to waive all questions of dowry, but to promise that our troops should evacuate all the places which they still held in Maine. Suffolk agreed to all ; he knew that he was treading a dangerous path, and he had obtained full pardon beforehand from the English Council for any terms that he might make. The truce was concluded at Tours on 24th May 1444, and eleven months later Margaret appeared in England. The expenses of bringing over this dowerless bride amounted to £5000, including £65 for the "keep, cage, and carriage of one lion " (apparently a wedding-present).

Of Margaret's character we may fairly judge from her letters and her history. She seems to have been always grasping, and, in the days of her prosperity, extravagant. She was passionately fond of hunting, and not averse to begging a week's sport from her friends. Indeed, she was an indefatigable beggar all round, both for herself and her courtiers. To contemporaries, and above all to the partisans of York, she was always the "outlandish woman," the pledge of a disgraceful peace, who was prepared to sell Berwick to the Scots and Sandwich to the French, and on whose shoulders the guilt of the civil war must ultimately rest. Brave in adversity, and horribly vindictive in her short-lived triumphs, she was no helpmeet for gentle Henry.

Suffolk did not dare to avow the terms of the marriage treaty until he had silenced Gloucester. He plunged into partisan schemes in England, and he and the Queen, who from the first seems to have taken complete control of Henry's policy, governed England most recklessly for five years. They early determined to remove Gloucester by fair means or foul, and, while avoiding for nearly two years the evacuation of Maine, they contrived to bring a charge of high treason against the Duke and his followers at a Parliament held at Bury, in Suffolk, in February 1447. Three days after his arrest Gloucester was "found dead." People talked about paralysis : it is one of those mysterious "removals" with which fourteenth and fifteenth century history abounds. We can hardly venture to acquit Suffolk, although Gloucester's death was not specifically laid to his charge at the date of his own subsequent impeachment. It seems dreadful to accuse the young Queen, but she certainly received a large share of the Duke's spoils. In spite of Shakespeare, we may unhesitatingly acquit Cardinal Beaufort, who had practically given up politics, and who died six weeks after Gloucester. Perhaps Gloucester had been meditating open treason ; and at any rate Henry, who had once really loved him, made no effort to save him.

But when the cession of Maine was made public, the outcry against Suffolk and Margaret was loud and instant. Suffolk at once became in popular song "Jack Napes," or

> "The ape with his clog
> Who hath tied Talbot, our good dog."

Every one, except the Queen's immediate *entourage*, joined in the cry. If York fanned the flame, he merely gave voice to popular disgust, and no one connected his complaints with any attempt against the house of Lancaster. Suffolk had but one policy—to keep York away from the King's ear. In December 1447 Richard was deprived of his command in France, and in the following July he was sent as Lord-Deputy to Ireland.

This was regarded as a sort of banishment; but he had inherited great estates in the north of Ireland from the de Burghs, and in Ireland the Yorkist cause continued popular even after the accession of the Tudors.

The truce with France lasted till 1449. It was then wantonly broken by the English, by the seizure of the Breton town of Fougères. But France had grown strong during the four years' peace; the germ of her standing army was already in existence, and she answered by sweeping Normandy from end to end. Somerset, after less than three weeks' siege, had to evacuate Rouen (Nov. 1449), and in April 1450 the decisive victory of Formigny finished the French task. Bayeux, Avranches, Caen, Falaise, Domfront, Cherbourg were the last cities to surrender.

The sense and the madness of England alike cried for a scapegoat—for many scapegoats; and we begin at once to realise the disturbed state of the country. Riots and private wars were raging everywhere. In December 1449 the Bishop of Chichester, who had held high office under Suffolk, was murdered by some mutinous soldiers, and was said to have accused "Jack Napes" with his dying breath of taking bribes from the French. Suffolk defended himself bravely in Parliament against this and worse charges. But the universal outcry was so great that, in order to save his minister's life, the King was obliged to banish him for five years. On his way across Channel the Duke was caught off the mouth of the Thames and murdered at sea. The murder was done on a King's ship. A Government which could not prevent its Royal Navy from being used for such a purpose was hardly a Government at all. Margaret evidently considered that York's friends had had a hand in the matter.

Next we have the fierce insurrection of Jack Cade

and the men of Kent in the very month of Suffolk's murder (May 1450). This was no mere peasant rising; there were substantial yeomen and squires in it; the insurgents demanded the recall of York to the King's Councils and the punishment of all Suffolk's friends. They put forward grievances, which the partisans of York eagerly took up. They forced their way into London and committed many murders in high places, at length agreeing to retire only on a promise of amnesty. Before it was well over York was announced as having landed in the west, and as coming to London to clear away aspersions on his loyalty. Edmund of Somerset was hastily recalled from Calais; but York arrived almost unopposed, with a large retinue. He raised no dynastic claims, but they were at once raised for him in the Parliament of 1451, when a private member moved that he be declared heir to the crown. At the same time the Commons tendered a bill for the removal from the King's Council of Somerset and all his party.

Meanwhile the last fragments of our possessions in Aquitaine were going the way of Normandy, though far less willingly. Bordeaux yielded in 1451, repented of having yielded, and called for English help. Old Talbot was sent out to his last field in October 1452, and fell at the battle of Châtillon in July 1453. The Hundred Years' War was over. But before this last news was known, King Henry's long-suffering mind had broken down; his malady seems to have been at first sheer melancholia. He could not speak or realise the presence of any one, and soon he became grievously ill in body also. The medical science of the age was exhausted upon him in all its horrible tortures, " electuaria, potiones, aquas, sirupos, confectiones, laxativas medicinas in quacumque forma, . . . clisteria, suppositoria, capudpurgia, gargarisimata, balnea, vel universalia vel particularia epithemata, fomentationes, embrocationes, capitis rasuram, unctiones, cerota, ventosa, cum scarificatione vel sine, emoroidarum provocationes," &c., &c. But all in vain. Probably his definite retirement from politics would have made little difference to Margaret, but for the position of York as next heir. But this position was suddenly changed. Three months after the beginning of King Henry's sickness his only son, Prince Edward of Lancaster, was born, October 1453.

The birth of a royal heir after eight years of childless wedlock naturally produces vague murmurs about " bastards and changelings." York had seriously to reconsider his position ; he was no longer the *heir* to the crown. He was either rightful king or a traitor. Probably his friends realised that he would only be safe as king. Dare he raise his claims ? We shall see that it took him several years to make up his mind.

For the moment he was content to be made Protector by the universal consent of Parliament, and he at once proceeded to sweep the Privy Council clear of Somerset and his friends (March 1454), and to fill their places with his own party. Among the members of this party we now begin to hear much of the enormous clan of the Nevilles of Raby, especially of Richard, Earl of Salisbury, and of his son, Richard, Earl of Warwick, later known as the " King-maker." He, " the most subtle man of his time," as a French chronicler calls him, devoted himself to the cause of his kinsman, York, from the first, and proved to be the mainstay of the house until his quarrel with Edward IV. The Nevilles were hereditary enemies of the Percies, and, though they were also divided into two separate factions among themselves, a series of fortunate marriages had left them very much the richest of English baronial families. York had married Cicely Neville, Warwick's aunt. It is difficult, if we consider Warwick's whole career, to conclude that he was anything but a self-seeking baron of rather superior political ability, who kept a retinue of over a thousand turbulent followers all emblazoned with his badge of the "ragged staff"; but he was undoubtedly a versatile man, a first-class sea-captain, something of a soldier, and a far-seeing politician. It was probably his prestige alone that saved Calais from sharing the fate of our other French possessions during the last years of Henry VI.'s reign. Possibly he acted at first as a moderating influence on the Duke of York until the time should be ripe for the final blow.

York's first protectorate was not much more successful in the way of keeping order than Henry VI.'s reign had been. He succeeded in reducing the King's enormous and wasteful household to "such a competent and reasonable fellowship as may worshipfully be found and sustained"; but even after the reduction it still comprised 413 menials and 123 gentlemen. There were still "31 cooks, 6 children of the kitchen, turn-broaches; 15 persons in the 'catery,'" including a groom-pig-taker, a tallowman, and a sea-fisher; in the laundry department economy evidently was effected, for there were but four persons there. Beyond this feat York did little but provide places for his friends. In January 1455 Henry began to come to his reason again, and "blessed God when he learned that his little son's name was Edward." By March the Yorkists were driven from the Council, and Somerset and his friends were in full power again. This revolution produced the first actual fighting in the field.

A writer who has endeavoured, however feebly, to render the earlier parts of English History interesting, must always feel that he owes an apology to his readers when he approaches the dreary period of the "Wars of the Roses." There is no known alembic for extracting interest from the characters, the situations, or the social life of the latter half of the fifteenth century. The sordid brutality of the principal actors in the drama is fittingly paralleled by the callous indifference of the nation to their acts; and the result is that, in default of any principles to trace, the historian is obliged to inflict on his readers a mass of details, which cannot fail to be tedious, and in which the main threads of history are very apt to get lost. If we look at the political map of England at this time we shall find that, on the whole, the south and east are Yorkist, the north and west Lancastrian; but this scheme must be modified in details, for the Yorkist branch of the Nevilles is strong in North Yorkshire; York city is Yorkist; Nottinghamshire is "Mowbray," and so Yorkist; the whole of the borders of Wales except Cheshire are "Mortimer," and so Yorkist; Wiltshire is "Neville" and Yorkist; but all west of that is Lancastrian; the Midlands are equally divided between the Leicester and Derby inheritance of the Lancastrians, and the Warwick earldom of the Nevilles; while Essex and Hampshire are partly Lancastrian. As for "the country," apart from the followings of the great lords, its apathy is startling. The mass of the gentry had indeed taken service with this or that great nobleman, and could bribe their tenants to follow them to battle; but the yeoman class is conspicuously absent from the field. The towns are sordidly indifferent: if the Red Rose won a battle, even London or York, though possibly at heart Yorkist, would be ready to open its gates without a struggle. There were no sieges, for no town cared to stand a siege. The House of Commons could easily be packed to register the decrees of either victorious party ; while all the great churchmen were either pledged partisans, or changed sides with cynical indifference.

It was clearly York who first drew the sword, and our view of his conduct must be coloured by our opinion on the question, "do the horrors of civil war outweigh the horrors of weak government or no government ? " If we could feel sure that it was no mere desire of saving his own head, and no mere dynastic ambition that prompted York to strike, but merely a desire "to help the King to govern better," we might believe in his patriotism. That was in effect the pretext he put forward : Henry IV. had also put it forward in 1399. It is true that York, after his victories at St. Albans and Northampton, did not at once depose Henry, but this was possibly owing to the influence of Warwick, who may have thought that England was hardly yet ripe for such a change.

The first battle of St. Albans, 22nd May 1455, a Yorkist victory, thinned the Lancastrian party by the deaths of Somerset, Clifford, and Northumberland ; the slaughter of the rank and file was, as in all the earlier battles, small ; a complete Yorkist ministry came in in November, and the King again lost his reason for a few months. York acted again as Protector from then till February 1456. Margaret, driven in her helplessness to negotiate with the enemies of England, had already offered Berwick to James II. as the price of a Scottish alliance ; but it should be stated that Somerset had repudiated this overture before his death. All 1456–57 we hardly see what is going on. Henry Beaufort, the new Duke of Somerset, took his father's place by Margaret's side ; Warwick entered upon his captaincy of Calais, and, though unable to prevent a French fleet from sacking Sandwich in 1457, victoriously defeated that fleet in at least one great naval engagement. There was an attempted reconciliation of parties at London in 1458, but both were steadily arming and both were intriguing for foreign help. In April 1459 Warwick threw off the mask of amity and brought the garrison of Calais over sea to help York.

There was a second Yorkist victory at Bloreheath in Shropshire in September, but its fruits were lost next month in an utter rout at Ludford in Herefordshire. From that field York fled to Ireland ; and Warwick and young Edward, Earl of March, York's eldest son, took ship for Calais, where they had to stand a long rambling siege from Somerset. In November Margaret called a Parliament, which attainted York and his followers of high treason.

The violence of this proceeding, though not unnatural, brought neither comfort to Margaret (for the Yorkist leaders were safe out of her reach) nor peace to the kingdom. In June 1460 Warwick again landed at Sandwich in some strength, and with a tame papal legate, pledged to the Yorkist cause, in his train. All Kent rose to greet him, and the Government abandoned London, where indeed King Henry had not ventured to reside since 1458. Much reinforced, Warwick advanced upon Northampton and utterly defeated King Henry at that place on 10th July, the victory being won mainly by the strategy of young Edward of March. They brought the captive king to London, though still treating him as King, and awaited the arrival of York from Ireland. York landed at Chester in September and came straight to London, having already quartered the arms of England. Arrived at Westminster, he in a hesitating kind of way claimed the crown ; that is to say, he put one hand on the throne, but did not sit down on it; he also turned the meek Henry out of the royal bedroom in Westminster Palace.   But, when he referred the question of his rights to Lords, Commons, and judges in turn, each body declared itself too "simple" to be able to settle so grave a matter; and it may have been Henry himself who suggested the compromise whereby he was to retain the crown for life, but York was to succeed him and to act as Protector meanwhile.   We can hardly suppose that, in such a bad age, King Henry's frail life would long have been allowed to keep York out of the promised inheritance.

Margaret and the young Prince were far away, raising the whole North for a last effort, and for the moment it became imperative for York to crush Margaret. He accordingly marched northwards and met a large Lancastrian force at Wakefield on December 30th, proved himself to be an utterly incompetent general, was defeated and slain. His second son, Edmund of Rutland, was stabbed after the battle, and Warwick's father, Salisbury, was beheaded. Margaret was not present at the battle; she was in Scotland, negotiating for Scottish help with the Regency of the new seven-year-old king, James III.; but her large army moved rapidly southwards under Lord Clifford, plundering and burning as it came.

Hitherto plunder had been avoided in the Wars of the Roses; and it was undoubtedly this march of the fierce borderers, to whom everything south of the Trent was like a foreign country, that turned all moderate people in the south into temporary partisans of the Yorkists. The rights of the slain claimaint had descended to his son, Edward of March, and he, while his father had hurried to his death at Wakefield, had gone westwards to crush the Western Lancastrians.

At Mortimer's Cross, in Herefordshire, he thoroughly effected this task (Feb. 2, 1461), and then marched back towards London. Warwick had been left in charge of the capital, and came out valiantly, with the captive Henry VI. in tow, to meet the Northerners at St. Albans. There he was utterly defeated on 17th February; Henry rejoined his Queen, who stained her victory by horrid executions, and the road to London was open. There was no sort of chance of the city making any effective resistance, and, considering the usual ascendency of Margaret, it is very strange that no further advance was made. Probably it was the gentle Henry who, for once asserting himself, determined to spare the capital the horrors of a sack such as the Lancastrian army had already inflicted on Stamford, Peterborough, Huntingdon, and many other towns on the North road.

So the great Northern army rolled back as it had come, plundering and burning. Warwick, surprised at his own good luck, called young Edward to London, and proclaimed him King on March 4th. No Parliament could be called quickly enough, but tumultuous bodies of citizens went about shouting "King Edward." A hasty proclamation in Westminster Abbey gave some sort of legitimacy to the title, and the new king at once marched northwards to avenge his father's fate. The one thing Edward IV. was really good at was war, and, though only nineteen years of age, he was already as far above any general in England in military talent as he was above most Englishmen in stature.[1] The swiftness of his march gave the plunder-laden Lancastrians no time to concentrate for the defence of the various obstacles which barred the North road, until the frontiers of Yorkshire were reached. There Edward forced them to give battle for the passage of the Aire, and there he

---

[1] Edward was 6 ft. 3 in., an unusual height for the Middle Ages.

utterly defeated them at Towton on 29th March. Both
armies were probably larger than on any other occasion
during the civil war, but we may safely divide by ten such
estimates as " 50,000 men a side." Edward signalised
his first battle as king by refusing quarter, and executing
wholesale the few prisoners that were taken. Apart from
the dynastic cause of the strife, Towton was distinctly
a victory of South over North, and one of the most
complete in English history. Henry, Margaret, and
the Prince fled to Scotland, and Edward carried the
pursuit almost to the border. In June he returned to
London for his coronation.

ENGLAND & WALES

IN THE

XVᵀᴴ CENTURY

Miles

0   20   40   60

δ Bishoprics
■ Religious Houses
○ Castles

To face page 350

CHAPTER XX

THE HOUSE OF YORK AND THE CLOSE OF
THE MIDDLE AGES

THE story of the Middle Ages in England hastens to
its inglorious and repulsive close. While the rest of
Western Europe is beginning to breathe the air of the
" new learning," which is wafted across the Alps, and
to taste the good peace that strong government alone
can give, England is still the prey of fierce baronial
factions yearly growing fiercer. Attempts have been
made to show Edward IV. as a patron of the " new
learning," because he once gave twenty pounds to
William Caxton, who set up the first English printing
press in his reign : attempts have been made to
prove that he anticipated the order-keeping Tudor
monarchs, because, like them, he dealt in wholesale
executions, torture, martial law, perpetual confiscations,
and the like. As a matter of fact he gave England the
bloodshed without the order. To my mind Edward
was nothing but the fitting head of a very bad political
faction, which had waded through blood to honours
and riches, and had to maintain them by more blood.
It is little justification to say that the usurpation of the
house of Lancaster had a precisely similar beginning.
Edward had some reasonable qualifications for this
position of party leader ; that is, he was faithful to those
few of his party who served him faithfully, and he gave
them rich rewards ; he was undoubtedly a first-class
soldier, and he was personally brave and careless of

danger ; he was utterly unscrupulous in deceiving, and utterly cruel in striking down both secret traitors and open enemies when he could discover them : but in the earlier part of his reign, being wholly given up to the grossest forms of self-indulgence, he often walked blind-fold into snares which both open enemies and traitors laid for him ; and so in his latter years he became a jealous and suspicious tyrant of an almost Italian type. The whole thing was to him merely a game played for the crown, and all that the possession of the crown meant in the way of riches and self-indulgence.   He was indeed, like Richard II., "landlord of England, not king."   To secure the greatest quantity of forfeited estates for him-self and his friends seems to have been his main object ; and, after lust, avarice was his ruling passion.   For external show he cared little ; he kept a frugal house-hold and a tight hand on his account-books ; left a surplus instead of a debt ; lent money on usury, and engaged in mercantile speculations on his own account. As for his abilities, they were mediocre ; in home politics he was a baby in the hands of the subtle Earl of War-wick, and in foreign policy he was tricked and outwitted again and again by the still more subtle King Louis XI. of France.   The treachery with which his throne was surrounded may be held to palliate some of his worst acts ; but it is evident that he disgusted the nation by his horrible executions (and the nation was by this time far from squeamish), in which very often the barest forms of justice were neglected.   His close friend, Tiptoft, the Earl of Worcester and Constable of England, was known as the " Butcher " for his cruelties, and deserved the name better than George II.'s son ever did ; he was the only man whom the restored Lancastrian government put to death in 1470–71.   So far as " the country " had any opinion, I take it to have been in the main Lancastrian.

It would have turned Yorkist readily enough if Edward's cruelties had given peace and order, but they did not; not even in the reign of terror which followed the destruction of the Lancastrians at Tewkesbury; though it is true that we hear rather less of private war then than in the years immediately following Towton.

The partisans of the house of York followed the normal rule of faction by quarrelling over the spoils of the house of Lancaster. If we bear in mind Henry IV.'s difficulties with the Percies (who had been his " King-makers "), we may indeed ask whether it would have been possible for Edward to keep upon good terms with the Nevilles. As Henry IV. had come to rely almost wholly on the Beauforts, so Edward came to rely wholly on the Woodvilles, the relations of his Queen. Neither faction enjoyed real national support, but there had been a curious magic in the name of " Lancaster " that prevented men from dancing to the tune of " York and legitimism." Yorkist Parliaments were very half-hearted affairs; they were few, short, and packed, and their main business was always attainders, confiscations, and resumptions of grants. From 1475 to 1483 there was only one little Parliament of a few days, called together solely to murder the King's brother, Clarence.

At first the Nevilles have it all their own way. Warwick is the " King-maker," and all powerful; one of his brothers will soon get the Percy Earldom of Northumberland, another is Archbishop of York and Chancellor; lands and cash are showered on the rest of them. The recognition of Edward by his first Parliament (Nov. 1461) takes the form of a restoration of a legitimate king, whose family has been "kept out of its own " by three successive usurpers; the Parliaments of these three are called "pretended Parliaments "; their Acts

z

therefore need confirmation and are confirmed, except such as were directed against the house of York. There is a fear that Margaret, " the pestilent indomitable woman," may get help from Scotland or France. She has indeed earned the former by the surrender of Berwick. But James III.'s Government is not really in a position to do more than accord a doubtful protection to Henry VI. and a few Lancastrian exiles, and that only until 1464. Margaret, therefore, turns to King Louis. Master as he is of all the baser forms of kingcraft, one would have expected this person to come to quick terms with Edward IV. ; yet until 1474 Louis remains on the whole, though with some wavering, a partisan of Lancaster. This is mainly because he lives in dread of the Dukes of Burgundy, Philip (died 1466) and Charles the Bold (1466–77), whose possession of Flanders makes it imperative for them to favour the man in possession of the English throne, whatever his name or origin.

The Civil War smouldered on till 1464, when the Percies were crushed at the battle of Hexham, and the Earldom of Northumberland given away to John Neville. In the following July King Henry VI., who had wandered from Scotland into various hiding-places in Cumberland and Lancashire, was betrayed by a ruffianly monk and some knights—ruffians, too, in spite of the honoured names of Talbot and Tempest which they bore—and brought to London, where Warwick ordered his legs to be bound to his horse's belly as he was taken to the Tower. There he was kept for five years. Visitors were admitted to see him, perhaps as a sort of show. Blackman tells us that during his brief restoration, in 1471, he pardoned a " certain wicked man " who had struck him with a dagger while he was in prison. However brutal the treatment he received, the conscience of the age obliged his enemies to allow him a chaplain to say mass.

In all this Edward and Warwick could perfectly agree; but already the rift between them had come. In 1464 Edward, for whose hand several European ladies had already been suggested, must needs go and marry a subject of his own, Lady Elizabeth Grey, widow of a slain Lancastrian knight and daughter of Lord Rivers of the Woodville family. This lady had sons and also numerous brothers and sisters, for all of whom she and Edward speedily provided rich marriages. At once within the Yorkist camp rose the spectre of division; at once Warwick's wrath blazed out: "he had two daughters; if the King must needs marry a subject, why had he not chosen Anne or Isabel?" There was no excuse for this outburst. Queen Elizabeth did turn out to be a shallow and grasping woman, but Edward would only have put himself in deeper bondage if he had married a Neville; while as for royal marriage with the native aristocracy, one could wish that it had been more frequently practised, for it would have improved the breed of kings. Warwick had, however, been duped, for he was in France at the time negotiating for a French lady for his master's hand. King Louis saw his displeasure, and at once marked him for his man. From that moment he never ceased to work upon the King-maker to induce him to unmake his creation. In whose interest this was to be done, and what king was to supplant Edward, was not at first made clear, even to Warwick himself. The historians of the period are so meagre and evidently so much afraid to tell truth, that it is not easy to say what other grievances Edward found against the Nevilles; it seems on the face of it as if the Queen industriously set to work to ruin them. Gradually they were weeded out of office; though the King-maker was obliged to stand godfather to the Princess Elizabeth (born Feb. 1466), he regarded with "great disapproval" the marriage of Edward's sister, Margaret, with Charles of Burgundy, 1468; and from this time regularly absented himself from Court, either at his Yorkshire castles of Middleham and Sheriff Hutton, or in France, where he fell deeper into the toils of the wily Louis. He had before the end of 1467 found a fellow-malcontent in the person of the King's brother, George, Duke of Clarence, a young man of eighteen, with all Edward's vices and none of his strong qualities. Little abortive movements against the King's government, partly perhaps Lancastrian, but partly also Neville in their origin, heralded this alliance during the year 1468. In July 1469, Clarence and Warwick fled to Calais together, and Clarence married Isabel Neville, the elder of Warwick's two daughters. It must be remembered that Edward had as yet no son, and that Clarence would probably have succeeded had Edward died before 1470. The marriage was immediately followed by a joint manifesto of Clarence and Warwick against Edward's misgovernment, and especially against the Queen's relations. The whole thing had evidently been carefully prepared, for there were risings in Lincolnshire and Yorkshire, with strings of grievances of which Warwick took hold, just as the Yorkists had taken hold of the "grievances of the Commons" at the time of Jack Cade's insurrection in 1450. Edward was taken completely by surprise; the forces which he hastily gathered to meet Warwick, Clarence, and their fellow-insurgents, were defeated at Edgcot, near Banbury. He was not present in the battle, but was taken prisoner the next day and carried to Warwick's castle at Middleham; and the Queen's father, and all the Greys whom Warwick could catch, were beheaded without any show of law or trial.

This was all very well, but was Warwick prepared to depose Edward and make George king? A very slight experience of George must have convinced him against this. Was he prepared to restore Henry VI.? Hardly, as yet. Therefore, a sort of compromise was patched up, and Edward, Warwick, and Clarence appeared in London as friends; two of them merely waiting their opportunity to strike at each other, and the third feeling that he was the dupe of both. Early in 1470 a Lancastrian rising blazed out in Lincolnshire, and this may have determined the King-maker to come to terms with Louis and Margaret. The wretched Clarence still followed him when he fled to France in July 1470, but was not present when he humbled himself at the feet of the haughty Margaret, with grim King Louis standing by. Margaret agreed to marry her son Edward—now a fine young man of eighteen—to Warwick's younger daughter, Anne; and Louis was to supply the wherewithal for a large invasion of England. Clarence thus saw his claims postponed to those of the hated Lancastrians, though it was agreed that, if their line should fail, his should come next in the English succession. Edward seems to have despised his enemies, and to have imagined that he had some real hold on the country. But he found himself almost alone; and when Warwick and Clarence landed in the west, to the tune of " King Harry," they carried all before them. Edward, who had gone to the north in anticipation of Neville risings there, fled to Holland with a few stalwart followers. Queen Elizabeth took sanctuary at Westminster, and there her ill-fated son, afterwards Edward V., was born in November 1470. Meanwhile Warwick proclaimed King Henry, and London looked on in sullen apathy.

All records of the brief Lancastrian restoration were destroyed by Edward on his return in the following

April, but we can make out that Henry VI. was taken from the Tower and treated as King, and that Warwick acted in his name; also, that some sort of a Parliament was held. But Queen Margaret and her son delayed their coming, and the delay was perhaps fatal. Edward had fled to the Court of his brother-in-law of Burgundy, who, much as he hated Edward, hated Louis more, and who recognised that this last job was manifestly of Louis' brewing. Warwick made no sort of attempt to conciliate the Burgundians; nay, with incredible folly, he proposed to aid France with an English force against Burgundy, thus losing for his party the hearts of all who cared either for English trade or English glory. Therefore, with a few ships, hired in Flanders with Burgundian money, but with no followers beyond his few exiled friends—little over a thousand men altogether—Edward resolved to make a dash for his crown again. Adversity had quickened his wits, and, landing at Ravenspur, where Henry IV. had landed in 1399, he proceeded, on the model of that king, to claim only his duchy of York. He received very little welcome or support from the districts through which he passed, but on the other hand neither Lancastrian nor Neville seems to have cared about facing him in open field. Various armies were reported to be advancing, but they always retreated before him. Clarence escaped from his unpleasant position and joined Edward. Why the King-maker (who advanced as far as Coventry) allowed Edward to proclaim himself King (at Warwick), and then to slip past him to London, one cannot say.

Just at the wrong moment for her cause, Queen Margaret landed at Weymouth, and the King-maker was obliged to detach considerable forces to meet and escort her; with the rest of his followers, which considerably outnumbered Edward's, he was at length compelled to give Edward battle at Barnet, eight miles north of London, 14th April 1471.   Barnet was a haphazard affair, in which each line outflanked the other at one end ; but it is evident that Edward caught Warwick napping, and the great King-maker was defeated and slain.   When Margaret landed on that same day she turned westwards to raise the Lancastrians of Devon, Cornwall, and Wales, and so allowed the victorious Edward time to gather troops.   Once he was sure of her objective, Edward, by incredibly swift marches, overtook her army at Tewkesbury, and simply annihilated it (4th May).   Prince Edward of Lancaster was either slain in the battle, or stabbed by Edward's orders after it ; and there followed a fierce massacre of Lancastrian leaders in cold blood.

In both these battles Clarence had fought bravely for his brother Edward, but the palm had been borne by the King himself, or perhaps by his youngest brother, Richard, Duke of Gloucester, a fiery-hearted dwarf of nineteen.[1]   Richard's steady loyalty to Edward had stood out in marked contrast to Clarence's shifts and vacillations.   He was zealous even to the shedding of blood ; doubtful tradition ascribes to him the stabbing of the Lancastrian Prince at Tewkesbury, but less doubtful tradition ascribes a more terrible murder than that ; on Edward's return to London King Henry VI. "died in the Tower":

---

[1] Richard is traditionally a "hunchback," and perhaps was really so; he certainly was very low of stature; the Scottish ambassadors once complimented him on the immense valour he possessed in "his tiny body." Specialist historians will say almost anything; we have been told that Richard had only "one shoulder slightly higher than the other," that he possessed great personal charm of face as well as of manner, &c., but certainly it is not easy to imagine a more evil-looking villain than is shown by his portrait in the Royal collection at Windsor.   It is, however, a more intellectual face than that of his brother Edward in the same collection.

> " When I was mortal my anointed body
> By thee was punchèd full of deadly holes,"

is not only Shakespeare's version of Gloucester's crime ; it is also that of the well-informed French chronicler, de Commines. Anyhow, he that was afterwards Richard III. had already graduated in murder.

The spoils go to the victors. Clarence, Gloucester, and the Woodvilles parted the vast Neville inheritance among them, and Gloucester married the widowed Anne Neville. Clarence, who had married her sister, at once began to be furiously jealous of him : the Nevilles were gone, but the house of York had to be still further split by intestine quarrels ere the end could come. The fewer men left to share the spoil, the greater greed each would display. It was perhaps to stifle their jealousies, perhaps in order to display on a wider field his really considerable military talents, perhaps as a measure of revenge against Louis, perhaps merely because he was beguiled by the Duke of Burgundy, that Edward resolved in 1474 to assert his claim to the French throne.

"The Kings of England," says de Commines, "make money out of their subjects for war and their enemies for peace," and so we see that John Bull has already got the reputation of loving his money-bags even at the expense of his honour, a reproach that could never have occurred to any critic of the earlier Edwards or Henries when a war with France was on hand. The moment the suggestion was made (1474) Edward found his hitherto stingy Parliament remarkably liberal ; and, not content with parliamentary grants, he went about in person soliciting free gifts from rich persons, which got the name of "benevolences" and became under the Tudors a regular means of extortion. Burgundy undertook to support the expedition with a large force ; James III. of Scotland was kept quiet with the promise of an infant princess of England for his son; and in March 1475 Edward transported to Calais the largest army that had ever left English shores at one time, no less in fact than 11,000 men (of whom 9000 were archers) and a large train of artillery. It was a different France that he was to find from the divided realm that Henry V. and Bedford had flayed bare. Thirty years of peace and order had worked the marvel which peace always does work on that wonderful country and her industrious peasants. Had King Louis been anything but a poltroon he might have faced Edward with double the English numbers, officered by paid captains who would not have repeated the mistakes of Crecy and Agincourt. Charles of Burgundy broke all his promises to Edward; he was already running his head against the hedgehog of Swiss pikes that was to destroy him two years later. Brittany was certainly disaffected to Louis, but not sufficiently so to move unless it was provoked. But Louis was a poltroon, and was besides a master of craft, while Edward was at the mercy of any diplomatic intrigue. Edward's nobles and Council, all but the stalwart hunchback Richard, were open to French bribes; and so, when the English army had advanced to the Somme, only to find all the country wasted before it and all the towns valiantly held against it, while tempting offers of peace were being whispered every day, Edward was not the man to resist. On 13th August Edward agreed to Louis' proposals, and a few days later the two kings had a carefully guarded interview at Pecquigny. From this interview Edward went home, outwitted and dishonoured, but with 75,000 crowns in his pocket, and a promise of a tribute or pension (whichever you like to call it) of 50,000 crowns a year, which Louis actually paid six years in succession.

By the treaty Louis further promised that his son, the Dauphin, should marry Elizabeth of York, a stipulation which he never intended to perform, but by which it is evident that Edward, and still more his Queen, set great store. For the kings of Europe, many of them connected by blood with the great house of Lancaster, evidently regarded Edward IV. and his house as *parvenus*, and such a marriage as this would at once have admitted that house into the charmed circle. Richard energetically protested against the whole business, and we may fancy that his protest was echoed in the hearts of many a stout yeoman whose father had reaped laurels under Bedford or Talbot thirty years before, and who looked on Frenchmen as his natural prey. Perhaps it was in wrath at the peace that Richard pushed on his quarrel with Clarence : perhaps it was Clarence's ambition and Edward's unquiet conscience that were again at work. More likely, however, the Queen and her relations were urging the King to get rid of Clarence, who in 1477 was accused of attempting the King's life by sorcery. The charges brought against him in order to justify fratricide are impossible to unravel; but fratricide it was, and Edward seems to have thrown his brother to the wolves without much compassion : after being attainted in Parliament Clarence "disappeared privately" at the Tower, February 1478. The greater part of his estates was resumed by the Crown, the rest divided between Rivers and Gloucester.

When one reads about the house of York thus preying on its own flesh and blood, one realises how great is the dramatic truth with which Shakespeare has drawn a shadowy figure of Queen Margaret hovering behind the doomed and self-dooming family of her rivals and teaching them how to curse each other and the wombs that bare them. " Margaret's curse " must have been felt by many who had never seen her face since Tewkesbury. Historically speaking she was not present, as she was sent back to France after the peace of Pecquigny. A small war with Scotland in 1481–82, partly stirred up by James III.'s traitor brother, Albany, is the last serious event of Edward IV.'s reign. It brought the recovery of Berwick and new fame to Richard of Gloucester, who conducted the campaign, but it interrupted the harmony which Edward had established between the kingdoms by the wise proposal of intermarriage : and the lad who was to have married Edward's daughter was destined to marry Henry VII.'s, and to bring, in the persons of his descendants, the two crowns to an ultimate union. In that year, 1482, Louis finally threw over the proposed marriage between Elizabeth and the Dauphin, to the bitter disappointment of Edward and his Queen. In April 1483 king Edward, probably the tallest and most robust king that ever reigned in England, died, worn out by drink and debauchery, at the age of forty.

As had been the King, so on the whole were his courtiers, his Queen, his nobles in general ; and, we must add, so were his enemies. Antony, Lord Rivers, the Queen's brother, is perhaps the most respectable of the lot, for he was a learned man and a patron of learning. The Bishops—Rotherhams, Nevilles, Mortons, Russells, Bourchiers (including the Archbishop, Cardinal Bourchier)—come very badly out of the story : they held high secular offices such as that of Lord Chancellor and Lord Privy Seal, and they made themselves the instruments of some of the worst acts of the Government. The whole of the Queen's large family was bitterly hated by the small remnants of the old Yorkist and Lancastrian baronage, whether of royal blood or not, as well as by the few new families outside the Woodville circle that had been advanced by Edward.

Chief among these last appears the Chamberlain, William, Lord Hastings. Both he and Lord Stanley had married sisters of the King-maker and been enriched out of Neville spoils. Lord Stanley's living wife was Margaret Beaufort, Countess of Richmond, who by her first husband, Edmund Tudor, was the mother of the fateful Henry, Earl of Richmond, then an exile in Brittany. This young man, of some twenty-seven years of age, was now the best heir of the house of Lancaster. Though the Beauforts had been only legiti*mised* (not born legiti*mate*), it was by this time an axiom that an Act of Parliament could do anything, and it certainly could legitimise bastards. There was a powerful tradition that Henry VI., as early as 1459, had prophesied that the boy Richmond would be King of England. Little as we know about the character of Henry VII. when King, we know nothing of him at all during his long exile in Brittany ; but we may fairly guess prudence to have been already his distinguishing characteristic. His new step-father, Lord Stanley, had been a loyal Yorkist ; his mother may possibly have encouraged her son's claims, but she seems to have avoided compromising herself with the Government. In learning and letters Lady Margaret was the first woman of the age, and has given her name at Cambridge to a divinity professorship and (as is perhaps better known) to a college boat-club.

Together with Hastings and Stanley we also begin to hear of the new family of the Howards, soon to be Dukes of Norfolk and Earls of Surrey. All three might be counted on to be fairly loyal to the sons of Edward IV., from whose side their greatest advantage might be expected.   It was otherwise with the two adult scions of Plantagenet blood, Richard of Gloucester, and Henry Stafford, Duke of Buckingham, representative of the youngest son of Edward III. Each of these might have something to say about the crown on his own account.   It must also be remembered that Clarence had left a son, Edward, afterwards Earl of Warwick, and a daughter, Margaret, afterwards Lady Salisbury.

Richard, in spite of his steady loyalty to Edward IV., had fallen under suspicion in his brother's last days; in his position as Warden of the North-Western Marches, he had kept himself or been kept away from Court; he had also been deprived of his office of Constable.   As a man of vigour and action with a biting tongue, he no doubt felt and expressed contempt for the sensual sloth in which Edward had been sunk; his bitterest hatred, however, he reserved for the Queen and the Woodvilles.   But if the young King, aged twelve and a half, must have a Protector, there was no possible reason for passing over Richard, and in his protectorate the remaining Yorkist lords (always excepting the Woodvilles) would certainly acquiesce. They did not trust him—it is obvious that nobody trusted anybody but himself—but they believed they could control him.   The young King and his brother, Richard, Duke of York (*aetat.* nine), were vigorous, healthy children, and the object of the Woodvilles was to do without a protectorate altogether.   Edward V. was at Ludlow with his uncle Rivers at the time of his father's death : a threefold struggle for the possession and management of his person at once began, and lasted from April to July : it was fought out by the Woodvilles, by Hastings backed by the wily John Morton, Bishop of Ely, and by Gloucester.   The latter relied for support on Buckingham, and perhaps to some extent on Henry Percy (who in 1470 had been restored to his Earldom of Northumberland), and on John de la Pole, Earl of Suffolk, who had married Edward IV.'s eldest sister, Elizabeth. Of these, Buckingham alone was likely to become a mere tool of Richard, but at what dates Richard's designs were successively unfolded to Buckingham it is hard to say. These designs were from the first for the crown, and nothing short of the crown : whether all the murders that must clear his way to it were already hatched in his scheming brain we cannot know. Contemporary authorities there are as good as none, for even the few chroniclers who note down facts are afraid or unable to clothe them in intelligible language. The Tudor historians (whom Shakespeare used) are wholly pro-Lancastrian ; but Sir Thomas More, who, early in Henry VIII.'s reign, wrote the " Life of Edward V.," had been brought up in the household of Morton, from whom he probably got the main lines of the story ; and Morton was likely to have known the truth.

Richard appears to have almost overdone the hypocritical business ; we read of the excessive blandishments he lavished on the young King and his brother, and of a disgusting amount of " kisses of peace." The first party to be eliminated were the Woodvilles, to whom it is probable that Edward V.'s affections were pledged. Before the King and his escort reached London, his uncle Rivers and his half-brother Grey had been seized by Richard's orders, and despatched to execution at Pontefract. Richard could apparently rely on a considerable following in Yorkshire and the North generally, and so he ordered up a large army of his northern friends to London. The Queen-mother fled with her younger children to the Sanctuary at Westminster ; and, thus disembarrassed of the whole Woodville connection, the Council, on 12th May, proclaimed Richard Protector, issued writs for a Parliament, and fixed Edward's coronation for June 22. But most suspiciously the royal residence chosen for the King (19th May) was the Tower, of which one of Richard's creatures, Brackenbury, was lieutenant.

The Protector proceeded to fill up the offices of State with adherents of his own, yet so carefully as not to excite much suspicion, and all seemed at first to be going fairly well. Hastings, however, must have been uneasy, for we find that before the end of May he, with Bishop Morton and the Archbishop of York, had a scheme for getting hold of Edward's person, perhaps even of reconciliation with the surviving Woodvilles. Richard, who always looked danger in the face, and sometimes even produced dangers by hasty actions, suddenly resolved to strike. On 13th June he accused the Queen-mother of attempting his life by sorcery, and Hastings and his friends of complicity. Hastings was arrested at the Council-Board and his head struck off in the yard outside; the bishops were imprisoned, and the astute Morton was given into the safe keeping of Buckingham, of whom he soon afterwards made a tool.

Next, by the disgraceful compliance of Archbishop Bourchier, Richard invested the Sanctuary of Westminster with armed men, and induced the Queen to surrender the little Duke of York. More disgusting kisses and blandishments, and we have the first act of the tragedy of the " Princes in the Tower " completed (16th June). Still aided by Buckingham, Richard now threw off the mask, and, after a farce of reluctance, "accepted" the crown, which a packed assembly of London citizens, overawed by Buckingham and the tidings of the coming army of the North, was induced to offer him. Charges of bastardy were then trumped up against the little Princes; clergymen were found to preach them openly at Paul's Cross. Richard was represented as the one man of action who could save the tottering State, &c., &c. One only wonders that any man should have cared to grasp at the crown of such a State. But Richard may fairly have argued that only as King would he be safe from the Queen-mother and her sons, who would otherwise one day call him to account for the deaths of their relatives.

Anyhow, on 26th June he was proclaimed, and on 6th July he and his Queen, Anne Neville, were crowned with all due and splendid formalities. Foreign countries, used by this time to English revolutions, took it on the whole quietly. Old Louis XI. was dying, and died in August, and the new King of France was a minor not without troubles of his own. We find a Spanish ambassador, who had been accredited to Edward V., calmly accrediting himself to the usurper and congratulating him. But the result was an immediate migration of malcontents to share the exile of Henry of Richmond, and this was a result that Richard could not afford to despise.

The new King set off on a series of royal progresses in the hope of winning "golden opinions from all sorts of people." The contrast of his public and active life to the retirement and sensual indulgence of Edward IV. was blazed abroad by his desire. One fancies Catesby, Ratcliff, and Lord Lovel, his chief confidants, going about before him organising pageants, and saying to the reluctant citizens of the towns through which he passed, "Shout, you dogs! why don't you shout?" Richard was for ever acting, for ever trying to justify his usurpation, and to take his people into his confidence; this attitude they rewarded by staring at him in sullen indifference and secret horror. This horror was soon deepened when whispers began to run that the Princes in the Tower had ceased to live. If there were ever any doubt upon the story as told by More, it was dispelled in 1674, when two skeletons, exactly corresponding to the age of the boys, were found at the foot of a staircase in the White Tower, exactly in the spot in which More says they were first buried.[1] They were murdered by two agents of Sir James Tyrrell in the first half of August. Probably Richard gave the bloody order when he was at Warwick, between the 7th and 15th of that month. His own son Edward, aged nine, was soon afterwards created Prince of Wales.

If we ask what moved the King to commit such a horrid murder, we must realise that his reign was never for a moment quiet. A great combination of Yorkist and Lancastrian exiles was afoot in July, and the captive Morton was pulling the strings of it; was inducing Buckingham to join it. Such a movement would have for its object either the liberation of the Princes, or the union of the houses of York and Lancaster by the marriage of Elizabeth of York to Henry of Richmond. Richard nervously resolved to cut away the first of these grounds from under the conspirators ; but in so doing he only planted their feet more firmly on the second. Buckingham had waded pretty deep in blood, since as a very young man he had presided over Clarence's attainder, but he was hardly prepared for this last crime of Richard's, and in September he raised the Lancastrian flag and invited Richmond over. Richard, however, struck swift and hard, and Buckingham, whose whole reliance was upon

---

[1] He wrongly says their bodies had been afterwards removed.

2 A

Wales and the south-west, found a heavy October flood on the Severn an impossible barrier to his men and his schemes.   He was caught and executed at Salisbury on November 2.   Richmond, who had actually reached the English coast, prudently retired to Brittany.

Richard professed to feel himself secure.   He opened his only Parliament in January 1484, and tried to play to the gallery by various useful law reforms, and a statute declaring benevolences to be illegal.   In the same connection we may notice his ostentatious devotion to the Church, and his translation of Henry VI.'s body from Chertsey to Windsor.   This hypocrisy did not pay him in the least.   Nor did the enormous gifts of Crown lands, which he made to possible friends and secret foes alike, win him a single heart.   His only son died in April 1484, and he fixed on John de la Pole, Earl of Lincoln, son of the Earl of Suffolk and his own eldest sister, as his heir.   While Richmond lived, such a man as Richard with such a history could not have known a quiet hour, and there is good evidence that he did not.   Once he very nearly bribed the Duke of Brittany (who was no better than his neighbours) into giving up Richmond ; but Morton sent timely warning, and Henry and his exiles fled into French territory.   How utterly blind Richard was to all sense of decency and honour may be seen in the consistent rumour (which he even took the trouble to contradict) that he intended to marry his own niece Elizabeth.   Certainly his wife died most opportunely, not to say suspiciously, in March 1485, and certainly, astonishing as it sounds, Elizabeth and her silly mother appeared in high favour at Richard's Court at the time.   Was the young lady privy to the design ?   We know even less of Elizabeth than of her subsequent husband, Henry VII., but the fact that she was the mother of Henry VIII. does not lead one to suppose that she would be horrified at the proposal on any moral grounds.

The mere rumour of it was, however, the beginning of the end. It endangered Morton's pet scheme for the union of the two houses, and it brought the cautious Richmond to the final stroke of action. With little force but that of his own exiled followers and hardly any aid from the King of France, Henry set sail from Harfleur, and landed in Pembrokeshire. His success would depend mainly upon the attitude of the Stanleys, Percies, and Howards, who were, nominally at least, on the side of Richard: the only personal strength he would be able to raise would be on the paternal estates of the Tudors in South Wales, and perhaps a little in Devon and Cornwall. But he knew that with few exceptions Richard's adherents would not fight seriously. Lords Lovel, Norfolk, and Northumberland did in fact respond to Richard's energetic appeal for men and arms ; but the armies that were to fight out the final struggle between York and Lancaster were probably little over two thousand men a side. Richard's was the larger, and would be overwhelmingly so if the Stanleys would join him ; the attitude of the Stanleys, however, remained mysterious. All the early summer Richard moved restlessly about the country, scattering proclamations and branding his opponents with various ugly names; and the strength that came in to Henry cannot be considered great. When the armies finally met at Bosworth in Leicestershire, on 22nd August, Lord Stanley looked on impassively at the battle ; but, strange to say, so did the Earl of Northumberland, whose troops were ranged on Richard's side. Sir William Stanley, with about one-half of the family forces, ended by striking in for Henry, and this finally turned the day. Henry's troops were skilfully managed by the Earl of Oxford, one of the exiles, and seem to have owed little to the generalship of their nominal leader. Richard, dwarf though he was, died fighting to the last. "King of England I will die this day," he is said to have cried; he also cried loudly on the treason of those who should have fought for him, treason which was only the due reward of the treason on which his own usurpation had been grounded. His crown was found in a thorn bush, and placed by Stanley upon the victor's head, after the battle.

One need not waste pity on the fierce, vigorous monster who represented the last pure Plantagenet blood in England; one may admit that as a statesman he would have been superior to Edward IV., as a soldier not much inferior; and that is about all one can say for him. Terror and blandishments were his alternate weapons, and the end of such a man, even in such an age, would surely not have been long deferred.

It is strange that, under kings who made so little attempt to govern decently, the economic and social condition of England was not worse than it was. But the fifteenth century, though not in any way a progressive or enlightened period, does not seem to have been a time of misery for the middle or lower classes. On the contrary, prices as a rule were low and wages were high in purchasing power. Wages were not paid in an increasing number of coins, for the stock of the precious metals in the Old World was running low, and the discovery of American mines in the next century came none too soon for purposes of trade. The battles of the Wars of the Roses, with the exception of those of the year 1461, disturbed neither town nor country very much. It must be remembered that the small armies which followed a Warwick or a Clifford were mostly composed of professional fighters, paid in meat and drink and clothing out of the estates of the landowners who raised them, and perhaps seldom altogether disbanded, or, if disbanded, rewarded out of the confiscated goods and lands of the defeated faction. As the century draws to a close, an increasing number of artillerymen is a marked feature in warfare, and these must always have been professionals. We even hear of hired bands of mercenaries from Burgundy, with "hand guns" of sorts; the dismounted knight begins to give place to the "billman," ancestor to the pikeman of the seventeenth century. The long-bow, however, still holds its own as the great weapon, and the proportion of bows to other arms even increases. But in a civil war the more professional the armies are, the less will the ordinary avocations of the peasant and the trader be disturbed, provided always that these armies do not subsist upon plunder, of which there is in this period no known instance except that of Margaret's Northerners in 1460–61. The summoning of the county levies occasionally took place for a Scottish war, but not for the faction fights themselves. It almost looks as if the kings and barons understood that they were to be allowed to go on with their bloody game only on condition of leaving the middle and lower classes alone.

The "yeomen," men of from fifty to two hundred acres, were beginning to enjoy the fruits of the land which they had been buying or renting steadily since the Black Death ; and the more successful of the ex-villeins, "copyholders" as they were now called, were becoming almost indistinguishable in point of wealth from the smaller yeomen. A decision of the law courts in Edward IV.'s reign laid down that a copyholder's title is good even against his manorial lord. Much of the land, in whosesoever hands, was beginning to be "enclosed"; that is to say landowners, of whatever rank, were beginning to put up permanent bits of fence and hedge to protect their arable, and still more their grazing lands. The process of enclosure was to go on, both with and without legal sanction, during the next three centuries; but the change was now just beginning. In the long run it was all to the benefit both of tillage and pasturage; but, of course, it was a fatal blow to the common village plough, and to many other cherished institutions of a conservative people. Moreover, the change from arable to pasture was going on rapidly, because wool was such a paying crop; and this led to the depopulation of villages, and caused the beginning of that crowding into towns which is such a distressing feature of our own days.

Wool was profitable now, not only as an export to the Flemish looms, but even more for the home manufactures, especially for those of Norfolk and Suffolk. Not long after the century closed we had almost ceased to export raw wool. We begin to hear of great fortunes made in the clothing trade, and the great clothiers were often great graziers as well. Statutes might, and did attempt to regulate and cramp these economic changes, but the blind goddess of Political Economy laughed at them, and went on her relentless way. Luckily for the clothiers, the woollen industry was exempt from many of the vexatious and petty regulations of the craft gilds in the towns; the Drapers' Company of London exercised a general supervision over it, but the Company of "Merchants Adventurers" was free to export English cloth to any port it pleased. In other industries and trades the restrictions of the gilds were everywhere maintained in the interests of the master-craftsmen; entrance fees were charged to those wishing to join a gild; privileges became hereditary in the families

of those who were "free of the gild"; the number
of apprentices began to be strictly limited, and "jour-
neymen" were employed (*i.e.* workmen paid by the
journée or day), who had no prospect, as apprentices
had, of one day rising to be masters. Thus the distinction between "capital" and "labour" was already
in existence, and to some extent also the antagonism
between them. To the gilds and their freemen was committed by fourteenth- and fifteenth-century charters the
municipal government of the towns, the right of electing
the town council, the aldermen, the mayor, and, if the
town were a borough, the members who represented it
in Parliament. Thus, while the county franchise remained fairly wide, that of the towns was distinctly
narrow; and we have no reason to believe that the
privileges and powers of a municipal corporation were
exercised by mediæval burgesses in any more intelligent
or honest spirit than they are at the present day.

Parliamentary legislation occasionally concerned
itself with these gild restrictions, but usually only to
support them and to prohibit aliens from setting up
new trades in England; thus there was a distinct slip
back from the wise commercial legislation of Edward
III.'s reign. One result of the restrictive action of town
corporations can be clearly seen, in that new trades
often took root in unchartered towns or in country
villages which had no gilds and no restrictions; and
hence we get the rise of such places as Birmingham,
Sheffield and Manchester. Far-seeing lords of manors
were thus often enabled to do a good turn for English
industries by encouraging artisans to settle in their
villages. London was even farther ahead of the rest
of the kingdom in population and prosperity than it is
to-day; it seems to have been decently governed, and,
after the great charter of Edward III., which put all

power into the hands of the twelve great "Livery Companies," no mediæval monarch dared to violate the privileges of the city. It was beginning to feel its way towards becoming the great emporium of Northern Europe. The jealousy of foreigners, however, was not much less in London than elsewhere ; the privileges of the great corporation of the German merchants of the "Steelyard" were several times in danger in the fifteenth century, and Londoners had already openly infringed the monopoly of the Baltic trade which these "Hanseatic" merchants had so long enjoyed. These had moreover been the great carriers of Eastern goods to our shores ; but the Venetians were now sending a fleet of galleys, laden with such goods, at stated periods to Southampton.

Probably all the ordinary "domestic" manufactures were supported by the raw produce of the land ; iron was being steadily worked, though the finer weapons and the very finest plate armour might still be imported ; glass was home-made, and windows were being regularly glazed ; tile and brick works were being set up, and many fifteenth-century houses and even castles were being built of red brick ; wooden houses were everywhere being superseded by stone or brick buildings, at least in the lower stories ; beautiful examples of the domestic architecture of the period may be seen in the streets of Shrewsbury, Tewkesbury, Chester, and above all of Ludlow. Your country house, whether of brick or stone, was still bound to be more or less fortified, but this was because, if you were rich enough to build a country house at all, you were sure to be an adherent of one or other of the dynastic factions, and might one day expect a visit from your opponents. The "perpendicular" style of church architecture has been called "unmeaning" and too symmetrical, and it is certainly

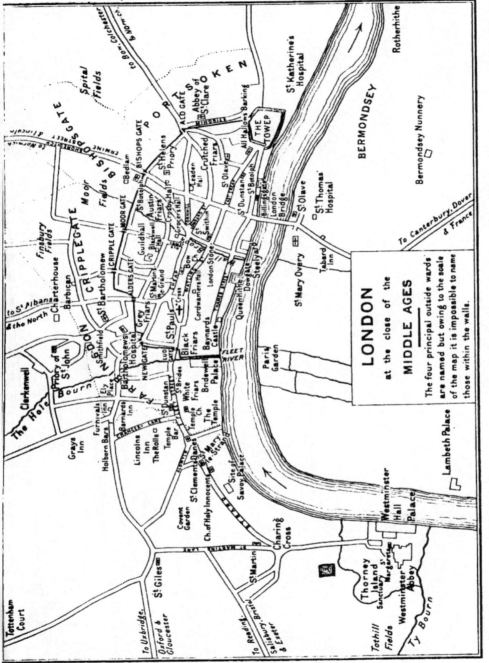

To face page 376

not of soaring beauty like the earlier Gothic ; but it has mellowed with time into the beauties of the Oxford of our own day and culminated in Magdalen College Tower. The Church was building and rebuilding very vigorously, perhaps, as I have hinted before, because it felt that the days of its riches were numbered.

The century was the great age of collegiate and scholastic foundations. The saintly Henry VI. founded no less than nine grammar schools in London alone ; I have already spoken of Winchester, Eton, King's, and All Souls' Colleges. Lincoln and Magdalen Colleges at Oxford and four of the Cambridge foundations date from the same period. The "Paston Letters," written by the various members of a Norfolk family of that name, are good evidence of the wide diffusion of a decent education in the upper and middle classes : the composition of the letters is uniformly good ; the spelling is of course purely arbitrary, and the handwriting as vile as fifteenth-century handwriting always was. The letters of William Paston the younger from Eton to his parents might, with certain necessary reservations, have been supposed to have been written under Doctor Warre instead of Doctor Barbour. Take the following extract : " I received a letter from you wherein was 8d., with which I should buy a pair of slippers. Also you sent me word in your letter of 12 lb. figs and 8 lb. raisins. I have not them delivered, but I doubt not that I shall have, for Alwedyr told me of them, and he said they came in another barge " (the Thames was, of course, the normal highway between Eton and London). Again he writes : "If it like you that I may come with Alwedyr by water and sport me with you at London a day or two this term time." He was an oppidan, and boarded for 13s. 4d. per half at his hostess' ; her name is not given, but she was probably the first "Dame" known to history. The badness of the elegiacs which he sends to his people as a specimen of his powers should afford hope to many a fourth-form boy that his "*carmina blanda*" may one day be preserved among the memorials of his country's history. The library of Sir John Paston contained more books than we should expect, and, though they were mostly works of chivalry and allegories, it would compare favourably with an average country squire's library in the eighteenth century.

People dined early in those days ; eleven is not infrequent, even ten is found. Their night was probably from eight till four, instead of from twelve till eight, and the practice of an after-dinner sleep was usual in the summer. Younger sons were almost invariably sent to some neighbouring great house to serve as pages and to learn manners, and the custom was occasionally extended to the daughters also. This points to rather an undomesticated life. "The Pastons," says Mr. Gairdner, the able editor of the letters, "may have been cold people, but one cannot help feeling that the lives of all in their station must have been too full of the harder business of life to allow of much time being lavished on the domestic affections." Margaret Paston complains of the bother of having a daughter at home, and wishes "hertily" she were rid of her. Margery, of the same family, is cast off by her people when she makes a *mésalliance* with a country tradesman and goes to "sell candle and mustard at Framlingham." A daughter was to a fifteenth-century mother legitimate capital, to be laid out to the greatest family advantage. It is obvious from the letters that, however dead feudal ties might be, feudal ideas were by no means dead ; order, reverence for age and rank and power in every shape, though constantly interrupted where the violent passions of the interrupter were concerned, were yet regarded as part of the divine scheme of the government of the world.

So, if the political life of mediæval England closes in fierce bloodshed on field and scaffold, we may think of her social life as continuing to flow in a stream somewhat narrow and somewhat sluggish, yet not without strength. Few tributaries are as yet feeding that stream, and there is little rain from above to swell it. But the sky is dark, and in a little time there will be the sound of abundance of life-giving rain. Then the windows of Heaven shall be opened, the dark Atlantic shall give up its secrets, the Gospel of Christ, stripped of Romish accretions, shall be open to all men to hear and read, the long-closed treasure-house of the ancient world shall be unlocked, and the study of Greek shall teach us what the study of Greek alone *can* teach, to bring everything once more to the divine test of reason.

INDEX

THE END

Printed by BALLANTYNE, HANSON & Co.
Edinburgh & London

Check Out More Titles From HardPress Classics Series In this collection we are offering thousands of classic and hard to find books. This series spans a vast array of subjects – so you are bound to find something of interest to enjoy reading and learning about.

Subjects:
Architecture
Art
Biography & Autobiography
Body, Mind &Spirit
Children & Young Adult
Dramas
Education
Fiction
History
Language Arts & Disciplines
Law
Literary Collections
Music
Poetry
Psychology
Science
…and many more.

Visit us at www.hardpress.net

CPSIA information can be obtained
at www.ICGtesting.com
Printed in the USA
BVHW081614220819
556561BV00018B/3974/P

9 781318 532667